PHILOPONUS

On Aristotle

On Coming-to-Be

and Perishing 2.5-11

PHILOPONUS

On Aristotle
On Coming-to-Be
and Perishing 2.5-11

Translated by
Inna Kupreeva

Duckworth

Ancient Commentators on Aristotle
General editor: Richard Sorabji

First published in 2005 by
Gerald Duckworth & Co. Ltd.
90-93 Cowcross Street, London EC1M 6BF
Tel: 020 7490 7300
Fax: 020 7490 0080
inquiries@duckworth-publishers.co.uk
www.ducknet.co.uk

A catalogue record for this book is available
from the British Library

ISBN 0 7156 3304 X

Acknowledgements

The present translations have been made possible by generous and
imaginative funding from the following sources: the National En-
dowment for the Humanities, Division of Research Programs, an
independent federal agency of the USA; the Leverhulme Trust; the
British Academy; the Jowett Copyright Trustees; the Royal Society
(UK); Centro Internazionale A. Beltrame di Storia dello Spazio e del
Tempo (Padua); Mario Mignucci; Liverpool University; the Leventis
Foundation; the Arts and Humanities Research Board of the British
Academy; the Esmée Fairbairn Charitable Trust; the Henry Brown
Trust; Mr and Mrs N. Egon; the Netherlands Organisation for
Scientific Research (NWO/GW); Dr Victoria Solomonides, Cultural
Attaché of the Embassy of Greece in London. The editor wishes to
thank Alan Lacey, Ian Mueller, Christopher Taylor, and Rosemary
Wright for their comments, Inna Kupreeva and John Sellars for
preparing this volume for press, and Deborah Blake who has been
Duckworth's editor for all volumes in the series since the beginning.

Typeset by Ray Davies
Printed and bound in Great Britain by
Biddles Ltd, King's Lynn, Norfolk

Contents

For further reading on the
ancient commentators on Aristotle see:

Richard Sorabji (ed.), *Philoponus and the Rejection of Aristotelian Science*,
London & Ithaca NY, 1987
Richard Sorabji (ed.), *Aristotle Transformed*, London & Ithaca NY, 1990
Richard Sorabji, *The Philosophy of the Commentators, 200-600 AD: A Source-
book*, vol. 1: *Psychology*; vol. 2: *Physics*; vol. 3: *Logic and Metaphysics*, London
& Ithaca NY, 2004.

Introduction

This volume completes the Duckworth translation of Philoponus' commentary on Aristotle's treatise *On Coming-to-Be and Perishing*. Since the publication of the two previous volumes,[1] new relevant scholarly work has appeared,[2] which (together with the two previous volumes) puts us in a better position to discuss the sources, language and structure of this commentary, considered to be one of Philoponus' earliest works.[3]

The title of the commentary as preserved by most manuscripts indicates that it is a set of revised lecture notes delivered by Philoponus' teacher Ammonius,[4] who is known to have cultivated interest in exact sciences[5] and medicine.[6] Lectures on Aristotle's *GC*, together with those on *Phys.*, *Cael.*, and *Meteor.*, formed the physics course which was a part of the 'Aristotelian' component of the Neoplatonic curriculum.[7]

Another important source for Philoponus was the now lost commentary on the *GC* by Alexander of Aphrodisias. Philoponus' dependence on Alexander had been argued by scholars previously on doctrinal and stylistic grounds; more recently, E. Gannagé has reconstructed fragments from the lost commentary preserved in the medieval Arabic corpus of alchemical works attributed to Jâbir b. Ḥayyân, where several passages explicitly attributed to Alexander show striking parallels with the passages in Philoponus' commentary in which Alexander is not quoted.[8]

The fact that our commentary is a compilation based on several sources should command special caution in the attribution of the post-Aristotelian doctrines presented in it. In each particular case, there is a question whether the view presented belongs to Philoponus himself, his teacher Ammonius, or Alexander, and one should not discount possible 'mixed' cases (e.g. Alexander in the interpretation of Ammonius and Philoponus).

The structure of the commentary corresponds to the pattern identified for the commentaries based on revised lecture notes.[9] One of the formal features characterising such commentaries is the style of their *lemmata*: they do not contain the whole text commented upon, but indicate the first line or the salient point of the discussion.[10] Commentaries based on lecture notes differ in this from the so-called *hupomnematic* commentaries written as scholarly notes,[11] and are closer to paraphrases, where *lemmata* are not distinguished, and Aristotle's text is stylistically integrated into the paraphrase.[12]

The text of Aristotle's treatise on which Philoponus' commentary is based usually shows agreement with some Aristotle manuscripts.[13] The structure of the commentary generally follows familiar division of Aristotle's text into chapters, although in some cases there are minor differences at the terminal points.[14] Exposition is divided into *theôria*, i.e. a discussion of the argument of the whole chapter,[15] and *lexis*, a detailed study of the text including the discussion of grammar and doctrinal consistency.[16] The combination of *theôria* and line-by-line exegesis in the same argument may lead to sometimes uneven coverage and repetitions of lemmata.[17]

The commentary is written as a continuous narrative, with frequent summaries of previous argumentation and cross-references to the earlier and later parts of the work. Its language contains many standard exegetical terms;[18] we shall notice the abundant use of logical terminology.[19] There is a tendency to present Aristotle's arguments in explicit syllogistic form, often with resort to hypothetical syllogism.[20] Some parallels in locution between Philoponus' descriptions of Aristotle's argument and Neoplatonic character classifications of Plato's dialogues (*gumnazein, anatrepein, huphêgeisthai, zêtein, theôrein*) may or may not be mere coincidences; but they are clearly rooted in a common school practice.[21]

The system of quoting the sources is notoriously difficult to track down. *phêsi* without a subject most frequently refers to Aristotle, although there are several rare cases where this is not entirely clear.[22] *phêmi* and *legô* normally refer to the author of the narrative and are not an indication of Philoponus' own contribution.[23] There are some instances where the first person singular seems to be used in emphatic constructions; and these might be cases where Philoponus' own additions are being signalled.[24] Several passages seem likely to be Philoponus' additions because they contain corrections or objections to the main line of the argument.[25] Other works of Aristotle are frequently quoted and alluded to.[26] At one point we find almost a verbatim quotation of Theophrastus' *de igne* 13.[27] Alexander is quoted by name 35 times in the whole commentary, seven times in this volume.[28] Apart from direct quotations, there are several passages where Alexander's discussions or concepts are taken up without explicit reference.[29]

On several occasions references to the Neoplatonic doctrines are made.[30] Pre-Socratic philosophers are quoted on the basis of the *corpus Aristotelicum*; the only exception I could spot is fr. B 115 DK (see below, 5 n. 56 and 266,4-5 n. 166).

Philoponus' commentary is mentioned by the Arabic bio-bibliographers, Ibn al-Nadîm and al-Qiftî.[31] It is likely that Avicenna knows it. In correspondence with Biruni, he compares Biruni's criticism of Aristotle with the objections raised by Philoponus in his polemic over the issue of creation, and points out (controversially) that Philoponus' commentary on *On Coming-to-Be and Perishing* testifies to the fact that he is in no disagreement with Aristotle on this matter.[32] We also seem to have extant a fragment of Olympiodorus' commentary *in GC*, which likewise comes from Ammonius' circle, is mentioned by both al-Nadîm and al-Qiftî,[33] and lost in Greek.[34] This, along with Avicenna's report, gives us some reasons to believe that Arabic translations of Alexandrian commentaries on Aristotle's treatise were in circulation, at least in the East.

There are some parallels with Philoponus in Averroes' *Middle Commentary*, but whether he actually had any access (direct or indirect) to Philoponus' commentary is hard to establish.[35]

The Latin Middle Ages seem to be largely unaware of this commentary, although some materials from it seem to be present in the marginal glosses to the *translatio vetus* made by Burgundio of Pisa.[36] The first Latin translation of Philoponus' commentary seems to be the one made by Hieronymus Bagolinus, from the Aldine edition of 1527, published in Venice by Hieronymus Scotus in 1540; the second, made by Andreas Silvius, was published by Valgrisius in 1564.[37]

The argument

In what follows I attempt to summarise the main points of Philoponus' commentary and signal some of its most striking features. More details can be found in the Notes to the translation.

2.5 Against Monists

Aristotle's goal in *GC* 2.5 is to show that his own doctrine of elements is incompatible with any version of the monist theory of elements. He argues against the notion that any proper subset of the four elements can play the role of the element for the rest, refuting as incompatible with his theory of change the views that any one of the four elements, or an 'intermediate body' can do so, and devoting a special argument to the distinction between the 'extreme' and the 'intermediate' elements by which the 'extreme' elements are exempted from change. His argument thus has the form of refutation of opposed doctrines (either historical, or as constructed for dialectical purposes); this form is underscored in Philoponus' commentary, where the *theôria* opens with a division of opinions about the elements (see pp. 27-9). This division has a number of affinities with other familiar 'divisions' found in the Aristotelian commentaries and in the doxographical sources.[38]

A remarkable feature of our division is that it seems to leave room (under number four in Philoponus' numeration) for the Stoics who are treated as the proponents of the view according to which one of the extremes (viz. fire) is the principle of other elements.[39] Aristotle himself does not spend too much time on this view,[40] but the Stoic revival of it accounts for the fact that in Philoponus' commentary we find an elaborate exposition of the theory, followed by several criticisms which are answered by a fairly sophisticated defence, before it is finally refuted from a 'catholic' Aristotelian standpoint.[41]

In his reconstruction of the theory, criticised by Aristotle, according to which the intermediate elements (water and air) do change into other elements, while the extreme elements do not, our commentary assumes a 'weaker' version of the theory in question (the extremes do change into each other not directly but through the intermediates),[42] thus siding with Cherniss and others[43] against Joachim (followed by C.J.F. Williams) who understood the criticised theory in a 'strong' sense ('change can occur "outwards" from the means but not "inwards" from the extremes').[44]

Philoponus' discussion of the monist views is characterised by a high degree of logical and exegetical precision in following Aristotle's arguments. The commentator and his sources do not refrain from criticisms where Aristotle's argument is unclear,[45] and develop ingenious and original arguments to strengthen Aristotle's position. The theory of change as linear infinite process in shown to be based on the treatment of change as an asymmetric relation – an interpretation which has potentially interesting philosophical implications.[46] In his critical analysis of Aristotle's point according to which 'as a new member is added to the series a contrariety attaches to the previous members' (333a5-6), the commentator shows his interest in investigating the concept of the infinite with the help of exact methods of logic and mathematics.[47]

2.6 Against Empedocles

Philoponus identifies Aristotle's goal as the criticism of the theory of four unchangeable elements. He elucidates Aristotle's discussion of several ways in which such elements can be commensurate while remaining unchangeable: (i) in amount; (ii) in power and quality, these being (iia) the same, or (iib) different. In the latter case our commentator distinguishes two further options: (iib′) when the powers are contrary,[48] and (iib″) when powers are not contrary but different in kind ('this is white as this is hot', cf. 333a29). In his discussion of comparison by amounts (i), Philoponus distinguishes two possible interpretations: (ia) comparison in an 'absolute' sense, i.e. between the total amounts of all the four elements, the case in which, he argues, comparison 'by masses' is impossible, meaning that these 'total masses' of the elements are unequal;[49] and (ib) comparison in terms of mutual change, which presupposes that a common substrate turns into one or another element, a process that involves its being contracted or extended. Philoponus describes contraction and extension of this common substrate as 'change', *metabolê*;[50] although it would be difficult to classify it within Aristotelian theory of change. The concept of common substrate is further developed by Philoponus in his discussion of case (ii), change in power and quality, where he points out that '[being] more and less in respect of the same power cannot happen except to that which is from the same matter: this comes about by tension and relaxing of powers; and this constitutes a change'.[51] Only once in this discussion is the substrate of change described as 'the three-dimensional', without an explicit link being drawn with contraction and extension;[52] nonetheless the immediate context is the 'qualitative' comparison of the elements (case (iib′)), and there is no reason to suppose that this description is purely coincidental and not implied in the concept of substrate through-out the discussion. Philoponus explains that Aristotle's example of *analogia* between the hot and the white falls under the case (iib″), the only case where Empedocles can legitimately compare elements, be-cause in this case the elements will lack the common substrate.[53] In this part of Philoponus' commentary we can see some preparatory work for the introduction of the concept of matter as three-dimensional.[54] Whether it is to be credited to him or to his predecessors must remain an open question; but his clear exposition of this view of matter indi-cates that he was at least comfortable with it.

In the rest of this chapter, Philoponus closely follows Aristotle's criticisms of Empedocles on the subjects of growth, nature vs. chance, and the source of motion. He explains Aristotle's distinction between growth and addition (333b3), citing the processes of alteration and assimilation of nourishment by the alterative power inherent in a growing thing, demonstrating again his Galenic background and refer-ring back to the discussion of growth in *GC* 1.5, the text which received most attention in the whole of this commentary.

There are no clear signs in the text that Philoponus himself is familiar with Empedocles' poem:[55] most of his quotations are taken from Aristotle. One notable exception is the already mentioned read-ing of fr. 115, v.13, but this may be taken from a closer Neoplatonic source.[56]

An excerpt from Alexander's commentary cited under the lemma 334a5-9 attributes to Empedocles the claim that 'the universe is in much the same state now under [the rule of] Strife as it was earlier under [the rule of] Love'. The text of quotation (268,1-14) is corrupt at 268,1-2, but the meaning of the discussion can be reconstructed.[57] Alexander asks in what sense the universe is 'in the same state', whether it is *qua* being the same, or *qua* being different each time. Two different (but not necessarily incompatible) solutions seem to be offered. Alexander says (i) that the universe referred to seems to be the same, since otherwise (if both periods of segregation and aggregation counted, each, as uni-verse) there would be no room for any other moving cause apart from these. If, on the other hand, the universe is a natural body which persists through the changes of segregation and aggregation induced by Strife and Love, respectively, then at some point it will move with its own proper motion as well. Further, he suggests (ii) that the expression 'in much the same state' (*homoiôs*) might be referring to the two 'passage'-periods, from the reign of Love to the reign of Strife and vice versa, in the sense that in both cases there is a struggle between the opposite forces of Love and Strife, whereas in the intervals between struggle (*en de tois metaxu dialeimmasi*) the universe is moved by some different movement not coming from Love or Strife.

2.7-8 Homoeomers

The problem of the formation of homoeomers, natural substances with homogeneous structure, is related to the problem of mixture discussed by Aristotle in *GC* 1.10.[58] In that chapter Aristotle outlines a general solution to the problem of status of the ingredients within mixture, according to which the ingredients cease to exist in actuality, but continue to do so potentially, so that in the appropriate circumstances they can be separated from a mixture again.[59] This solution, being quite general, leaves open a number of important philosophical questions concerning the precise nature of this 'potentiality' and also the ontological status of the transformations taking place in the processes of being mixed and being separated from a mixture. Alexander of Aphrodisias, in his treatise *On blending and growth* (= *Mixt.*), sets out to clarify these important concepts, in a polemic against the Stoic theory of blending (*krasis*) according to which the qualities of the ingredients were preserved when they were mixed. Alexander in his discussion draws a distinction between numerical and specific persistence and argues that qualities potentially preserved in a mixture are to be treated as specifically, though not numerically, identical with the qualities of the individual ingredients, so that on separation these specific qualities are restored, but their instances are not numerically identical with the corresponding qualities of the ingredients.[60] He thus recognises a special ontological status of the process in which the ingredients are recovered from a mixture, because in this process their original forms are restored. However, he draws a distinction between a specific (universal) and individual (particular) sense of form, pointing out that in the latter sense, i.e. in the sense of individual identity, there is no persistence either of an individual ingredient as a composite substance, or of its form insofar as that characterises this individual.[61]

The potentiality that characterises the ingredients in their mixed state is described earlier in our commentary as a potentiality of a 'third' type, lying somewhere between the 'first' and the 'second' potentialities familiar from the Aristotelian metaphysics.[62]

The discussion in *GC* 2.7 is focussed on the crucial case (addressed neither by Aristotle himself in *GC* 1.10, nor by Alexander in *Mixt.*), where the four elements serve as the ingredients of a mixture. Aristotle's task in *GC* 2.7 is to show that only his theory of elements *qua* changeable can provide a good explanation of elemental constitution, whereas the Empedoclean view according to which the four elements do not change into each other fails to do so. Perhaps the new, refined conditions of the problem as it is stated in Aristotle's text account for some further doctrinal innovations that we find in this part of Philoponus' commentary.

Philoponus begins the *theôria* by outlining the problem and briefly expounding Aristotle's criticism of the doctrine of unchangeable elements for its failure to explain natural compounds in general and more specifically, the fact that each element can be separated out of any part of a homoeomer. Readers' attention may be arrested by a passage at 269,25-270,6 containing a defence on behalf of the proponents of the view that elements are unchangeable: they are said to argue that the homogeneity of organic homoeomers is merely an appearance – in fact, in each case there is a very fine particulate structure – without, however, denying the homogeneity of each of the four elements. This defence is left without a direct response in the commentary,[63] and its exact source and purpose are unclear, but it shows an interesting parallel with Proclus' and Simplicius' criticisms of Aristotle's and Alexander's theory of mixture.[64] Whether Philoponus' argument was a part of Ammonius' lectures or whether he himself inserted it as a student's 'doubt', should remain an open question.[65]

Philoponus goes on to present his solution to the problem of the status of homoeomers within the Aristotelian theory by applying to the case of mixed elements a distinction of the three kinds of potentiality already familiar to the readers of *in GC* 1.10. He explains that the forms of the elements are the extreme states of the four elemental qualities, and in a mixture only the extremes are destroyed, which does not involve a complete destruction of the quality in question. Thus, when fire, whose form is the extreme of heat, enters a mixture, that extreme heat ceases to exist, but the 'relative' heat continues, and so 'pure fire' ceases to exist, though fire continues to exist in an 'inhibited' or 'restrained' mode (*kekolasmenon*).[66] Philoponus' language in this exposition is a bit vague: he does not explain in precise terms the distinction between 'pure' and 'inhibited' fire, and on the whole prefers to speak of pure and inhibited forms.[67] The presentation is followed by a critical remark to the effect that if fire means 'extreme heat', and the 'extreme heat' has been destroyed, then fire has been destroyed accordingly, continuing to exist in matter only in the first degree of potentiality; whereas the third degree of potentiality applies only to the 'extreme heat' (271,25-272,10). The source of this remark is uncertain,[68] but it should be noted that later in the commentary the idea of mixture containing 'inhibited' elements is used to explicate a distinction (drawn by Aristotle) between the prime matter and the proximate (elemental) matter of a compound (274,21-275,9; 275,31-276,30).

Aristotle's argument in 2.8 (each element is present in every homoeomer) goes as follows: (i) earth is present in every homoeomer, because each element is present to the greatest extent in its own place, i.e. here on earth, 'around the middle place', earth must be present in all compounds; (ii) water is present because '(iia) the composite must be bounded, and (iib) water alone of simple bodies is easily bounded; and (iic) because, moreover, earth itself cannot keep together without the wet, this being what holds it together'; (iii) air and fire are shown to be present because they are constituted by qualities contrary to those of earth and water, which have already been proved to be present. Philoponus follows this reasoning fairly faithfully, making a pedantic remark at (ii), that in the description of water as 'easily bounded' (*euoriston*), 'easily bounded' should be taken in the active sense of 'providing with bounds' (*horistikon*) rather than in the passive sense of 'being bounded'. Thus the principle of 'causal transmission', according to which the cause must itself possess the property which it causally imparts, seems to be violated.[69] In (iii), where Aristotle says that 'earth is the contrary of air and water of fire', Philoponus points out the imprecision of the expression (drawing an appropriate distinction between the elements *qua* substances and elemental qualities), and (with clear reference to Aristotle's *Categories*) makes allowance for it as a way of speaking ('in respect of powers').

2.9 Counting causes
Aristotle sets out to show that efficient cause is not reducible to either formal (which he here identifies with the final cause), or material. At the beginning he draws a general distinction between things eternal and those that are generable and perishable, and states that the principles (*arkhai*)[70] of these two classes of things are equal in number and the same in kind, specifying briefly at 335a30 that by 'principles' he means form and matter.

Philoponus' discussion of the matter of eternal things shows a number of parallels with *Quaest.* 1.10 attributed to Alexander of Aphrodisias. Philoponus explains that by 'matter' Aristotle means the underlying substrate in a general sense (*to hupokeimenon koinôs*), the concept which is also used by Alexander who contrasts it with the notion of matter as receptive of the contraries.[71] In our commentary this contrast between the two kinds of matter is described as that between 'superior' and 'inferior', where superiority of heavenly matter consists in its always being in actuality, never in potentiality (283,4-10). The commentator next raises a difficulty similar to the one raised by Alexander in *Quaest.* 1.10 and discussed in *Quaest.* 1.15, as to whether the difference between the two kinds of matter is not due to different forms inherent in the same matter underlying both.[72] The solution consists of a statement that 'difference comes about not only through form, but also through matter itself ',[73] followed by a *reductio ad absurdum* of the main premiss of the aporia. This argument is too compressed compared to the array of proofs we find in Alexander's *Quaest.* 1.15.[74] Nonetheless, it is

possible that Alexander's commentary here served as a template either
to a lecturer, or a note-taker, or both. It is also well-known that in his
later work Philoponus came to deny that heavenly matter in any way
differs from the sublunary.[75] Furthermore, in a number of recent publi-
cations attention has been drawn again to a fragment preserved in the
papyrus PSI xiv 1400 containing an argument against the position
defended in our passage and Alexander's *Quaestiones*.[76]

Aristotle's argument for the necessity of the third kind of cause
besides form and matter is expounded by Philoponus in the form of a
reply to a question why two principles (form and matter) are not
sufficient if in natural substances matter receives form of its own
nature, without an intervention of a third party. The argument establishing that an efficient cause is needed to make matter suitable for
working upon is illustrated by the example of a sculptor who produces
a sculpture by removing the impeding parts of matter rather than by
imposing a form from outside. This seems to be a somewhat convoluted
statement in which two principles are not properly distinguished: the
notion that efficient cause imparts suitability to matter corresponds to
the transition from first to second potentiality (on Aristotle's view); but
the example of a sculptor removing the extra chunks from the rock's
'inherent statue' seems more apt as an illustration of the passage from
second potentiality to act (second actuality).

Aristotle's criticism of Plato's failure to attend to the problem of
efficient causation in the *Phaedo* is countered in Philoponus' commentary by a defence put forward on Plato's behalf by 'some' who say that
'creative forms (*ta dêmiourgika eidê*) are efficient causes, by participation in which things come to be and by the loss of which they perish'.[77]
The concept of *dêmiourgikoi logoi* is a part of the philosophical vocabulary of Proclus and Ammonius, both of whom also use the term
'demiurge' to designate the second principle in the Neoplatonic triad;
but significantly, the defence reported by Philoponus does not mention
the Demiurge. In fact, he goes on to suggest that the reason why
Aristotle criticises Plato at this point is that the Demiurge is not
mentioned in the *Phaedo*, where all the efficient causal power is rele-
gated to the forms. This (Neoplatonic) interpretation is supposed to pass
smoothly into the following argument ('and therefore he says a doctor
and a knower are also needed'), perfectly Aristotelian in itself, but which
could be interpreted also as a reference to the Demiurge of the Neoplatonic triad.[78] Perhaps we are dealing here with a deliberate ambiguity
stemming from a tendency to reconcile Plato and Aristotle on the basis
of Neoplatonic metaphysics.[79]

In Philoponus' presentation of the materialists' position we can notice
the use of the term *tropê* as a synonym for *kinêsis* (on account of which
they are said to have posited matter as a cause),[80] and a remark that
they consider fire to be the most active (*malista drastikôteron*, 287,28).
Both points could be the traces of a 'Stoic presence' in one of the sources;

in his later work Philoponus acknowledged his debt to the Stoic system.[81] Aristotle's contrast between Plato and materialists, with the former completely omitting the account of a causal mechanism of production, while the latter concentrate exclusively on the 'instrumental' causes, is underscored by Philoponus (who probably uses the term 'instrumental' in the technical sense it receives in the Neoplatonic theory of causes).[82]

2.10 Efficient cause

Aristotle fulfils the task outlined in the preceding chapter and provides an elaborate account of efficient causes operating within his system of cosmology. This account is also a further development of the account of motion in *Physics* 8, in application to the whole of cosmology. The efficient cause of coming to be and perishing should be the cause of uninterrupted motion, able to impart the character of eternity to these processes. The sun which moves in an inclined circle around the earth satisfies the requirements for the 'global' efficient cause stated in the theoretical discussion.

In his commentary on Aristotle's chapter, C.J.F. Williams duly draws attention to the parallel discussion of double motion in Aristotle's *Metaphysics* 12.6, 1072a9-17, where this motion is said to be the cause of the processes of coming to be and perishing. In the fragment of Alexander's commentary preserved by Averroes (fr. 27 Freudenthal), Alexander refers to the discussion in *GC*, saying that the *Metaphysics* passage is a shorter version of the account found there; presumably, the step missing in the *Metaphysics* has to do with establishing the rotation of fixed stars on the one hand and the axial inclination on the other as two causes of the sun's motion.[83]

In this chapter Aristotle also presents his view on the relation between the heavenly motions and natural processes in the sublunary world, especially biological processes. Philoponus discusses several problems arising from this view. Rendering the sun's motions of approach and retreat as two respective causes of coming to be and perishing raises the problem of the processes of coming to be and perishing that happen 'out of season': both kinds of processes are seen to happen both in summer and in winter. This problem is discussed in *Quaest.* 3.4 attributed to Alexander of Aphrodisias, and the solution found there coincides with the solution stated by Philoponus in his *theôria* at 289,27-290,7, according to which the approaching and retreat of the sun directly cause, respectively, the coming to be and perishing of the superior substances. The latter class is detailed by Philoponus (but not in *Quaest.* 3.4) as including 'fruits and animals and the superior elements, fire and air' (290,2-3).[84] In the discussion of the *lexis* (336b8-9), a different version of this solution is put forward: since for many substances the process of coming to be and perishing is extended over many approaches and retreats of the sun, the meaning of the causal dichotomy initially proposed is that the sun contributes more to the coming to be of a 'strengthened' nature (i.e. the one that is young and growing), which is also less affected by its withdrawals; and the substances that are in the phase of decay are more affected by its withdrawals and less liable to benefit from its approaches. This version is further countered by the objection that the retreating motion of the sun also contributes to the coming to be in a positive way. This objection is apparently based on the Aristotelian sources,[85] and is left without an explicit response, although the general conclusion is modified to say that the approach of the sun is *more* the cause of coming to be, and the departure *more* that of perishing.

Philoponus discusses several questions concerning the life-span of living beings and its dependence on the structure of the universe at large. Aristotle's claim that 'the perishing and the coming to be that occur by nature take place in equal time' (336b9) is first interpreted as being really about the processes of growth and decrease, which are to be substituted for 'coming to be' and 'perishing', and which take place over equal time-intervals under normal circumstances, in accordance with nature, to exclude any kind of anomaly (293,11-21). This explanation is then faced with a further difficulty: that even if it is assumed that in an average case the acme divides the life-span exactly in half, we have to accept that some individuals live longer than the average, whereas their acme falls on a standard average age and not later, as one would expect on this theory. Two solutions are proposed to meet this difficulty: Aristotle may speak of elemental transformations, such as air into fire, where the coming to be of fire happens over the time interval numerically the same as the perishing of air; or by 'coming to be' he may mean gestation rather than growth up to the acme. Both solutions are rejected: the first, because it does not preserve the unity of the subject of change; the second, because it is not clear what kind of decay might correspond to perishing in the way in which gestation corresponds to coming to be. This discussion may be an illustration of a layered composition of the commentary: first there is a positive elaboration of Aristotle's point (going beyond the scope of the text),[86] and then there is a critical discussion of this point that effectively discards the 'positive' interpretation.

Philoponus points out that when speaking about a certain 'number' which defines the life spans of living things Aristotle has in mind species rather than individuals (294,14-26). This is in agreement with the position presented in several works attributed to Alexander, according to which the divine providence reaches as far as the species.[87] Aristotle's explanation of premature perishing in individual cases by the 'mingling of things with one another' (336b20), a notoriously difficult text, receives three different interpretations derived from two different manuscript readings 'mingling' (*sunkrasis*) and 'collision' (*sunkrousis*).[88] The first (reading *sunkrasis*) accounts for premature perishing (perhaps taking its cue from Aristotle's text at 336b21-4) with a bad mixture due to the 'unsuitability or inappropriateness of matter' (295,16). The text does not make it entirely clear whether the unsuitability (*anepitêdeiotês*) of matter is to be understood as referring to individual anomalies or to the general characteristic of matter which, in turn, creates the possibility of such anomalies. Both 'general' and 'individual' interpretations of this statement are found in Alexander's texts on providence preserved in Arabic.[89] The second and third interpretations are based on the reading *sunkrousis*. The second suggests that *sunkrousis* ('collision') should be understood in a broader sense of 'coincidence' of individual material and efficient causal factors. The efficient cause is divided into the proximate (in animal generation, the father) and first (the heavenly bodies), and the anomalies of individual comings to be are explained by the fact that the joint effect of proximate efficient and material causes counteracts the action of the first efficient cause. This interpretation seems to be a more technical elaboration of the view presented in the first one;[90] both may go back to Alexander. The third interpretation is 'astrological': according to it, 'collision' refers to combinations of heavenly bodies that act on the sublunary comings to be and thus affect the length of life of living beings that are generated. This interpretation is probably not Alexander's, although it could have been critically discussed in his commentary.[91]

Philoponus interprets Aristotle's claim that 'god has filled up the whole in the way that remained' (336b31-2) as implying that god created the heavenly bodies as well as the sublunary ones. This interpretation of Aristotle's god as efficient cause is characteristic of Ammonius and differs from the interpretations given by both Alexander and the Athenian Neoplatonists Syrianus and Proclus.[92]

Aristotle's argument for the unmoved mover (337a17-20) is described as 'rising to the transcendent causes' characteristic of Aristotle's method, with *Physics* 8 and *de Anima* 3.5 cited in parallel (299,12-21), a juxtaposition probably Neoplatonic in inspiration.

2.11 Necessity in the sphere of coming to be and perishing
In the final chapter of the treatise Aristotle considers the question whether heavenly motion, which is the cause of all coming to be and perishing, while being itself regular and continuous brings it about that some things come to be necessarily, or whether all coming to be is contingent.

In setting out the problem, Aristotle draws a distinction between things that 'will be', i.e. will come to be necessarily (the form he uses (*estai*) is the future tense of the standard verb 'to be', *einai*) and those that 'are going to be', i.e. whose coming to be is possible but not guaranteed (the verb used is *mellein*, which has the meaning of intention with animate subjects). Philoponus in his commentary explicates *mellein* as signifying the possibility whose criterion is not 'outcome, but

... unimpeded disposition' (302,30-2). This concept of possibility is found in the works of Alexander and Simplicius where it is presented as a Peripatetic elaboration on the definition of the possible based on 'mere suitability' given by Philo the Megarian.[93]

Aristotle distinguishes between two classes of things: those capable of both coming to be and not coming to be, and those incapable of not coming to be, and goes on to state the argument according to which for two connected processes of coming to be, what is earlier necessarily involves what is later only if what is later is necessary *per se*, i.e. without qualification. This argument makes use of a distinction between simple necessity (*haplôs, simpliciter*) and conditional necessity (*ex hupotheseôs, ex hypothesi*). With this result in hand, Aristotle goes on to prove that necessary coming to be is only possible in a circle, not in a straight line.

The proof proceeds by eliminating simple necessity in linear succession. Aristotle (338a5-6) considers two cases, of infinite and finite straight line. In the case of infinite line, he argues that necessity simpliciter is impossible in the direction from the earlier to the later (*eis to katô*), because in such a sequence for every 'earlier' event there is a 'later' event on account of which the earlier one must come to be; so no event seems to be free from hypothetical necessity, and thus, presumably, nothing can be necessary simpliciter.[94] In the case of a finite line, Aristotle cites an example of a house and its foundations and points out that the coming to be of the house does not always follow upon that of the foundations, whereas simple necessity is equivalent to always coming to be (337b29-33). Thus what remains is circular succession.

The proofs that Philoponus gives in his *theôria* (304,16-32) are different. Aristotle in his argument about the infinite line considers the case when coming to be is directed from the present to the future. Philoponus starts with a past-to-present direction. The key assumption of this proof is that it is impossible for anything to come to be in an infinite open line. In this, he makes use of Aristotle's argument in *GC* 2.5 and his own (or his sources') elaboration on it, according to which coming to be on an infinite straight line involves traversing infinity, which is impossible.[95] This assumption is clearly much stronger than needed for this argument. Later in the commentary we find a criticism of this interpretation of Aristotle's argument,[96] which says that Aristotle's denial of coming to be in an infinite straight line can be accepted as long as its ground is the absence of the end in an infinite linear sequence, because all coming to be presupposes the end. But insofar as such denial is based on the notion that along the infinite straight line there can be no proper succession (of 'the earlier' and 'the later'), it is not sound, and in fact contradicts Aristotle's own views on time and temporal succession in *Phys.* 4.11.

Philoponus elaborates on Aristotle's elimination of simple necessity along a finite straight line by distinguishing between the two meanings in which coming to be is said to be 'always' (*aei*): one referring to the continual character of a single coming to be (by which he understands an uninterrupted circular motion), and another referring to the repetition of one portion of circular movement, as in the case of the Sun coming to be in this sign of zodiac at regular intervals), and constructing separate proofs for each of these meanings. This distinction may go back to Alexander's commentary.[97]

In the line-by-line commentary, there is another objection out of tune with the generally favourable presentation of Aristotle's conception of hypothetical necessity.[98] The author argues that it is not true to say that nothing is necessary simpliciter unless there is a circle: weals are necessarily caused by blows, and emaciation is necessarily caused by starvation, although neither weals in the first case nor blows in the second case are necessary simpliciter; and moreover, the conditional sentence 'if a blow, then a weal' does not convert into 'if a weal, then a blow'. The objection is left unanswered. An Aristotelian reply to it might be constructed with the help of a more restricted metaphysical definition of 'things that come to be', to exclude accidents, such as weals, illnesses, and other anomalous cases that cannot be treated as proper products of any regular causal processes. The fact that 'chance' occurrences can have regularity may be due to the regular character of natural causes (e.g. dynamic properties of the elements, and properties of organisms) which operate independently from each other but whose coincidence with respect to a particular instance will produce the anomalies.[99] It is remarkable that the argument against Aristotle in support of simple necessity *a tergo* is based on medical examples. We have an argument of this kind earlier in the commentary where an attempt is made to reduce the external causal power (of a powder) to the power of an organism to receive a certain type of causal action.[100]

The final problem considered in this chapter (338b6-19) has to do with two different types of recurrence: one that preserves the numerical identity of the subject of recurrence (as in the case of heavenly bodies which come to be in the same positions preserving their individual identities), and one that preserves the same kind, but not the numerical identity of the subject of change (as in the case of men and animals). The open question, to be resolved at the end, is about the status of the sublunary elements. Aristotle starts out on the assumption that they belong to the first type of recurrence, and ends with the conclusion that they should probably be referred to the second type.

In Philoponus' commentary, we find two discussions of this problem, first as an aporetic appendix to the discussion of Aristotle's argument according to which there is no simple necessity in an infinite straight line (337b25-31, Philop. *in GC* 310,1-24); next, at its proper place in the order of Aristotle's text (338b8, Philop. *in GC* 312,5-32). The two discussions show no major doctrinal differences. The first one has the character of a paraphrase, supplying an explanation of the way in which the coming to be of man from man is cyclical and explaining the difference between the recurrences performed in a circle and in a finite straight line, and illustrating the 'numerical' recurrence with the example of sun's being in different signs of zodiac, and individual descent by the progeny of Tantalus. The second discussion follows Aristotle's text more closely, without drawing on any external literary or scientific material. It is not clear that the two discussions come from different sources, but the fact that there is a considerable overlap, if not direct repetition, deserves notice.

Philoponus gives his explanation of Aristotle's enigmatic last sentence (338b18-19) which says that the elements do not recur as numerically the same, and even if they do recur the same in number, it is not those whose substance is capable of not being; he says it refers to the elements of Empedocles which have been shown to be unchangeable. At the end he reports a remarkable problem stated by Alexander who asked why individual recurrence cannot take place, given that the matter and the efficient cause are always the same. The solution given to this problem – namely, that the recurring individuals even in this case will be recurring only in kind not in number, 'because a thing that is one and the same in number cannot have intervals' (314,18-19) agrees with Alexander's general approach to the problem of identity and persistence elsewhere.[101]

Text and translation

The translation is based on the Greek text published in *CAG* 14.2, edited by the great Italian philologist G. Vitelli (1849-1935). Vitelli lists twelve manuscripts he in some way consulted for this edition:

A   Oxoniensis Colleg. Nov. 237, s. XV
F   Ambrosianus F 113, s. XIV-XV (no. 937 Wartelle; cf. Rashed 2001)
G   Ambrosianus G 51 sup., s. XIII[4] (no. 939 Wartelle)
V   Paris. Coislinianus 166, *c*. 1360 (no. 1588 Wartelle, see below)
P   Vaticanus gr. 312, s. XIV-XV (not in Wartelle)
Q   Vaticanus gr. 499, s. XIII (last third, cf. Rashed 2001; not
      in Wartelle)
R   Riccardianus 63 , s. XIV (no. 642 Wartelle, cf. Vitelli 1894)
S   Laurentianus 85,1, s. XIV (no. 555 Wartelle)
T   Marcianus Ven. 232, s. XIV (no. 2133 Wartelle, cf. Mioni 346)
U   Marcianus Ven. 233, s. XV (no. 2134 Wartelle, cf. Mioni 347)
X   Vaticanus Gr. 2168, s. XV) (not in Wartelle)
Z   Marcianus Ven. 230, s. XIV (no. 2131 Wartelle).

and the Aldine edition (a) published in Venice in 1527.[102] Vitelli worked on the basis of collations (his own and J. Tschiedel's) of GRSTZ and the Aldine edition, while consulting other manuscripts selectively.

In the Preface to his edition Vitelli says: 'Besides, I have found many pages of the Aldine edition[103] collated with the codex V; had the collation of this codex been complete, the lacuna signs would have been less frequent in my edition (cf. 32,6 sq., 33,19 sq., 37,16 sq.), and I could have fixed other minor faults of the text (cf. 130,23; 134,25; 135,27). But since it is mainly for the sake of Aristotle that we deal with these less subtle (*phortikôtera*) commentaries, lacunae and corruptions are related to the commentator's words in such a way that almost never is it unclear what he says about Aristotle, and Philoponus, too, I believe, will not be very angry with me because of the received injustice.'

I leave it to the reader to judge whether Vitelli's assessment of the intellectual value of the commentary was right. In any case, since the scholarly goals of this translation are not restricted to a mere task of providing an exposition of Aristotle's text, but include an approach to the study of its *Wirkungsgeschichte* in new intellectual milieux, I thought it right to check the manuscript V (Paris. Coisl. 166), which was not used by Vitelli (except for several readings), and which I consulted in the microfilm. Some relevant results of this will be found in the Appendix devoted to textual questions and in the notes to the translation. It will be clear that Vitelli's conjectures often anticipate the readings of V.

The manuscript itself is an interesting document of Byzantine Aristotelian scholarship.[104] Together with Paris. gr. 1921, Coisl. 161, and Hieros. Sancti Sepulcri 150,[105] it forms a part of an important edition of Aristotle undertaken in the third quarter of the fourteenth century in Constantinople[106] under the supervision of an Aristotelian scholar whose identity (and also the hand of his scribe, if it was a different person) is still unknown,[107] who is called, after D. Harlfinger, 'Anonymus Aristotelicus'. This scholar seems to be particularly well informed in the field of philosophy. D. Harlfinger has argued that he was familiar with the now lost *Topics* commentary by Michael of Ephesus.[108] Moreover, this is the only source which has preserved the end of the *Metaphysics* commentary by Ps.-Alexander and also attributed it to Michael of Ephesus.[109] The latter attribution has now been argued for in a recent study by C. Luna.[110] The 'Anonymus Aristotelicus' is described as an intelligent and erudite reader and editor,[111] and thus V should be a respectable manuscript source to consult.

In my translation I have tried to be consistent with C.J.F. Williams's translation of the two previous volumes in this series. I have also kept his 1982 translation of Aristotle's text in the lemmata, although I have made some adjustments. Details of translation are discussed in the notes.

Acknowledgements

I am grateful to Richard Sorabji for the opportunity to work on this translation, and for his encouragement and support throughout the project. The final draft was produced during my tenure of the V.H. Galbraith Research Fellowship at St Hilda's College Oxford, hereby gratefully acknowledged. Thanks are due to many colleagues for their assistance at different stages. I am particularly grateful to Marwan Rashed for providing me with information about the readings in his forthcoming edition of Aristotle's treatise, to Emma Gannagé for the opportunity to read and discuss her forthcoming work on Alexander, and to Heidrun Eichner for showing me her forthcoming study of Averroes' *Middle Commentary* in advance of publication. All this material proved invaluable. I am grateful to anonymous vetters, Alan Bowen, Heidrun Eichner, Alan Lacey, Bob Sharples, and Simon Trépanier for written comments on parts of the text, to Sylvia Berryman, Frans de Haas, Marwan Rashed, Bob Sharples, Richard Sorabji, and Bob Todd for comments on the Introduction, and to Natasha Alechina, Alan Bowen, Heidrun Eichner, Edward Hussey, Alexander Jones, Peter Pormann, Will Rasmussen, Bob Sharples, Anna Somfai, Bob Todd, and Simon Trépanier for discussions and correspondence on specific issues. Their contributions improved the original draft and saved me from many errors. The ones that remain are my own. Special thanks are owed to my family and friends back in Russia for their love and support. The dedication is to the memory of my grandparents, Sergei Vasilyevich and Maria Korneevna Volkovs.

Notes

1. Williams 1999a, 1999b.
2. I mention only five most relevant studies of which I was able to take account in the course of preparation of this volume: Moraux 2001, Rashed 2001; Luna 2001; d'Ancona and Serra 2002; Eichner 2005 (this valuable work first came to my notice only when this volume was essentially completed; I still benefited from reading the introductory essays and the commentary, but was not able to see the edition of the Arabic text); Gannagé 2005 (forthcoming).
3. Todd 1980, 159, n. 34; K. Verrycken 1990b, 254-7.
4. On the characteristic features of style, language and structure of the commentaries produced in the school of Ammonius, see Richard 1950; Westerink 1964; Évrard 1965; C. Luna 2001.
5. Mathematics and astronomy: cf. Philoponus, *On astrolabe*, 143,9-11 Hase (in Segonds 1981); on teaching mathematics in Alexandria, cf. Mueller 1987, 306-7; on astronomy, Westerink 1971.
6. Todd 1976; 1984. The question of authorship of the medical treatises and commentaries transmitted under the name of John of Alexandria, or John the Grammarian (Yaḥyâ al-Naḥwî) should remain open until all relevant texts have been edited and studied (see Garofalo 1999, esp. 187-93; id., 2000; Pormann 2003; Schiano 2003), but medical references and allusions in Philoponus' Aristotelian commentaries should not be overlooked (cf. *in GC* 4,32-5,1; 7,26-7; 106,33-5; 308,13-28).
7. See Westerink 1971, 18-21. Recent discovery by the Polish-Egyptian archaeological expedition in Kom-el-Dikka of what seems to be the site of the school may cast new light on the history of the Alexandrian school in the fifth to seventh centuries AD (see A. Bowman in Bagnall and Rathbone 2004, 62-7).
8. The annotated translation of these fragments is forthcoming in this series

(Gannagé 2005). For the argument, see Gannagé 1998; and on *GC* 1.5, Kupreeva 2004, 314-16; Eichner 2004.

9. On the differences between this genre (designated by the term *skholai*, cf. *skholikai aposêmeiôseis* in the title of Philoponus' commentary) and the proper writings of the commentators (*hupomnêmata*), see Lamberz 1987, with reference to Philoponus 6 and n. 21.

10. On truncated lemmata in the commentaries, see Wittwer 1999, cf. Kupreeva 2001.

11. On this difference, see Lamberz, 7-16.

12. 'Embedded' quotations in Themistius' paraphrases are a good example of this. On the method of Themistius' paraphrases, see Todd 1996, 2-7.

13. Parallel readings listed in the *Appendix* are based mainly on Joachim's text; a new edition of Aristotle's treatise is now being prepared by Dr Marwan Rashed.

14. e.g. between chapters 8 and 9, 9 and 10.

15. Or in some cases, perhaps, part of the chapter (e.g. in *in GC* 2.10, the discussion on life-spans is not included in the *theôria* at the beginning of chapter, but is paraphrased in what seems to be another *theôria* (293,11-294,11), before being commented upon line by line. I am grateful to the anonymous reader for this observation). From Olympiodorus on, the structure of the commentary is more explicitly tied to the structure of the lecture course than to that of the text commented upon; *theôria* and *lexis* become clearly distinguished as parts of a *praxis* (working session) rather than (in a vague way) of Aristotelian chapters. See Westerink 1971, 6-10.

16. For the meaning of *lexis*, see Lamberz 14, n. 53, Westerink 1971, 8.

17. As in our commentary, 277,11-12/277,20; 281,1-2/282,19-20; 299,11/299,30-1; 302,11-13/306,1-2; 307,19-21/307,25. For more examples see Lamberz 14 and n. 52. Short lemmata excerpted for the purposes of a briefer explanation of lexis (306,1) (sometimes coinciding verbally with the 'long' lemmata, but serving a different purpose; still marked as lemmata).

18. This terminology has been studied in detail by C. Luna; our commentary shows many parallels to her analysis of Neoplatonic exegetical vocabulary, as will be clear from the word indices.

19. For the logical terminology used by the commentators, see useful Introductions and notes in Barnes et al., 1991; Mueller and Gould 1999a,1999b.

20. cf. 300,5-26 with notes below.

21. cf. D.L. 3,49; Albinus, *Prologue*, 148,25-9; Proclus *in Remp.* 15.19-27 Kroll; Alcinous, *did.* 6, 158, 27-31 and n. 91 (Whittaker); discussions in Opsomer 1998, 27-33; Reis 1999.

22. There are several cases where *phêsi* without a subject (and determining context) seems to refer to the source other than Aristotle (Ammonius or Alexander): 253,11; 265,28; 302,3.8-10; 314, 21 (*eipen* probably refers to Alexander, although the immediate reference may still be Ammonius); cf. 295, 26 (*phasi*).

23. *phêmi* occurs 31 times in the whole commentary; five times in the part translated in the present volume: 251,28; 292,7; 295,21; 299,25; 314,5; in only one case, 251,28, it may have something like personal reference (in other cases meaning 'i.e.') .

24. cf. *emoi (de) dokei* at 8.2, 255,21.

25. See 269,25-270,6; 271,25-272,10 and n. 206; 308,13-28 and n. 464; 309,20-31 and n. 473

26. See Index of Passages.

27. *In GC* 2.10, 292,31-2.

28. 249,18; 255,18; 268,1; 287,10.26; 291,19; 314,9.

29. 241,27; 243,29-244,2; 263,11-12; 264,18; 275,24; 279,26-8; 282,32-283,2 (*Quaest.* 1.10); 289,27-290,7 (*Quaest.* 3.4); 291,12-15 (*Prov.* 45,1-7 Ruland); 292,30-1; 293,2-3 (*Prov.* 37,1-10 Ruland); 295,16-17 (*Prov.*, 103,2-9 Ruland; D15 103,3-105,4 Ruland); 297,27 (*Fat.* 22, 192,1; 25, 195,19); 298,10 (*de An.* 4,27-5,12); 298,10-12 (*de An.* 4,27-5,12); 302,31-2 (*in An. Pr.* 183,29-184,8); 304,29 (*Quaest.* 3.5, 88,22-89,2); 304,35-7 (*Quaest.* 3.5, 87,32-88,4); 306,22-3 (*Quaest.* 3.5, 89,2-18); 310,21-4 (*Quaest.* 3.5, 88,17-21); 311,19-21 (*Quaest.* 2.22, 71,10-12; 3.5); 312,25-8 (*Quaest.* 3.5, 89,18-24); 313,9-13 (*Fat.* 24, 194,8-15); cf. 296,7-8 (*Fat.* 6, 170,4 and 169,23-5).

30. 286,2.7-10; 288,24-6; 297,17; cf. 269,25-270,5 and n. 193 below.

31. Fihrist: 'There is a complete commentary by Yaḥyâ the Grammarian on the *De generatione et corruptione*. The Arabic version is worse than the Syriac version' (Flügel 251, trans. in Peters 1968, 37); al-Qiftî: 'Yaḥyâ the Grammarian commented on it and his commentary is extant in Syriac and was translated into Arabic. Those skilled in Syriac say that the Syriac version is better than the Arabic version' (Lippert 40,18-41,2, trans. in Peters 1968, 38). On the Arabic tradition of Aristotle's treatise and its commentaries, see Rashed 2003, Eichner 2004, Gannagé 2005.

32. cf. Nasr and Mohaghegh, 1972, [13,7] 'And you must have taken this objection from Yaḥyâ al-Naḥwî, who was pretending for the Christians to declare his disagreement with Aristotle in this argument, whereas for anyone who looks into his commentary to the end of the *On Coming-to-Be and Perishing* and other books, his agreement with Aristotle in this question cannot but be obvious.' For discussions, see Rashed 2003, Eichner 2004.

33. 'There is a commentary by Olympiodorus in the version of Astât' (Peters 1968, 37).

34. It is signalled in Dietrich 1966, 182, and its English translation will appear in Gannagé 2005.

35. See Eichner 2002 and 2004; cf. Kupreeva 2004, 315 n. 56.

36. MS Bodl. Selden. Sup. 24. I am grateful to Marwan Rashed for drawing my attention to this fact. See also Yudycka 1981, XXXIX-XLVII; Durling 1994, 320-30; Besnier 2003.

37. For a brief survey of the fortuna of Philoponus' commentary in Renaissance Latin, see de Haas, 2004, X-XII; useful material and a list of sixteenth-century editions of Philoponus' Aristotelian commentaries is to be found in Schmitt 1987.

38. cf. Rashed 2001, 8-13.

39. 237,29-238,7; 244,29-245, 8; 245,18-246,19. Whoever included it in the division, the discussion of Stoic cosmology probably has Alexander's commentary as its source. Gannagé, sec. 94 (*ahl al-riwâq*).

40. As our commentator notes, 248,13-14.

41. cf. 193, 28-9 with Alexander *Mixt.* 2, 215,13-18, with Todd's notes ad loc. I am grateful to Sylvia Berryman for her suggestions on the argument of this paragraph.

42. 247,22-5.

43. Cherniss 1971, 123, Verdenius and Waszink, Migliori ad loc. (references and discussion in C.J.F. Williams 332b5), all of whom attribute this theory to Anaximenes. In our commentary, this attribution is not made: the arguments are developed against 'those who posit air as principle' (247, 5) and 'those who say that water is the principle' (247,13-14) alike.

44. C.J.F. Williams ad loc.

45. cf. Philoponus' comment on 332a13-17 (240,25) with C.J.F. Williams' remarks ad loc.; reported Alexander's criticism of Aristotle's argument for the change of the extremes (249,18-24 with n. 77); 251,1-252,6.

46. 257,8-13, with n. 109.

47. 251,1-252,6 with nn. 83, 85.

48. 258,12-13: 'as when I say "water is as cold as fire is hot" ', the case not considered by Aristotle and not appearing in the line-by-line discussion of the text, but only in the *theôria*.

49. 260,14-20, Philoponus or his source draws on *Meteor*.1.3, 340a11f., cf. 258,33-259,3 and n. 120.

50. 260,20-7.

51. 262,5-7, cf. 262,19-25.

52. 259,22: the three-dimensional is described as the matter (*hulê*) of contrary qualities.

53. 262,5-9.

54. On the role of the conception of matter as three-dimensional in Philoponus' later philosophy, see Sorabji 1983, 23-43, de Haas 1997, Sorabji 2004, vol. 2, 17(g)-(h) (263-8).

55. In fact, there are some indirect signs to the contrary, cf. 265,15 and n. 160.

56. See 266,4-5 and n. 166. O. Primavesi in a recent publication credits Philoponus' teacher Ammonius with five 'new' verses of Empedocles (i.e. not found in the earlier sources). This does not necessarily mean that Ammonius quotes those verses from a primary source, but at least indicates a certain breadth of his textual basis (for comparison, Alexander has one 'new' verse and one 'new' half-verse on nine verses and six half-verses, according to the same calculations, Primavesi 2002).

57. For the reading, see 268,1-2 with n. 177. For discussion of this passage, see Frohn-Villeneuve 1980, 124-36.

58. A mixture in a strict sense must itself be homoeomerous (*GC* 1.10, 328a10-11).

59. *GC* 1.10, 327b27-9.

60. For discussion, see Kupreeva 2004, 308-12.

61. *Mixt*. 15, 231.22-30, discussion in Kupreeva 2004, 310.

62. *in GC* 1.10, 188,17-30; de Haas 1999, Berryman 1999b. It should be noted that although it is to be understood as being 'lower grade' potentiality compared to the 'second potentiality', in the sense that its operation is inhibited by the conditions of mixture, nonetheless, in terms of its own coming to be, it is as well-formed as the 'second potentiality': there is no additional immanent process for it to undergo before being released into action.

63. The transition is in fact rather abrupt; having stated a strong defence of anti-Aristotelians on mixture, Philoponus continues blandly: 'In this way then, Aristotle proves that it is impossible to make flesh, bone and each of the others from the elements if they are unchangeable' (270, 6f.) This summarising remark would have been more appropriate at 269, 5.

64. Simplicius, *in Cael.*, 659,11-661,14, discussion in de Haas 1999, 40-4, cf. also 270,2-5 with n. 193. For the discussion of the idea of *minima naturalia* in Philoponus, see Berryman 1999b, 8; in Averroes, Glasner 2001.

65. cf. n. 25 above. In the former case, we might suspect some kind of an omission or transposition in Philoponus' notes.

66. 270,16-271,7.

67. 'Pure fire' (*qua* substance rather than any of its characteristics such as 'heat' or 'the form of fire') features only three times in the passage 270,16-271,25, neither of which seem to me to contain a definitive doctrine of fire retained *qua* substance: 270,21: denial that there is pure fire in a compound; 271,5-7: a composite is said to have an inhibited form of fire, and therefore the whole fire, not pure, but inhibited (here there is a commitment to the view that some substance 'inhibited fire' is preserved in a mixture); 271,11-12: in a description of the kinds of potentiality he says that a compound does not have a disposition and potentiality of pure fire, because it does not have a power of fire. Later in the commentary we find a more definitive statement of the conception of 'inhibited fire', but it is defined as 'what is hot relatively to something else' (276,18-23), and one can wonder how much difference this second view really involves.

68. And so is its force, I would argue. It could be (a) a request for a more precise account of 'inhibited fire' in which case it might be reconcilable with the account found later in the commentary (cf. previous note), or, alternatively, a difference could be stated more explicitly; (b) a denial of a distinction between prime and proximate matter, a stronger claim, for which a stronger argument would be expected. With regard to the sources, Frans de Haas has suggested 'that Ammonius relied on Alexander for most of his account, and that Philoponus added this criticism as a consideration of his own .... Alternatively, the remark may simply derive from Ammonius' lectures' (de Haas 1999, 35, n. 51). The question is perhaps best treated as empirical, to be decided by forthcoming research on the Neoplatonic use of Alexander's commentaries.

69. For the exposition of this principle on the basis of Aristotle's *Metaph*. 2.1, 993b24, see Alexander, *in Metaph*. 147,15-28 (I am grateful to Frans de Haas for this reference); for further instances of violation of causal transmission, see Sorabji 2004, vol. 2, 6(f) (141-8). Cf. Lloyd 1976, and 278, 29-279,2 with n. 240. Philoponus apparently is on record for this discrepancy with the Neoplatonic 'mainstream'. The examples he cites (as in the case of the cold causing solidification) may indicate his (or his source's) stronger dependence on a certain group of Peripatetic texts in this matter rather than any original 'schismatic' tendency (cf. Aristotle *GC* 1.5, 320b21; on the role of heat and cold in Aristotle's *Meteorology*, Solmsen 1961, 412-20; Furley 1987; on Theophrastus, Steinmetz 1964, 123-6, Federspiel 2003).

70. On the use of the term *arkhai* for causes, see C.J.F. Williams ad loc.

71. *Quaest*. 1.10, (20,32-21,5 Bruns). Cf. Alexander, *in Metaph*. 1.3, 22,3-4; cf. *in Metaph*. 2.3, 169,17-19; 5.8, 375,37-376,4; *Mixt*. 13, 229,8; discussions in Sorabji 1988, 42 and n. 69, Sharples 1990, 59, n. 169, de Haas 1997, 286 n. 21, Fazzo 2002, 114-45 (Philoponus' text is not discussed).

72. 283,10-15, cf. Alexander, *Quaest*. 1.10, 21,5-7 B.: the difficulty is implicit in the statement ('it is not the case that, if two matters are different from each other, that which is the substrate in the divine body and that which is in the things subject to coming-to-be and passing-away, therefore they are compound', Sharples trans.)

73. 283,15-17, cf. Alexander *Quaest*. 1.15, 26,29-30, where the problem is formulated in terms of difference because of either form or matter.

74. 283,15-25: the solution says that the matter of sublunary things must be characterised by potentiality, because otherwise it could not have received the opposite having lost the form it had, and the matter of heavenly bodies must not have the potentiality of losing the form, because if it does it will lose it (the principle of plenitude at work here). This argument is not on the list of solutions in *Quaest*. 1.15. We should note Alexander's argument preserved by Simplicius according to which heavenly bodies do partake of potentiality to a degree, but do not change into a contrary because there is no contrary to a circular movement (Alexander ap. Simpl. *in Phys*. 1218,20-36, discussion in Fazzo 2002, 141-4); cf. Michael of Ephesus, ('Alexander') *in Metaph*. 9.8, 592,39-40.

75. Philoponus *Contra Aristotelem*, fr. 59 Wildberg; Sorabji 1988, 15; Wildberg 1988, 181-5, de Haas 1997, 286 and n. 21.

76. For most recent edition of the papyrus and the account of *status quaestionis*, see Medri 2003; for attribution to Philoponus, see McCoull and Siorvanes 1990; discussions in Falcon 2003; Wildberg 2003.

77. 286,1-2; on Ammonius' metaphysics, see Verrycken 1990a, 1990b.

78. See 286,10-16.

79. This interpretation, if it could be established as definitive, would be in a fairly close agreement with the attested view of Ammonius (cf. Verrycken 1990a, 208-10). In other commentaries based on the works of Ammonius' circle this tendency sometimes gets a more explicit rhetorical elaboration. Cf. Michael of Ephesus ('Alexander') *in Metaph.* 8.6, 1045a36, 563,24-564,22, especially 563,29-32 for distancing from those, who, like Plato, say that participation is the cause of unity, but fail to explain the cause of participation; and further 564,16-22: 'And behold the divine power of teaching that is in this man [viz. Aristotle], how – because it was not possible to do it differently – from the last things, and those known to us he skilfully contrives to lead us on to the much esteemed father and creator (*poiêtên*) of all, in showing that just as the copper-smith is the cause of the bronze and sphere being one, so too his unifying and creative power is the cause for all things that are to be the way they are.'

80. 286,19.29 (see n. 296 ad 286,19).

81. *de Aeternitate mundi contra Proclum* (=*Aet.*) 11.3, 413.21-414.10 Rabe.

82. 287,19-20; for Neoplatonic theories of causes and causation, see now Sorabji 2004, vol. 2, 6(f-g).

83. Williams 1982 dismisses the account in *Metaphysics* as unsatisfactory; Alexander apparently treats it as an elliptic statement of what he takes to be the same argument of *GC* 2.10 (see nn. 326, 327 below).

84. See 289,27-290,7 with nn. 315-17.

85. See 292,13-293,8 with nn. 333, 334.

86. This 'positive' interpretation seems to be resumed without any reservations at 294,30-295,5.

87. cf. *Prov.* 87,5-89,7 Ruland; *Quaest.* 2.21 (68,5-15).

88. See text at 295,8-296,10, Appendix at 336b20 and nn. 350-8.

89. Cited in n. 356 ad 295,16-17.

90. The unsuitability of matter plays a substantial part here, too, cf. 296, 2-3.

91. As it is in *Fat.* 6, cf. n. 368 ad 296,7-8 (cf. also Averroes, in n. 358). L.G. Westerink argues that astrology, along with astronomy, might have been a regular part of the scientific quadrivium in the school of Alexandria in mid-sixth century, cf. Westerink 1971, 18-21, on the time of Ammonius 19-20.

92. See Verrycken 1990a, 215-26, on Philoponus 223-6 and n. 189. Cf. Philoponus *in GC* 1.7, 152,23-153,2 (Williams 1999b, 55 and nn. 47-9).

93. Alexander, *in An. Pr.* 184,6-10; *Quaest.* 1.4, 1.18; Simplicius, *in Categ.* 195,32-196,3; discussions in Todd 1972, 26-7; Sorabji 1983, 78-9; Sharples 1992; Bobzien 1998, 108-16. It is clear from Philoponus' own commentary *in An. Pr.* 169,19-21 that he is aware of Philo's definition.

94. 337b25-9 (cf. 338a6-10). My interpretation seems to be different from that of C.J.F. Williams (who takes *emprosthen* at 337b26 to mean 'before', i.e. referring to the preceding member of the succession) and in agreement with that of Joachim.

95. *GC* 2.5, 333a8-13, Philoponus *in GC*, 254,17-255,28.

96. 309,20-31. Again, we can think of Philoponus' authorship, although there is nothing to indicate this in the introductory phrase (*isteon de hôs dokei mê* *katôrthômenon einai to toiouton epikheirêma*). Only the fact that this criticism (as several others in the commentary) is left without response can suggest this.

97. cf. Alexander, *Quaest.*3.5, 87,32-88,4; Philop. *in GC* 304,35-7 and n. 441 ad loc.

98. 308,13-28: introduced by the phrase: *doxei de polla antipiptein tois pros Aristotelous legomenois*. As in several other cases noted above, this objection is left without reply.

99. cf. Sharples 1979,33 and n. 98; for this interpretation of Aristotle and for a detailed argument in support of Aristotelian position, see Sorabji 1983, 3-69.

100. *in GC* 1.5, 97,15-99,5.

101. I discuss Alexander's position in Kupreeva 2004. Richard Sorabji kindly draws my attention to the related discussion of the individuation of change by Aristotle in *Phys.* 5.4.

102. On the text of the Aldine, see Vitelli's Preface in *CAG* 14.2, x. The Aldine editor completely overhauls the original lemmata of his MSS. He expands Philoponus' truncated lemmata in such a way that all of them taken together would give a full text of *GC*; where the expanded lemmata incorporate several of the old truncated ones, he eliminates the division of argument and combines separate arguments into a single one under his new longer 'lemma', sometimes inserting connecting sentences in place of the old lemmata to make the argument run smoothly.

103. *complures praeterea editionis Aldinae paginas cum codice V collatas inveni.* The Latin is ambiguous as the term *editio* in the textual criticism may refer generally either to the edition proper or to the copy of edition (I owe this point to Bob Todd), and in this case it must refer to the copy that Vitelli used, as his examples of readings make clear. I am grateful to Bob Sharples for discussion of this point.

104. Apart from the *GC* with Philoponus' commentary (ff. 252r-302v), it contains Aristotle's *Physics* with scholia from Philoponus' and Simplicius' commentaries, the *Cael.* with Simplicius' commentary, the *Meteor.* with commentaries, the *de Mundo*, a part of the *de Motu Animalium* followed by the *Long.* See Mondrain 2000,20; cf. Rashed 2001, 229-36.

105. Mondrain 2000, 20.

106. See Mondrain 2000, 20-1.

107. Cacouros 1998 argues for his identity with Neophytos Prodromenos; Mondrain 2000 associates him, without a more precise identification, with the circle of Philotheus Kokkinos, the patriarch appointed by John Cantacuzene.

108. Harlfinger 1996, 49, plate 20.

109. In Paris. gr. 1876, Mondrain 2000,19; Rashed 2001, 230.

110. Luna 2001.

111. On him as a textual critic, cf. Harlfinger in Hadot 1987, 244-5; Mondrain 2000, 19-21.

Conventions

< > = additions to the text made by Vitelli; in the lemmata, additions made by Williams
[ ] = English or Greek supplied by the translator
*** = lacuna in the Greek text

Transliterations of the Arabic are given as in J.M. Cowan (ed.) *Hans Wehr, A Dictionary of Modern Written Arabic (Arabic – English)*, 4th ed., Urbana, Ill., 1994, except for the following letters:

th:	ث	s̲:	ص
ḥ:	ح	d̲:	ض
kh:	خ	t̲:	ط
dh:	ذ	z̲:	ظ
sh:	ش	gh:	غ

PHILOPONUS
On Aristotle
On Coming-to-Be
and Perishing 2.5-11

Translation

On the Second Book of Aristotle's
On Coming-to-Be and Perishing

<2.5. NO FIRST ELEMENT>

332a3 Furthermore, let us consider them also this way.   237,4

Having shown that the elements are four and all change into each   5
other, and having explained, further, the mode of their change into
one another, he now sets out, as though having made some sort of a
fresh start, to apply himself to another study which is appropriate in
the analysis of the elements. It should be explained what this [study]
is.[1] At the start of the book, he had expounded some opinions that the
ancients had about the principles, not discussing all of them, but only   10
briefly refuting that of Anaximander,[2] and had criticised Timaeus[3] for
not defining clearly [his concepts] about matter [GC 2.1, 329a13-24].
Now, after the demonstration of the elements that he laid down
himself [GC 2.2-4], he expounds all the views about the elements,
both the ones that the ancients held, and the ones that it is possible
to posit as following from the division; and refuting all the others,
leaves to stand as true the one that was stated by himself.[4]   15
    The aim of the proposed study can also be defined as follows.[5]
Having stated that there are three principles – matter, contrariety,
elements [GC 2.1, 329a27-35] – and having after that treated of the
contrarieties, hot/cold and dry/moist, and moreover, of the elements,
he now wants to treat also of the matter underlying the elements:
whether one of these underlies all of them, or whether something   20
other than these [does].
    So, in order that we would more easily follow each of the [teach-
ings] handed down, a division should be additionally assumed, in
which everything that will be said is embraced.[6]
    For, someone who posits corporeal principles of things must say
either (Ia) that there is one or (Ib) that there are more. And if one, it
must be either (IIa=1) different from the four, as Anaximander said,
or (IIb) one of the four, as Heraclitus, Thales, and others [did].[7] And   25
if one of the four, either (IIIa) *qua* unchangeable or (IIIb) *qua* that
which is subject to change.[8] And if unchangeable, either (IVa) as
holding the status of matter with respect to the three others and the
things that are composed of them, as those said who assumed air or
fire to be the principle of existing things; or (IVb=3) as not having
even the relation of matter towards the others, [a view] which no one
held. If, on the other hand, someone were to say that (IIIb) it is one

Philoponus' *diairesis* of views on the elements

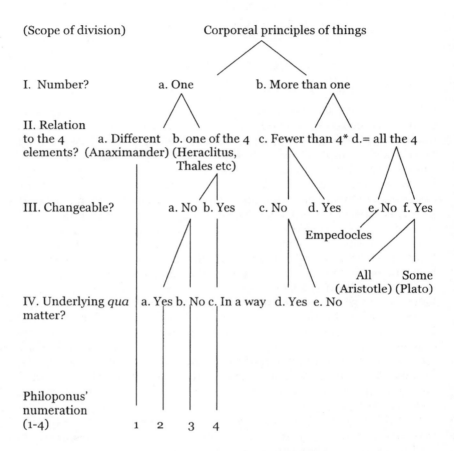

(Scope of division)   Corporeal principles of things

I. Number?   a. One   b. More than one

II. Relation
to the 4   a. Different   b. one of the 4   c. Fewer than 4* d.= all the 4
elements? (Anaximander) (Heraclitus,
                          Thales etc)

III. Changeable?   a. No b. Yes   c. No   d. Yes   e. No f. Yes

                                                      Empedocles

                                                              All   Some
                                                           (Aristotle) (Plato)

IV. Underlying *qua* a. Yes b. No c. In a way d. Yes e. No
matter?

Philoponus'
numeration
(1-4)   1   2   3   4

Roman numerals with letters are used for the reconstructed steps of
Philoponus' division. Arabic numerals (1-4) correspond to Philoponus'
own numeration which he uses discussing some doctrines from the
division.

*II-c: 'Fewer than four'. Earlier in the commentary (*in GC* 2.1, 207, 15-20,
see Williams 1999b,117), Philoponus attributes to Parmenides the doctrine
of two elements (fire and earth), and to Ion of Chios that of three elements
(earth, fire, air).

[of the four] and changeable, (IVc=4) that [entity] cannot be possibly 30
assumed to be the principle *qua* matter, but perhaps it is possible to 238,1
say [about it] that it is the principle in a different way, a kind of more
proximate matter, as e.g. nothing could come to be from prime matter
unless fire came to be first, if fire is the principle, and without being
changed through the medium of that [i.e. fire] into the nature of the
others, i.e. air, water, earth. So what comes to be air must prior [to 5
this] have come to be fire, and in the same way too water must come
to be water by virtue of having earlier passed through the [stage of]
fire, and similarly with the others.[9] This, then, is the case if the
principle were one. If (Ib) there are more, they are either (IIc) fewer
than four,[10] or (IId) all four; for no one has suggested a greater
number. Now, if we posit (IIc) *some* of the four as the principles, then
again it is necessary to say that those are either (IIIc) unchangeable
or (IIId) changeable. And if (IIIc) unchangeable, then either (IVd) 10
underlying the others *qua* matter or (IVe) not. And generally, all that
was said about one [of them] can be said about more, as long as they
are less in number than four. If, however, (IId) they are four, we shall
either say, (IIIe) as Empedocles [does],[11] that they are unchangeable,
or (IIIf) that they are changeable. And if changeable, either all of
them, as is his [viz. Aristotle's] opinion, or some [changeable] and
some not, as Plato said who thought the earth to be unchangeable.[12] 15
The whole division, then, is something like that.[13]

Now, he first turns to the second branch of the division, the one
according to which one of the four, being unchangeable, is the material principle of the others [332a4-20]. Then, having refuted that, he
will also make some objections to the view of Anaximander, which he
has refuted in the preceding [*GC* 2.1, 329a10-12], and refutes now
again by some further arguments [332a20-30]. And after this he turns 20
to the fourth branch, which assumes [as the principle] one of the four
[*qua*] changeable.

As to the third branch – the one that says that a certain one of the
four is the principle, being unchangeable and not underlying in the
status of matter – he does not even consider it worthy of discussion,
since it is plainly foolish. For if it is unchangeable and does not
underlie *qua* matter, how will it be the principle of the others, having
no relation to them? 25

And by the same arguments [as those] by which the previous
branches are refuted, the assumption that takes [only] some of the
four to be principles is refuted.[14] For it too assumes [them to be] either
unchangeable or changeable, and either having the relation of matter
towards the others or not. So the refutations will be common too, as
we show in the course of the argument.

30   **332a4** For if some[15] of the natural bodies are matter, as some
            believe, water, air, and such.

            He now refutes the branch according to which a certain one of the
            natural simple bodies is the matter of the others.

239,1   **332a5-7** It is necessary that this be either one or two, or more.
            [But everything cannot be one, e.g. everything be air or water or
            fire or earth]

            Having said that someone who assumes the principle of the other
            [elements] to be unchangeable and to have the relation of matter [to
            them] has to assume [that it is] either a certain one of the four, or two,
            or more, he next goes on to expound[16] the argument for the case of
5   one, when he says 'but everything cannot be one'. For by the same
            arguments by which we prove that a certain one [of the elements]
            cannot be the matter of the remaining four, we prove that neither two
            nor three [can be that]. This is why he makes an argument as if for
            the case of one.[17]

            332a7 If change is to contraries.

            He says that if it has been agreed that change is to contraries, then
10   it is impossible for either air or water to be the matter of the
            remaining [elements]. For it is using this [thesis] that he sub-
            sequently proves the impossibility, as we shall learn.

            332a8 For if it were air, given that it persisted.

            Saying 'given that it persisted', he allows supplying in thought an
            alternative, namely 'given that it did not persist, but changed'. For
15   this is the opposite member of the dichotomy;[18] he examines it next,
            as the fourth branch of the received division [of opinions].[19] But we
            must now consider the way in which he refutes, prior to that, the
            present [thesis], [as he argues] that it is impossible that a certain one
            of the remaining four should be the unchangeable matter of the rest.

            332a8-10 Given that it persisted, what there would be would be
            alteration not generation; although it does not seem possible
            even on those terms for them [to exist] at the same time,[20] so
            that water was at the same time air or anything else.

20   He says, if it is the case that from one of the four, which is not
            undergoing change, and yet is underlying in the status of matter and
            persisting, others are produced, then first of all, he says, this will no
            longer be generation, but alteration (for change which comes about in

that which is being made to have form in respect of quality is alteration, and all the elements, of which a certain one has been assumed to produce the others, being [itself] persistent, are made to have form).[21]

Further, he says, if air (for let this be assumed to be the principle) while being persistent comes to be fire, fire and air will be the same thing. But this both militates against the evidence and will involve [as its consequence] that contraries are present in the same [substratum].[22] For suppose, on this assumption, that air, while being persistent [*qua* air], has become fire. Since, because the opposition 'hot/cold' is tangible, one of the contraries has to be in the fire, let us assume that it is hot. Then air which has become fire will be nothing but hot air, and therefore it would be true that [the process that] comes about is not coming to be but alteration. Further, it [air] will also necessarily have contraries in the same [substratum]. For if air by having become hot has been completed as fire, it is clear that prior to that it was not hot. For had it been hot [before], how has it become hot? And if it did not have the [quality of] heat, then it was completely occupied by the contrary quality. For change is from contraries, and it has been previously assumed that [these] contrarieties are common, occupied by all. Accordingly, if air, not being hot, has become hot, by changing into fire, then it surely was cold. But even now, being fire, it has preserved the nature of air; hence it will have in the same [state] coldness *qua* air and heat *qua* fire.

The same [conclusion follows] too if air, persisting [*qua* air] and changing into fire has become dry. For it was moist too. Hence it will be at the same time both dry and moist. And he proves this for the converse case. For fire, he says, reverting into the substance of air loses heat, and having lost it, necessarily acquires coldness, by the additionally assumed axiom. But if air, cold by its nature, has become fire, and not changed (for this has been the assumption), then it has therefore acquired heat and coldness in the same [state] which is impossible. And he called air 'cold' continuing the argument in accordance with the assumption. For in truth in the coming to be of fire from air, the change is in respect of the moist and the dry.[23]

332a13-17 And vice versa, if there is to be air from fire, this will happen through the heat changing into its contrary. This [contrary] will accordingly belong to the air[24] [and the air will be something cold, so that it is impossible for it to be hot air because the same thing would then be simultaneously hot and cold].

The conversion does not seem to me necessary.[25] For fire is not assumed to persist also when it has become[26] air, but to change.[27] And if so, then it does not change *qua* hot, in order to become air, but *qua* dry. And perhaps the previous statement is not necessary either.[28]

For let air, while persisting, come to be fire and thus undergo alteration. But it must not undergo alteration in respect of the hot, so as to
30   become both cold and hot (for it is hot), but in respect of the dry, the
[resulting] incongruity being that it is both dry and moist, not cold
and dry.

241,1   **332a17-18 Both therefore[29] will be some other identical thing
[and some other matter common to them both]**

He says, if the air persisting unchanged cannot possibly produce fire,
it is clear that some other underlying thing, while remaining the
same, will be both fire and air, becoming at one time this, and at
5   another time that, and that is matter.

**332a20-2 Nor for that matter is there anything else besides
these [as it were some intermediate between air and water, or
air and fire, coarser than air and fire and finer than the others].**

From what has been said, he says, it is clear that none of the four can
be the matter of the rest, nor in fact can anything else be the matter
of the four while being a body and subsisting apart from the four. And
10   here he turns to the view of Anaximander, which assumes a certain
body that subsists as an intermediate between air and fire or water
and air,[30] which he already refuted earlier, but refutes now again, by
different arguments.

**332a22-3 Fire and air will in that case be that [intermediate
thing] together with a contrariety.[31]**

As to the intermediate [thing] of Anaximander, he says, if being a
15   subsistent body it persists in the change in respect of each of the two,
it will of necessity have contrariety in relation to each of the two, and
will be hot and cold in the same respect.[32]
    (i) For if it has been agreed that what changes does so from
contrary to contrary [*Phys.* 1.5, 1.7-9], it is clear that this body of
Anaximander becoming hot in its change into fire, comes to be hot
from [being] cold. Therefore coldness is considered to be present in it
20   in accordance with its essence [*kata ousian*]. And if this has become
fire, while having persisted, it is clear that it has become hot without
losing coldness. Hence it will have the contrary in the same [substra-
tum]. For insofar as it has become hot – clearly, from cold, because
change must come about from the contrary – to that extent we retain[33]
coldness in the intermediate body. But insofar as we say, again, that
it produces fire, while [itself] persisting – to that extent we are
25   constrained to say that in the same way as the heat, the coldness is
also present in the underlying [body], which is impossible.[34]

It is better to establish the proposed thesis in the following way.[35] (ii) If this intermediate [body], which, as they say, is denser than fire but thinner than air,[36] differs from fire in no other respect except density, so as to make fire by adding only rarefaction, then clearly all the other [properties] assumed to be present in fire belonged to it as 242,1 well. So it would have been dry by nature; for it is by condensation and rarefaction that they generate the rest from it. But in the same way, if it became air by having added only density of texture, as many other [properties] as there are in air belonged to it. But moisture is one of these [properties] that belong to air. Hence moisture was in the 5 intermediate body. But by the previous assumption we have also posited dryness. Hence, the same [thing] is both dry and moist, which is impossible.[37]

(iii) Or in a third way, more briefly, as follows.[38] If this [body] intermediate between fire and air comes to be each of them, and every change is from contrary to contrary, and fire is hot, then it [the intermediate body] was cold. But changing again into water it be- 10 comes cold; hence it was hot. Consequently it will be cold and hot simultaneously. The case will be the same with the dry and the moist. For insofar as it changes into fire in respect of the dry, [the interme-diate body] will be moist; and [insofar as it changes] into air in respect of the moist, it will be dry. Hence it will be dry and moist simultane-ously.

And this is [the meaning of the sentence]: 'Fire and air will in that case be that [intermediate thing] together with a contrariety.'[39]

332a23 But one of the pair of contraries is a privation. 15

He brings this up as though in order to amplify the impossibility. For if it has been agreed that it is impossible for a state and its privation to be in the same [substratum] then it is also impossible for the contraries to be in the same [substratum]. For indeed one of the contraries, the better one, bears analogy to form, while the other one does so to privation.[40] And it has been also said previously that the 20 better of the contraries bears analogy to form, e.g. of the white and black, the white to form and the black to privation.[41]

332a24 So it is not possible [for this thing ever] to be isolated.

By 'to be isolated' he means 'to subsist by itself'. He says that it was thus made clear from what was said that apart from the four ele- 25 ments there is not any other body subsisting by itself. Or perhaps 'to be isolated' means rather 'to subsist without some quality of other [elements], e.g. heat or coldness'.[42] But it has been shown that these have to be assumed [as being] in a body that subsists by itself, in accordance with what those people say.[43]

243,1   **332a25-30** It must then be any one of the elements indifferently,
or nothing. If, then, nothing perceptible at least is prior to these,
these will be everything. [Necessarily, therefore, they will either
be such as always to remain and not change into one another, or
such as to change; and either all of them, or some but not others,
in accordance with what Plato wrote in the *Timaeus*.]

Having shown that it is not possible that any of the four [elements]
should be the matter of the rest, and having added the counter-argu-
ments against Anaximander, he now says concluding that because
5   the status of each of the four elements has equal importance, either
each of them must be matter and a corporeal principle, or none of
them. Now, since we have proved in the case of one [of them] that it
cannot be related to the others as matter, it is clear that none of them
will be the matter of the rest. We have shown, too, that nor will any
body different from the four generate the others as matter, as Anaxi-
10   mander believes. And by the same arguments by which we have
demonstrated that one of the four [elements] cannot be the matter of
the rest, it will be proved that nor will [any] two of them, e.g. fire and
earth, as Parmenides said,[44] be the matter of the rest, viz. air and
water. For if fire and earth produce air and water, while persisting
15   and not changing, the arguments stated earlier will apply. Similarly,
nor will the three be the matter of the remaining one. So, since
neither any other body apart from the four is the material principle
of things, nor any one of the four, nor any two or three of the four, and
[yet] there must be a corporeal principle of things, 'all these four', he
says, 'will be' the principle,[45] not of each other (for this has been
20   shown to be impossible), but of the composites. The matter of these
[viz. the four elements] is not corporeal, but incorporeal and formless.[46] But all these four are the matter of the composites that follow
upon [them]. But if all [four] are the principle and matter of the
composites, is it *qua* unchangeable, he says, as is Empedocles' view,[47]
or *qua* changeable into each other? And if they change into each other,
25   is it that some change and some do not, as Plato said, who assumed
that earth is unchangeable,[48] or do all change into each other, as we
have shown, because all have contrariety in relation to each other?

    332a30-4 That it is in fact necessary that they should change[49]
    into one another has been proved above [and it has been said
    above that different ones do not come into existence from each
    other equally fast, since those that have a counterpart come into
    existence from each other quicker, and those that do not have
    one, slower].

He recalls what was said earlier, taking up the argument that all of
30   them change into each other because all of them have contrariety in

relation to each other, and that some [of them] change more easily, 244,1
[namely] those that have some association with each other, and some
more slowly, [viz.] those that have no kinship with each other;[50] and
that the simple bodies must be four, because there are two contrarieties in respect of which they change into each other, [i.e. the one] of
the hot and the cold and [the one] of the dry and the moist. When the 5
two contrarieties are combined with one another, there come to be six
pairs, of which two are incapable of being composed,[51] while the
remaining four when composed give form to the four elements.[52]

332a34-b5 So, if there is just one contrariety according to which
they change, there will have to be two of them [; for the intermediate is the matter which is imperceptible and inseparable.
Since, however, there are seen to be more than this, two contrarieties are the least there could be. And given two of them there
cannot be three <elements> but four, as is obvious; for this is the
number of pairings, since, of the six there are, two cannot occur,
as comprising qualities contrary to one another].

What he says is the following. If the contrariety in respect of which 10
the elements change is one, e.g., that of the hot and the cold, then
there would have been only two elements, viz. one hot and another
cold. For matter, he says, does not make something third, because it
is intermediate, i.e. underlying the contrariety and receiving each of
the contraries in turn, being itself imperceptible and formless,[53] and 15
never subsisting by itself.

332b5-7 These matters have been spoken of earlier. What follows will show that it is impossible, given that they change into
one another, for any of them, [whether one of the extremes or
one of the intermediate ones] to be their principle.

After proving that some one of the four [elements] cannot be the
principle of the rest while remaining unchanging, he now proves that
even if it is changeable, it will not be related to the rest as principle. 20
[He proves this] in order to have it proven that neither *qua* unchangeable, nor *qua* changeable, can any one [of the elements] be assumed
to be the principle of the others. What is being expounded now is the
fourth branch of the division set out in the beginning,[54] the one that
claims some one of the four [elements] to be, *qua* changeable, the
principle of the others.

We should realise, as we have also said above,[55] that those who 25
assume this to be changeable, cannot preserve the concept of the first
and real principle; for the principle must remain unchangeable, since
[otherwise] it would not be the principle. Further, it is not possible to
grasp that *by which* it is changed as it produces the other elements,

if it alone is underlying. For it is impossible to say that it is changed by itself.[56]

30
245,1   But they might say[57] that a certain one [of the elements] is the principle of others in the sense that they pass through it, i.e. all come to be from it in the process of change and pass away by being resolved into it; for instance, if they said that fire is the principle of the others, so that none of the others can be without coming to be from it in the process of change, but air, water, and earth come to be from fire and
5   are resolved into it, and neither does anything become air not having become fire first, nor again water, so that it [viz. fire] is prior in the order of generation, and it is the first to come to be from the formless matter (if this is how [the coming to be] happens), and other [elements] come to be from it and are resolved into it.[58] The assumption, then, being something like that, let us now see how Aristotle responds
10   to it.

332b7-10 It will not be the case where the extremes are concerned, because everything[59] would then be fire or earth, [and this view is the same as the view that everything comes from fire or earth[60]].

He says that neither any of the extremes, nor [any] of the intermediates can be the principle of others *qua* changeable. And he calls fire
15   and earth 'extremes' and air and water 'intermediates'. And first he shows that none of the extremes can be the principle. For if, he says, we assume fire or earth as the principle then everything will be fire or earth.

Let us now examine the way in which from the claim that from fire being changed other [elements] come to be he draws the conclusion
20   that everything is fire. For if it is in changing and not persisting that fire makes air and each of the others, how would air and each of the others still rightfully be fire? But perhaps someone will say that although it does change it still does not change all of [its] nature, as we say in the case of the four elements. For although, when being changed into one another and mixed, they make composites, yet they do not completely pass away, but whereas the purity [of constitution]
25   is destroyed, it is still not the case that all of their nature is changed.[61] To someone who says that it is in this way that fire changing makes other [elements], and concludes that everything is fire, it should be replied that when a certain *composite* is produced from the simple [bodies], it is reasonable that it does not completely abandon the proper nature that pertains to the qualities by which the simple bodies are characterised; but when *simple* [bodies] come to be from
30   one another it is impossible to assume this. For each of the simple [bodies] has its qualities extreme and unmixed, and not suppressed by the admixture of the contraries, as is the case with the composite

[bodies].[62] How, indeed, can fire, while being dry and somehow remaining in its proper nature, produce air, which is moist? Air is not an intermediate between the moist and the dry, but moist in the extreme, as fire too is dry in the extreme. Consequently, all of the   35
nature of fire has to undergo change in order for air to come to be,   246,1
unless we assume that the contraries are present in the same, which is an impossibility.

So, according to this understanding, it is not plausible to conclude that everything will be fire, if fire has been posited as the principle; but apparently the text is rather hinting at something else.[63] 'For this view', he says, 'will be the same with the one that says that everything is from fire or from air',[64] meaning that when we say that everything   5
comes to be from fire undergoing change we assume that everything is fire[65] because everything comes to be from it undergoing change, as if we were saying that [everything] comes to be from fire as matter. But in this way no incongruity at all will ensue. For what incongruity is there in saying that everything is fire in the sense of a substrate, just as everything is [said to be] matter in the sense of a substrate, or a three-dimensional?[66] And generally, as it is not incongruous to say   10
that all generated things are the same in substrate, namely matter, so it is not incongruous, as far as the present discussion is concerned, having posited everything to be fire *qua* matter, to assume the difference to be only in accordance with form. And if it is not incongruous to say that everything is from fire as from matter, since it, being matter in a universal sense, would be able to receive different   15
forms, it is clear that neither will it be incongruous to derive the rest from the fire that undergoes change and to say that everything is fire on that account. For similarly, he says, it is incongruous to say both that the others come to be because of fire undergoing change and to say that the rest come to be from fire as matter.

Now, then, as far as what has been said is concerned, the refutations do not seem to have too much rigor. But it is possible to destroy   20
completely in one argument, as he himself will proceed to do in what follows, the assumption that makes a certain one of the four [elements] the principle of the rest. For if all have contrariety in relation to one another, and it has been shown that those that have contrariety in relation to one another change into one another, it is clear that all change into one another. But if all change into one another, then neither will it be the case that a certain one of them is the first, while   25
another one second, nor will it be the case that one of them is the principle, while another one is that which is [derived] from the principle. Now, with respect to the thesis that none of the extreme [elements] is the principle, he was content with saying only this much, that all will be fire. And that any of the intermediates will not be the principle either, he establishes through some further arguments.

332b10-12 Nor will it be the case where the intermediates are
30   concerned, as[67] is the view held by some, that air changes both
          into fire and into water, and water both into air and into earth.

He now sets out to show that neither will any of the intermediates be
the principle, as some believed, who regarded it more reasonable to
posit as the principle some one of these, because each of these changes
in both directions and into contraries, which is a special charac-
247,1   teristic[68] [of the principle], viz. changing into contraries, while the
extremes, according to them, are not suited to change in both directions. But this will be examined shortly afterwards. Now it must be
said that if it is reasonable to posit as the principle those [things] that
change in both directions, one should not posit [as the principle] this
5   intermediate rather than that, but both equally. How then do they
say that some *one* is the principle of the rest?
          Further, as regards those who posit air as the principle, arguing
that both it changes into fire and water and these latter into air, and
through it into one another, while fire and earth too do not change
into each other without mediation, but through the medium of air,
and therefore it must be the principle, since everything gets trans-
10   formed from it, first going through it, and everything is dissolved into
it, – now, as regards those who claim this, – what would they say
about the transformation of water into earth? For this one comes to
be without mediation, not passing through [the stage of] air, as it
should have been if the air indeed were to have the nature of the
principle of every change. In this way, too, against those who say that
water is the principle, the difficulty should be raised about the change
15   from air into fire and from fire into air: for these too will be without
mediation, not passing through [the stage of] water.[69] So much will
do for now, by way of criticism of the *assumption* from an external
standpoint.[70] Let us see, next, in what way they say that the extremes
do not change into each other, and how their *arguments* are to be
refuted.

20   **332b12-30** But the extremes do not similarly change into one
          another. For the process must come to a halt and not go on to
          infinity in a straight line [in both directions: that would involve
          an infinite number of contrarieties belonging to one <element>.
          Let E stand for earth, W for water, A for air, and F for fire.
          Now, if A changes into F and W, there will be a contrariety
          between A and F. Let the contraries in question be whiteness
          and blackness. Again, if A changes into W, there will be another
          contrariety, since W and F are not the same thing. Let these be
          dryness and moistness: D for dryness and W for moistness. If
          whiteness remains, water will emerge as white and moist; if it

does not, water will be black. Change is from contrary to contrary, so water will have to be either white or black. Let it be the first. Similarly, D, i.e. dryness, will belong to F. So there will, after all, be such a thing as a changing of F, i.e. fire, into water. This is because they possess contrary qualities: we saw in the first place that fire was black, then that it was dry, that water was moist, and then that it was white. Obviously, then, change is possible from every element to every other element, and in the terms in which we conducted the argument E, i.e. the earth, will have the remaining pair of counterparts, black and moist, since these have not yet been paired.]

The extremes, they say, no longer change into each other. For being extremes they have not anything further into which to change, but revert back to air and water. For if, they say, the extremes do not revert[71] [to the means they come from] but keep changing further, the   25
process of change will go on to infinity. So, being wary of assuming the process of change which goes on to infinity, and not being able to understand that coming to be accomplishes a circle, coming to an end at the point from which it started out (for from fire comes air, and then water, then earth and again fire, since change always comes to be in a succession and does not go on to infinity because it does not come about in a straight line but circles back), they, as we have said,   30
not realising this were afraid to assume that the extremes change into each other; for they believed that change must come to a halt once it has gone as far as them [i.e. the extremes], in order not to proceed to infinity. This is why Aristotle says, addressing himself to them: 'for the process must come to a halt and not go on to infinity in a straight line in both directions: that would involve an infinite number of   35
contrarieties belonging to one [element]'. He says that one should accept that change does not proceed to infinity as though going on in   248,1
a straight line. For although change does proceed to infinity, yet it is not in a straight line, but by a circular recurrence of the same things into the same.[72] For [change going on] in a straight line stops when it reaches the extremes. So, for this reason change of the extremes into each other is not impossible – rather it is in fact necessary, in order   5
to preserve the circle of coming to be. And intending to explain immediately afterwards that change cannot proceed to infinity in a straight line, he has now brought this up,[73] as he hinted at the incongruous consequence that necessarily follows [from the opposite view], namely that an infinite number of contrarieties belongs to one [element].

And he shows next that the extremes too change into one another. He proves this by using the additional assumption mentioned above,   10
that all the things which have contrariety in relation to one another

change [into one another], and he shows that each [element] has a contrariety in relation to the rest, in order to show, generally, as we said, that all change into each other, not just the intermediates, but the extremes as well. And perhaps since he did not adduce any exact
15   refutations of the previous view, the one that posited a certain one of the extremes as the principle, therefore he now sets out some sort of a universal refutation [to establish] that none of the four [elements] is the principle of the rest. For if he proves that all have contrariety in relation to each other, it is clear that all change into each other. But if this is the case, then none of them will be singled out as primary or the principle, neither the extremes, nor the intermediates, but all
20   equally change into each other, the extremes, and the ones that are contrary [to one another], and those next to one another in order.[74]

The mode of proof is of some such kind. Assume, he says, earth, water, air, and fire, each of which he designates by the letter at the beginning of the name. (a) Now, if you say that air, being intermediate, changes into both fire and water, it is surely not in accordance
25   with the same opposition that it changes both into fire on the one hand and water on the other hand. For this way fire will be the same as water. For if the air, changing into water, undergoes transformation in the same respect in which it, in the process of change, has come to be fire, then it follows that it differs from water in the same respect in which it is at variance with fire. But if fire and water differ from the same thing, e.g. from air, in the same respect, fire and air will
30   have to be the same as each other, which is incongruous. Hence it follows that air changes into fire and water not in respect of the same opposition; so, in respect of a different one in each case. (b) Let it be assumed that it changes into fire in respect of white and black, so that fire is black and air is white; and into water in respect of a different opposition, say, of the moist and the dry, so that air is dry, while
35   water is moist. But, he says, having changed into water in respect of
249,1 the moist and the dry, it can preserve its whiteness as well as it can change it, too. (c) Suppose it has preserved it. Air then must be white and dry, and water white and moist.[75] So water will have contrariety in relation to fire, since the former is white, and the latter black, by
5   assumption; and so they change into one another. For it has been previously assumed that those [things] that have contrariety in relation to each other change into each other.

And let the argument be the same, again, about water. For although it does change into both air and earth, it does not change into each of these in respect of the same [contrariety] since [otherwise] air and earth will be the same thing; and so in one respect [it changes] into air, in another, into earth. Therefore it changes into air in respect
10   of the moist and the dry; so it remains that it will change into earth in respect of the black and the white, since there are only two oppositions. This has been obtained from granting that there are four

simple bodies; for if there are four bodies, two oppositions are to be seen necessarily. So, if water is white and moist, air, as has been said, will be white and dry (for its difference from water is in respect of the 15 moist and the dry), and earth black and moist, if it is in respect of the black that water changed into it. Consequently, air will have contrariety with earth, and so it will change into it.

The proof of the argument is, then, of some such kind. But Alexander inquires how comes it that having proposed to prove that the extremes change into one another, he apparently has not proved *that*; but rather has demonstrated instead that contraries change into one 20 another. And he says: 'Perhaps in the beginning too he referred by 'extremes' to contraries; and after that, as is also more adequate, he proved from the terms set down[76] that all [elements] have contrariety in relation to each other. And if this is the case, it is clear that all will change into each other too.'[77]

And it is manifest that he has proved the extremes, viz. earth and fire, to have contrariety in relation to one another, since he has 25 assumed fire to be black and dry, and earth black and moist.[78] So by this argument earth changes into fire in respect of the moist and the dry. Accordingly, from what has been proven, we have that not only none of the intermediates is the principle, but that none of the extremes is, either. For if the extremes and generally all [the elements] change into each other in equal degree, there will be no more 30 reason for any one to be the principle than for any other.

332b30-2 That it is not possible to proceed to infinity – the thesis we were going to prove, but then first dealt with this [– can be shown from the following].

Having shown that unless it is assumed that coming to be proceeds to infinity in a straight line, it is necessary that all [elements] should change into each other, since it is also shown that all have contrariety in relation to each other, he now deals with this very point that it is 250,1 impossible for change to proceed to infinity, having already previously alluded to this impossibility, when he said, 'for that would involve an infinite number of contrarieties belonging to one [element]',[79] so that when this is refuted, it will become clear that all [elements] change into each other.

And perhaps someone will object that even if we do assume that 5 change proceeds to infinity, there will be change not only of [the elements] that follow upon each other in a straight line, but the ones that are remote from each other will change into one another as well, if, that is, we take it as agreed that all the ones that have contrariety in relation to each other change into each other.

But it should be realised that he [Aristotle] now expounds this very [argument], that if anyone assumes the elements to be infinite, where 10

one element changes into another in a straight line, what has been assumed will be brought round to its contrary, namely that none of the elements changes into any of the rest – neither the remote ones into one another, nor the ones that are proximate [to each other] – so that the assumption will be completely impossible. For if, he says, we assume that a certain one of the extremes, either fire or earth, does
15 not turn back making a cycle, but [proceeding] in a straight line changes into some further fifth [element] in sequence, then there will be a certain contrariety in respect of which it has undergone change, other than the ones in respect of which the four elements have changed [into each other] in sequence. And let it be assumed, he says, that fire neither turns back again into air, nor comes round in a circle, [changing] into earth, but changes into some fifth thing, let us say, X. Then there will be some contrariety in respect of which F changed
20 into X. Let us assume it to be the one between [qualities] G and B, in respect of which none of the other [elements] (A W E) have changed, but only F and X. In that case, one [part] of an opposition will belong to X, e.g. B (suppose it stands for 'bad'), whereas to fire and all the rest G will belong (let us call it 'good').[80] For the contrarieties partaken of by all [the elements] were assumed to be such. And so on in
25 sequence: if X, in turn, changes into some other thing, then another contrariety will be added; and if that one, again, [changes] into yet another one, a third contrariety will be added. And if this proceeded to infinity in sequence, there would be an infinite number of contrarieties. Now, first, it is incongruous to assume the infinite to be in actuality; further, if the contrarieties are infinite, and the qualities of the contrarieties are double (for there are two qualities per each
30 contrariety), there will be twice as much as the infinite. But if, he says, these things are assumed, it is neither possible to define any of these and comprehend the infinities by a rational account, nor is it possible for them to subsist or come to be from each other; but the mutual change will be completely destroyed.[81] And it will also follow, he says, that all are the same.[82] But how each of these is proved, we
35 shall examine afterwards in a close study of the text.
251,1 And the following is worth an enquiry: how one contrariety is added per each element. Now, it is clear that if the elements are infinite, the contrarieties must be infinite, too. For if the contrarieties were limited [in number] it would be necessary for combinations and
5 pairs, although much more numerous than the contrarieties themselves, to be limited nonetheless. For just as it is possible to grasp, by means of a systematic procedure, how many pairs come to be from two contrarieties, namely four, so too for any arbitrary number of contrarieties, as long as it is countable and rational,[83] the pairs must necessarily be countable and limited [in number]. If, however, the
10 elements are infinite, clearly, the contrarieties will not be limited [in number].

But this is not what the [present] argument queries; rather [it is] whether with each added element one contrariety is added too – something that no longer holds true. For when one contrariety is added the elements become greater in number; thus when there are two contrarieties the elements will not be just two, but four. And if the contrarieties are three there can be eight elements. And so on in 15 this way, always, when one contrariety is added, the elements will be much more numerous.[84]

Now, to this it should be replied that even if with the addition of one contrariety the elements will grow more numerous [than by one element], what was initially proposed [in Aristotle's argument] is not barred from being logically conclusive. For since it has been shown that if the elements are infinite [in number], contrarieties in each of them are infinite [in number], an impossible conclusion follows in a 20 similar way, whether one element is added per one contrariety, or whether more [elements than one are added]. For, as it was said before, he proves the impossibility of the premiss using as an additional step the claim that the contrarieties are infinite.[85]

But to say that with each element one contrariety is added is neither true nor [logically] necessary. For it is not the case that if, let us suppose for argument's sake, air changes only into fire in respect of the moist and the dry, and not into any other of the elements, it is 25 by the same token necessary that nothing else changes in respect of the contrariety of the moist and the dry, for water and earth change in respect of these.[86] Why then does Aristotle add one contrariety per element? Well, I should say,[87] [he does so] because he follows through the premiss of those who say that the change of the elements proceeds only in a straight line; for if this is what has been laid down as a 30 premiss, it is impossible for there to be two changes in respect of the same opposition, as for instance in respect of that of the moist and the dry, both air changes into fire, and water into earth. So, if it has been assumed that change of the elements occurs only in a straight line, it is absolutely necessary that when an element is added in all cases a contrariety should be added, in respect of which the preceding element changes into the following one. And that Aristotle adds one 35 opposition per each element in response to the assumption that the coming to be does not turn back, is clear from this: after saying that 252,1 F changes into X in respect of the contrariety of G and B, i.e. of good and bad, where G belongs to F and to all [the elements] under it, and B to X and all the elements after it, he still assumes that only F changes into X, but not any of the other [elements]. So it is necessary that for each 5 addition of an element in all cases a contrariety should be added.

332b32-33a1 If the next move of F,[88] i.e. fire, is to change[89] [into something else] (and not turn back), e.g. into X, [there will be a contrariety between fire and X other than those mentioned, because *ex hypothesi* X is identical with none of the group EWAF].

If fire, he says, does not turn back, when it happens to change into air
10 or earth or water, but changes into some X different from these, it is absolutely necessary to assume, beside the two contrarieties, the one of the hot and the cold and of the dry and the moist, a third one, e.g. of white and black, in respect of which F changes into X. For X was laid down as different from the four elements.

15 **333a1-2** Let G belong to F, B to X.[90] G will belong to the entire group EWAF [this, however, ought not at this stage to be taken as proved].

Let F, he says, changing into X in respect of the contrariety of B and G, be changed in respect of the contrariety in respect of which none of the elements preceding F changed.[91] So if B belongs to X, and G to
20 F, that very G which belongs to fire, will also belong to air and water and earth, because none of these differed from fire in respect of this contrariety, but in respect of a different one, viz. that of the hot and the cold and the dry and the moist. But this should be given proper attention: that G belongs to all those preceding F follows from Aristotle's premiss, according to which in respect of every one opposition
25 there is one change.[92] For none [of these] will have yet changed in respect of it until F changes into X. So, where does G in the fire come from if not from those? In the same way, too, B [belongs] to all those after X, since none [of these] after X changes in respect of this opposition any more.

However, if we grant, as has been said previously, that the ele-
253,1 ments come to be more [viz. than one] in number when one contrariety is added,[93] and that different [elements] change in respect of one contrariety, it is no longer necessary for G, because it already belongs to F, to belong as well to all the elements that precede it.[94] How so? Because another element, too, has changed in respect of this contrariety, as it is the case with fire and air. For air changed into fire
5 in respect of the moist and the dry. And it is not the case that since it has moisture, by the same token also all those preceding it [have moisture]. For earth is dry. And the cause of this is that not just air has changed into fire in respect of this contrariety, but also earth into water.

So Aristotle, as I said earlier, in following the premiss that makes change proceed only in [linear] sequence, and having assumed that a
10 contrariety is added with each element, said rightly that G belongs to all [the elements] preceding fire, particularly if, he says, they change into it.[95] For if [fire] F has one [part] of the contrariety according to B

and G, viz. G, then those preceding fire also necessarily must have
G, if fire came to be from them and they changed into it. For if [the
elements] preceding fire do not have G, where does fire have G   15
from? For none of them differed from fire in respect of G, as has
been said.[96]

'This, however', (viz. that the four elements change into each
other), 'ought not at this stage to be taken as proved' [333a3], he says
referring to the premiss that is currently being expounded, since if we
say that the four elements all change into each other, we will be
importing [the view] that the process of coming to be is circular; [the
view] that is destroyed by the premiss now posited, which states that   20
change proceeds only in a straight line and in succession. For that
reason it has to be posited as not yet proved. However, one ought to
realise that what we need in order to prove that G belongs to F and
all [the elements] preceding it, is neither destroyed nor impeded by
the assumption saying, 'let it not be the case that all change into each
other'.[97] For that the change of each of the four proceeds in a sequence   25
ending in fire is sufficient to prove that G belongs to all [the elements]
preceding F, from whose change in sequence fire came to be. For if G
had not belonged to them then fire would not have come to be from
them as having G. Now, that G, one part of the contrariety of G and
B, belongs to AWE, is proved from this, not from [the assumption]   30
that all change into all. And that G and B belong to them is proved
from [the assumption that] none of the rest has changed in respect of
this contrariety except F and X. So in respect of this [contrariety] F
does not at all differ from those [elements] that precede it. Hence, G
belongs to them as a common [character].

333a3-6 But that much, at least, is clear; if X in its turn is to   254,1
change into something else, another contrariety will belong to
both X and F, i.e. fire. [Equally, it will always be the case that
as a new member is added to the series a contrariety attaches to
the previous members]

That is if we add another element after X, e.g. V, and X changes into
V, yet another contrariety is needed again, in respect of which change
occurs, apart from the one [already found] in F and X. The case will   5
be similar with as many other elements as we might posit.

333a6-8 So that if the series goes on to infinity the number of
contrarieties [which attach to a single member] will also be
infinite. [In this case it will not be possible for anything either
to be defined or to come to be]

Now the incongruous conclusion is being drawn. For if a contrariety
is added with [the addition of an] element, and the elements are

infinite [in number], then the contrarieties will be infinite, and in
10   each element, of the infinite [number] of contrarieties there will be
one part [of each pair], these [parts], too, being infinite. Now, if in
each [element] there will be an infinite [number of] parts, see what
will follow. For it will not be possible for anything, he says, either to
be defined, or to come to be. And it is manifest that infinities can
neither be embraced by a definition, nor subsist.[98] It is now to be
considered in what way he says that neither do they come to be from
one another.

15   **333a8-13** For, if it is to be from one another, it will be necessary
for that many contrarieties to be gone through, and still more.
[So there will be some things into which there will never be
change. This will happen if the number of intermediate stages
is infinite, and this will necessarily be the case if the elements
are infinite in number. Again there will be no change from air
into fire if there are infinitely many contrarieties.]

If, he says, the contrarieties in each [element] are infinite, it will be
necessary for that which comes to be to go through as many contrarieties as each one has (but [each one] has an infinite number). This
is impossible, for the infinite is not traversable. But since he said 'that
20   many', – and this seems to be indicative of a limited number, whereas
the infinite is always greater or more numerous than every given
[number], – for that reason, putting his point in a precise way, as it
were, he added, 'and still more'. Now, it must be considered how that
which comes to be must go through infinitely many contrarieties. For
if we take several intermediates as changing in sequence, in order to
come before the extremes and change into these latter, they [viz. the
25   intermediates] will have to go through an infinity in order to change
into the extreme. But this is impossible. Consequently, they will
255,1 neither change into it, nor even arrive at it at any time, if the distance
between that which is changing and the extreme is infinite. But just
as the intermediate does not change into the extreme because of not
being able to arrive at it at any time, nor does anything else at any
time change into the intermediate, e.g. that which is in the beginning
(something it is not even possible to conceive, for the infinite has no
5   beginning), in a similar way neither will that[99] reach any point
in-between, because the distance from the middle to the beginning is
infinite. It is thus manifest that none of the [elements] posited in the
middle changes into the extremes. And he says that neither do the
elements next to each other change into each other. For 'again', he
says, 'there will be no change from air to fire if there are infinitely
10   many contrarieties' [333a12-13]. It is worth an inquiry, why exactly
he says this. For in order for fire to come to be from air it does not
[have to] go through all the contrarieties, but comes to be by changing

in respect of only one contrariety, the rest of them remaining the same. So perhaps it is on a general ground that the infinite cannot subsist, that [he says that] none[100] of those [elements] that have [an] infinite [number of] contrarieties would come to be.

But perhaps someone might say: *assuming* that they do subsist, 15 see if they can come to be from one another. And they can, since the coming to be of the adjacent [elements] from each other in accordance with the change of one contrariety is observed.[101] Therefore it is better, as Alexander says, to take this as said with reference to what follows. And in what follows he shows that all the elements will be the same with one another. But if all are the same then [they] would not come to be from one another, nor will there be change from any 20 one into any other: for nothing comes to be what it already is.

It seems to me, the proposed thesis should be understood as follows. Given that the change of the elements infinite [in number] is in a straight line, and we have shown that some intermediates do not change into anything, because [for this] they must traverse the infinity, and the infinity is not traversable, – let us suppose now the intermediate to be air. Then it will not change into fire: for in order 25 for a change to result from it an infinite number of changes will be necessary, and this is impossible. So, if the change into air cannot arrive at it[102] in the first place, then neither will air change into fire, which is the next after it.

333a13-15 Furthermore, everything will come to be[103] one; because those members lower[104] in the series than F will have 30 necessarily to possess the contrarieties[105] that belong to those above F, and these latter will have to have the ones that belong to those below. [So everything will be one.]

His purpose now is to show that from the assumption that change is in a straight line to infinity it follows that all [elements] are the same. 256,1 For, he says, to all of them, below and above F, belong the same contrarieties. Now, it is manifest that if all the elements preceding F have the same contrarieties as all those after it, then all turn out to be the same. For if all the [elements] on both sides of F have the same 5 contrarieties then the ones that start from X and proceed upwards and the ones that start from A [air] and proceed as far as the lower ones will be the same as one another. So that A, i.e. air, will be the same as X, and speaking generally, all those above [will be the same] as those below. And in this way, again, if we take [the elements] on either side of A to be, by the same argument, the same as each other 10 then F will be the same as X, and all those above. And in this way, again, having shown that [the elements] on either side of X are the same with each other, he proves that fire is the same as air. So, accordingly, [it is the same] as all [the elements] after it. And it has been shown through the preceding [argument] that [it is the same] as all [the elements] before it, and all [the elements] before air are the same as all the ones after it. So it is clear from this that fire and all

15　[the elements] on both sides of fire, will be the same as each other.

Now, from what has been said it is clear that if we grant that all [the properties] that belong to the [elements] above are the same as [the properties] that belong to the [elements] below it will follow that all are the same as one another. But that the same contrarieties belong [to these elements] can no longer be taken as a true consequence from the assumption that change is in sequence and in a

20　straight line. And this is clear from what he said previously explaining the assumption. For if[106] F changes into X, he says, it changes in accordance with the contrariety in accordance with which nothing else has changed,[107] for instance the one [between] B and G, and B will belong to X and G to fire and all the [elements] below [fire]. And

25　when X again changes into [the elements] that are after it, the B remains as a common [character] in all those after X. So that all [the elements] after fire have been contrary to all the elements before fire with the contrariety of G and B. And when X again changes into another element, in accordance with another contrariety, those after X will again have contrariety in relation to those before X. So it is clear from this that everything will not be the same, but on the

30　contrary, everything will have contrariety in relation to everything.

Now, it should be examined how Aristotle maintains this as true. Perhaps, then, (a) he establishes this on the basis of [the assumption] that in each [element] there is an infinite number of contrarieties. For if you say that each one has an infinite number of contrarieties, and it is impossible to assume more than the infinite, then there will be

257,1　no such contrariety that will not belong to every one [of the posited elements]. So all will be the same. But this does not make sense, either. For (b) having assumed an infinite number of contrarieties he makes the [number of the] qualities double infinite. So that when each is said to have infinite contrarieties, it is not said as though it

5　has both sides of a contrariety, but one of the two members of a contrariety, and only one. Consequently, it is not incongruous to observe in these ones one part of the contrarieties, in the other ones, the other part.[108]

But it is best to understand this argument in this way, as elaborating the theorem *per se*, in its own nature, rather than as continuous with the preceding argument. (a) For if you say that (i) F

10　changes into X and (ii) X neither turns back to F, nor changes [into it] then (iii) X has no contrariety in relation to F. (iv) For had it had one, X would have been liable to change into F; (v) it follows that it will be the same [as F]. In this way going through the sequence [of elements], you will prove that all [the elements] are the same with one another.[109] (b) But if someone says, 'I have assumed this very thing from the beginning, that these, F and X, have contrariety in relation to one another, when I assumed that F changes into X', I will say to him: 15 'This very contrariety that you assumed you yourself are destroying when you say that X no longer changes into F. And in this way, in general, having assumed that the [elements] above do not change into the ones below you destroy their contrariety which you assumed in the change of every one in relation to the following one. And the contrariety having been destroyed, all will be the same with each 20 other, as he has reasonably concluded.'[110]

<2.6. REFUTATION OF EMPEDOCLES>

333a16-20 One might well be surprised at those who say that the elements of bodies number more than one while denying that they change into one another [as on Empedocles' view. How, one may ask, is it open to them to say that the elements are susceptible of comparison? And yet Empedocles speaks in this way: 'For all these things are equal'.[111]]

After he has shown that one of the four cannot be the element of the others, either *qua* unchangeable, or *qua* changeable, and since it has been shown through the same arguments that it is not the case that 25 any [several] of them are the elements of the rest, the next thing it remains to examine is whether all the four are elements.[112] For it has been said by him above that 'if nothing perceptible, at least, is prior to these, all of these will be' [332a26]. Since, then, these must be the elements of other things either *qua* unchangeable or *qua* changeable, it is his task in the present [argument] to show that they are not unchangeable, so that, once this is refuted, there will remain the true 30 opinion, namely that all [the four] are the elements *qua* changing into one another.[113] And since Empedocles is the champion of the opinion set out for refutation, he refers to him, showing that according to him, neither coming to be and perishing in accordance with nature are 258,1 possible, nor growth, nor movement in accordance with nature.[114] But before refuting his view of the elements, [Aristotle] shows him to be contradicting himself; for having assumed them to be unchangeable, [Empedocles] says that they are comparable, writing 'for these are all equal'.[115] So [Aristotle] first demonstrates that it is impossible for 5 Empedocles to say that they are comparable, as long as he holds the elements to be unchangeable, for if they are comparable with one another, they must be comparable with one another either (i) *in amount*, so as to say, [for instance,] that fire is *equal* (*ison*) to air;[116] or (ii) *in power and quality*, (iia) quality being either the same, as when I say, for instance, 'fire is similar (*homoion*) to air in that air is as hot as fire'; or (iib) the comparison is drawn from a collocation of 10 qualities different from each other, 'different' meaning either (iib')

contrary, as when I say 'water is as cold as fire is hot', or (iib″) not
contrary but different in kind, as when I say, for instance, 'this is as
white as this is hot', the juxtaposition being made on the basis of
proportion.

15   He shows, then, that first of all it is not possible to understand
their comparability in terms of *amount* [(i)] if they are unchangeable,
for to understand their equality in this way, viz. as that of the wholes
that are the same amount as each other, is silly. With some [ele-
ments], e.g. earth and water, this clearly appears not to be the case,
since water is seen in the hollows of the earth, and air is larger than

20   both.[117] With other elements the demonstration of equality is unclear,
as with air and fire, and water compared to each of them. So it is not
possible to say that the elements are equal to each other in this way.

But then, if he says that they are comparable *in amount*, he would
mean by this that they would change into each other if equal matter

25   were underlying each of them; for example, if we were to say that the
whole of water is equal to the whole of air because in each there is
matter equal [in amount] and the same [in kind], which can, if
extended, produce air, and if contracted again, [produce] water.[118] But
it is impossible for him to consider this, except on the basis of the
parts changing into each other. For when we see, say, a pint of water

30   change into ten pints of air,[119] if it turns out like this, we say that the
ten pints of air are equal to one pint of water in this way, namely that
both are from the same matter, rarefied [in one case] and condensed
[in the other], and that the same proportion of prevalence is preserved
in the wholes as is seen in the parts. Aristotle, too, in his *Meteorology*,

259,1   derived the proportion of water to air from the changing of their parts,
for, he says, it is plausible that the proportion of water to the air
coming from it is the same as that of the whole of air to the whole of
water.[120] Now, it has been sufficiently established that it is not
possible [for any two things] to be comparable in amount unless

5   because they have equal the matter which can receive the amount of
each of the two things compared,[121] and that such comparison is
necessarily understood on the basis of the changing of the parts [viz.
of things compared] into each other. It is a contradiction, therefore,
to say that the elements are comparable in amount while preserving
them unchangeable.[122]

Let us see, then, whether we can say [(ii)] that they are comparable

10   *in powers*, for instance, ten pints of air are as hot as one pint of fire,
drawing the comparison in terms of the same power [(iia)]. But if the
elements are unchangeable this cannot be assumed, either, for the
same quality has one and the same underlying matter. So if you say
that ten parts of air are equal in power to one part of fire, you will

15   judge the power of air as relaxed, and that of fire as intensified. But
since the underlying matter is one and the same, it is possible for the
relaxed power to be intensified and for the intensified one to be spread

out. Since there is one matter common to both, what each of the two is must be assumed [as being present] in it 'potentially'.[123]

The same reasoning will hold again if the comparison is taken in terms of [(iib')] contrary powers, should we say 'air is as moist as fire 20 is dry', or 'water is as cold as fire is hot'. For someone who has claimed that there are contrary powers and one matter [common] to both, namely the three-dimensional,[124] must also adduce change, for contraries necessarily act upon each other and are affected by each other, since [otherwise] they would not have been called contraries.

Now, if neither in terms of amount, nor in terms of power (whether 25 the same or contrary), is it possible to conceive of a comparison of the elements, as long as they stay unchanged, we should find out whether Empedocles can maintain the comparison of the elements in a third way,[125] [(iib'')] according to the *proportion* of powers of *different kinds*, so that one could say, 'this is white as that is hot'. And Aristotle says 30 that only in this way is it possible for him to say that the elements are comparable, while assuming that they are unchangeable, for it is not possible to say that powers of different kinds act upon, or generally change into each other, for example whiteness into sweetness. So, insofar as [it] does not revoke the assumption of unchangeable elements, the comparison considered in this way would be legitimate, 35 since it does not introduce change of the elements, as others do. However if this belief is tested on its own, it is not exempt from a criticism, [namely,] whether [on this view] one would not be considering only one power of a co-ordinating pair as present in the elements, but not the other one, as if it were said that whiteness belongs to the elements, but not blackness, or that they partake of sweetness but in no way of bitterness; and so with hot and cold. First 5 of all, it is incoherent[126] that one set should belong but not their corresponding opposites, and secondly [the former] will exist in vain, if there is nothing to act upon or to be affected by. And if the contrary [powers] were there, but he were to claim that comparison is being assumed as present only with respect to [powers] of *different* kinds, then the arguments previously given would apply, for where there is contrariety there must also be affection and change, since [the pow- 10 ers] would not be contraries if they were not fighting and trying to destroy each other.[127]

333a20-3 If they are [comparable] in terms of quantity there will have to be some identical thing belonging to all the things which are comparable by which they are measured [: for instance, ten pints of air might come from a pint of water. In this case there would have to be some one thing that both were, if they are measured by the same thing].

He proves (i) that [the elements] cannot be comparable in amounts

15   and masses.[128] For, (ia) it has been agreed from sense perception that
       they are not all equal in masses. For air is greater than [both] earth
       and the confluence of water in its hollows;[129] and the comparison in
       terms of quantity of fire and air with each other is unclear, not to say
       that it is plausible that the inflammable substance[130] surrounding the
       air is greater than the air and everything within. Consequently it is
20   impossible to take equality in terms of masses. But then [any two
       elements] could be said to be equal in masses in the sense (ib) that
       change bringing about each of the two came from an equal substrate
       – a substrate of a certain size could produce ten times the amount of
       air when rarefied, and when condensed a tenth of the mass of water.
       This for him is what is indicated by the phrase 'by which they are
       measured', i.e., according to which they are equal with respect to the
25   substrate. And if such is the case, the elements would not be un-
       changeable, as long as they have a common substrate, which produces
       water when contracted, and air when extended, by rarefaction; for
       this is change.[131]

261,1   **333a23-9** If, however, they are not comparable in terms of
          quantity in this way – such and such a quantity being derivable
          from such and such – but according to the amount of their power
          [(e.g. if a pint of water had the same cooling effect as ten of air),
          in this way too they are comparable in terms of quantity, not *qua*
          quantity, but *qua* possessing such and such powers. It would
          indeed be possible to compare these powers, not by a quantita-
          tive standard of measurement, but by way of a proportion: e.g.
          as this is hot, so this is white].

       He has passed from equality in masses to that of powers. If, he says,
       they were not speaking about equality in terms of quantity [for the
5   elements] – the larger and the smaller of them arising from some
       equal substrate, as we mentioned earlier – what is left is to say that
       they are comparable in respect of powers, because their powers are
       equal in proportion to their quantity. And here let the same power be
       assumed, so that the heat which is in, say, ten parts of air, would be
       equal to that in the part of fire which is one tenth of this mass. And
       [the phrase] 'not ... as such-and-such a quantity being derivable from
10   such-and-such a quantity' indicates that [the elements] do not change
       from a certain equal quantity into a greater by rarefaction and lesser
       by condensation, but equality is to be understood in respect of power.
       And before mentioning the incongruities that follow from this as-
       sumption, he moves over to the equality of powers *in proportion* (iib″),
       in which he takes those differing in kind, e.g. white and hot, to have
15   some likeness and proportion to each other in respect of powers of
       their qualities, so that we may say that this water is as white as this
       fire is hot. Only so can Empedocles say that they are comparable,

while holding that they are unchangeable. For white does not change into hot, or *vice versa*, since [things] that belong to different kinds do not change into one another.

333a29-30 But the 'as this' [in quality] signifies likeness and in quantity equality. 20

If the elements are not comparable in respect of quantity, but in respect of the proportion mentioned, Empedocles put it badly when he said 'for these are all equal'; for 'equal' is according to quantity and 'like' is according to quality; so he should have said 'like', not 'equal'. 25

333a30-2 Indeed, it appears absurd for bodies which are incapable of changing into one another to be comparable, not by way of proportion, but by a measurement of their powers.

If, then, he says, Empedocles states that the elements are comparable, while at the same time maintaining that they are unchangeable, 262,1 it is impossible for him to say that they are comparable by a measuring of their powers, as, say, ten times this [amount of] air is as cold as this [amount of] water. For to say that [the elements] differing in respect of an equal quantity[132] are empowered by the same powers is impossible for someone who keeps them unchangeable, as we have already proved. [Being] more and less in respect of the same power 5 cannot happen except by virtue of <being> from the same matter; this comes about by tension and relaxing of powers; and this constitutes a change.[133] So, it is only in terms of a proportion of powers that belong to different kinds and therefore do not change into one another, that Empedocles can say that the elements are comparable.

333a32-4 A given quantity of fire and a multiple of this quantity 10 of air being [said to be] equal[134] or similar in respect of heat. [For the same thing, which is greater, will have such an proportion because it is of the same kind.]

After he had said 'equal in respect of heat', [meaning] the equality of quantity, he immediately changed to 'similar', saying 'a given quantity of fire [and a multiple of this quantity of air being equal], or similar'. And he shows how it is possible for there to be similar heat in a small mass of air and an even smaller one of fire by adding 'for 15 the same which is greater will have such a proportion because it is of the same kind'[135], taking 'the same' as referring to power (for according to our assumption air is hot as well as fire), and 'greater' as referring to the respective masses; for by assumption air is many times the mass of fire, but equal to it in heat. But it is impossible for the same power to be in different amounts, unless there is one and 20

the same matter underlying both. And if the unequal masses of fire and air are similar in heat, then if I take the mass of air to be equal to fire, the heat in the air will be less than that in the fire. So it is by relaxing and tension that the same substrate becomes more and less hot; but this
25   is change; hence the elements will not be kept unchangeable.[136]

333a35-b3 Moreover, there would be no such thing as growth according to Empedocles, except by way of addition. [Fire will grow by means of fire, 'earth will make its own body grow and aether, aether', but these are additions. Things which grow do not, in our view, grow in this way.]

After showing that Empedocles makes a self-contradictory assumption in saying that the elements are both unchangeable and comparable with each other, [Aristotle] now shows that according to him
30   there is neither growth, nor coming to be according to nature, if the elements are unchangeable. And here he argues that there is no
263,1   growth – except that spoken of in the homonymous sense of addition. For if someone were to add water to water and make[137] more of it, we would usually say, 'water has increased',[138] and similarly with house-building or sculpture, when something is added from outside. This, however, is not growth, but adding like to like. For he has shown
5   before in the first part[139] what growth according to nature is, [namely] that [it takes place] when the matter providing growth (I mean food) is being altered, added to the [bodily] parts, and assimilated to them by the alterative power inherent in them,[140] and the growing thing[141] increases in all dimensions.

333b3-12 It is much more difficult to give an account of genera-
10   tion in so far as it occurs by nature. [Everything that comes to be naturally comes to be always in a particular way, or for the most part: those that do so contrary to the 'always and for the most part' do so spontaneously or by chance. What, then, is the cause of a human being's always or for the most part coming to be from a human being, or wheat, rather than an olive-tree, from wheat? Furthermore, if things are put together in a particular way, will it not be bone? For nothing comes to be when things come to be as it may chance, as he says, but only when they do so by a certain formula.[142] What, then, is the cause of this? Because fire, for certain, will not do, or earth.]

He said 'by nature', because some things also come to be by art, or choice, or chance.[143] Empedocles says that different things come to be at different times, as the elements chance to come together, and Aristotle has pointed this out when he said 'but nothing comes to be
15   when things come together just as it may chance, as[144] he [Empedo-

cles] says'.[145] Things that come to be by chance and spontaneously are rare, but those by formula[146] and nature are so always or for the most part, for man always comes from man and grapevine from grapevine. If chance is concerned with things that are rare, then what is not seldom, but comes to be always or for the most part is not the result of chance, but formula and nature. And besides, if the elements are   20
not subject to affection there will be no coming to be of anything, 'but only mixing and separation of things mixed.'[147] But this apparently is not the case; for where would the diverse forms of compound bodies and the structural differentiation[148] of animate beings come from? For mixing produces only the intermediate state of the ingredients, not a change of substance or a shaping of organs.[149]

But 'nothing comes to be as a result of things coming together just   25
as it may chance, as he [Empedocles] says, but according to a certain formula. What, then, is the cause[150] of this? Because fire, for certain, will not do, or earth'. If it is not the case that a chance mixture produces bone or sinew[151] or flesh or anything else,[152] that may chance, but [this production happens] according to a formula of mixture in each part, what is the cause of coming to be in accordance with formula and in a certain order? It most certainly is not fire or earth,[153] he says, i.e. [not] the gathering of the elements. For as I said,   30
the elements coming together produce some blending and intermedi-ate state of powers, but surely not the substance of bone or nerve or   264,1
vein or any other homoeomerous or organic parts. The production of these therefore is to be explained by formula and nature, [the kind of account] he does not provide.[154]

333b12-19 What is more, nor will Love and Strife, for the former is the cause only of aggregation, the latter of separation. The   5
cause is in fact the essence of each thing, not simply 'mixing and putting asunder of things mixed', as Empedocles says. [Chance 'is the name given to these processes', not proportion; for it is possible for mixing to take place merely by chance. The cause of things which exist according to nature is their being such and such, and this is the nature of each thing, about which he has nothing to say. So in fact he says nothing 'About Nature'.]

'Nor yet are Love and Strife', he says, the cause of coming to be according to formula, for on his account Love is the cause only of combining and Strife, of separation. So what does produce mixture   10
according to formula? For even in the artisan's mixture, the powers of the ingredients are indeed the causes of simple mixture, but art is responsible for assembling them according to a formula and combin-ing to a certain degree. Consequently there is something other than Love that is responsible for mixing according to a formula, and this is what we call 'nature', i.e. the essence of each thing. Empedocles,

15 however, says that only the mixing brought about by Love and the separating by Strife can be termed 'nature'; and in the same way, according to him, also chance mixtures without any proportion would have to be called 'nature' and separations similarly. Since, then, these things include[155] also what is contrary to nature, therefore it would not be right for either mixture resulting from chance or again sepa-

20 ration to be called 'nature', but mixture according to formula, about which Empedocles has nothing to say.[156]

333b19 Furthermore this is for each thing its well-being and its good; but Empedocles praises only mixture.

Mixture according to formula, [Aristotle] says, which characterises the essence of each individual, is the well-being and good of that individual, for good for each is that which is according to nature, that

25 is according to formula. But Empedocles, having omitted that, 'praises mixture alone'. [157] Yet, if it is not according to formula, it deserves censure more, for it becomes the cause of perishing.

333b20-2 In fact it is not Strife but Love which dissolves the elements, which are by nature prior[158] to God – although they too are gods.

30 Empedocles, calling the Sphere god, praises Love as being its cause
265,1 through bringing all things together, and censures Strife as causing the god to disintegrate, for the elements, being prior to the sphere, produced it as they were brought together by Love. Aristotle, there-fore, turns Empedocles round to [make] a contrary [claim], that according to him Love is rather the cause of disintegration, for if the

5 Sphere has come to be from the elements it is surely not through the persistence of the nature they have. So, [Love] was separating from them the qualities which characterise each before the Sphere, [viz.] from the substrates underlying these [qualities], for otherwise they would not have all taken on the one form, that of the Sphere. If therefore disintegration is to be understood as the separation of form

10 from matter, and this is what Love has done, then she is the cause of disintegration rather [than bringing together]. And the phrase 'these too are gods' means that the elements and not only the Sphere are gods. Perhaps he said this to indicate that Love is no more to be praised for producing the Sphere-god than censured[159] for separating out and destroying the elements, for these too are gods. [And he says this] either because Empedocles [actually] claims that these too are gods or, more probably, because this is implied by his assumption,[160]

15 for if [the elements] are prior to the Sphere and unchangeable, what inconsistency is there in saying that they too are gods?

333b22-6 And his discussion of movement is too general. It is not sufficient to say that Love and Strife cause things to move, unless to be caused by Love is defined[161] as [being moved] with this type of movement, and to be caused by Strife, [as to be moved] with this [other one]. [What was needed was to give definitions or assumptions or proofs, whether rigorous or more relaxed or of some other variety.]

He says that Empedocles, having given no definitive account of 20
movement, what it is, or of what things, simply states that Love and Strife cause movement, the latter by separating and dissociating the elements from each other, and the former by fitting [them] together from the state of being set apart. In the first place, [Aristotle] says, he should have given either definitions relating to movement, or assumptions, or demonstrations; for these are the tasks of knowledge.[162] For they assume and define principles, e.g. that the point has 25
no parts, that there are three kinds of triangles (equilateral, isosceles, and scalene), that circle is a plane figure contained by one line such that the lines drawn from the centre to meet it are equal to one another; and they demonstrate what follows upon the principles.

Unless, he says,[163] Love is self-movement, and similarly Strife.[164]
But Empedocles does not say this, but that Strife and Love are causes 30
of movement. So he said nothing about movement.

333b26-33 Again, since it is apparent[165] that the bodies are 266,1
moved both from constraint, i.e. against nature, [and in accordance with nature (e.g. fire moves upwards without constraint, downwards if constrained), and that which is according to nature is contrary to that which is by constraint – so there is such a thing too as to be moved in accordance with nature. Is it this movement, then, which Love sets in motion? Or not? For, on the contrary, it moves earth downwards, and resembles segregation, and Strife rather than Love is the cause of that movement which is in accordance with nature; so that in fact Love would be altogether against, rather than in accordance with, nature].

When Empedocles praises Love as the cause of movement according to nature and censures Strife as [the cause] of contrary [movement] (for he says, 'as I too am here now, an exile from the gods and a 5
wanderer, trusting in mad strife'),[166] Aristotle again brings him round to a self-contradiction, proving that according to his own assumptions, Love is the cause of movement contrary to nature, and Strife is the cause of movement in accordance with nature. But before this he proves that there does exist movement both in accordance with nature, and contrary to nature. For he has proven that there is forced movement, such as that of fire downwards and a lump of earth 10

upwards; and also the movement that is not forced, as of fire upwards
and a lump of earth downwards, and these are contrary to each other,
the forced against nature, and the unforced in accordance with nature. So, if Strife is the cause of separation, and the elements that are
separated out from the Sphere are borne up and moved, earth down-
15   wards and towards the centre, fire upwards and towards the periphery, and these are their movements in accordance with nature, then
Strife is the cause of the elements moving in accordance with nature and
Love, in combining them and bringing them into one, keeps the earth
away from the centre, and the fire from the periphery, so that she can
bring them together into the same; but this is to move fire and earth
20   contrary to nature, driving them out of their natural places. The movers
will have the same dispositions as the movements, and so Love will be
contrary to nature and Strife according to nature.[167]

333b33-5 But without Love or Strife to move them, there is
absolutely no movement of the bodies themselves, nor rest; but
this is absurd.

According to Empedocles, he says, movement and rest according to
25   nature will be completely destroyed. For if there were no Love and
Strife and the elements were moved by themselves, Love and Strife
would not be the cause of their movement. But if these are the only
causes of their movement, then we shall take away from them movement in accordance with nature, for movement coming from something else and not from itself is, for what is being moved, contrary to
30   nature. But if there is [movement] contrary to nature, then there will
certainly also be[168] movement in accordance with nature; for 'in
accordance with nature' and 'contrary to nature' are terms relative to
each other.[169]

267,1   **333b35-334a2** Moreover, it is apparent that they do move – for
though it was Strife that separated them out, aether was borne
upwards not by Strife.

And even if [Empedocles] himself, he says, does not give them movement from themselves, he does not stand by this, but says that Strife
5   alone separated out the elements from the sphere, but once they are
separated, earth[170] is brought downwards by its nature and fire[171]
upwards. So, they do also have movement that is from themselves
and according to nature; Empedocles thus did not stand by his own
assumptions.

34a2-5 But as he sometimes says, as if by chance, 'for so it
chanced then to meet them running, but often in a different

way',[172] while at other times he says it is the nature of fire to be   10
borne upwards, whereas the aether, he says, 'sank into the
ground with long roots'.[173]

He says that the elements are moved by Strife and Love, and then, as
if not standing by what he says, he sometimes claims that they are
carried along by chance, and at other times [that they are carried
along] according to nature. Consequently, when these statements are
now set down side by side, he does give [the elements] movement from   15
themselves. Empedocles then has not said anything definite or clear
either about movement in an unqualified sense, or about the movement of the elements.

334a5-9 At the same time he says that the universe is in the
same state now under [the rule of] Strife as it was earlier under
[the rule of] Love.[174] [What, then, is the first mover and cause of
movement? It cannot, evidently, be Love and Strife: rather these
are the causes of particular movements, if that other is the
principle.]

Again he charges Empedocles' assumptions with another incongru-   20
ity. [Empedocles] kept saying that the universe is in a similar state
and is similarly moved 'now under Strife as earlier under Love'. If
therefore Love and Strife cause different, in fact, contrary, movements, one causing the Sphere to disintegrate,[175] the other bringing
the elements together, and the universe is now as it was earlier, then
it has a different <movement>, from itself and eternal, with neither   25
Strife nor Love moving it. There will, therefore, be some explanation
for the movement of the universe apart from them. This, then, will be
the principle, as [it is] eternal, and neither Strife, nor Love for each
of these causes movement [only] sometimes.[176]

Alexander inquires in what way he says that the universe is in a   268,1
similar state now as it was earlier, whether *qua* being [the same][177]
or whether *qua* being different each time.[178] And, he says, (i) the
universe he speaks of seems to be the same. For, he says, if someone
were to say that both the separation under Strife and the uniting
under Love were the universe, how would there still be another
source of motion for the universe, apart from Strife and Love? But if,   5
[Alexander] says, [Empedocles] means that it is a natural body, it will
indeed be undergoing uniting and separation, being a substrate for
both the elements and the Sphere, but as a natural body it will be also
moved in some respect[179] by its proper motion. Or, says [Alexander],
(ii) according to Empedocles the universe is and is moved in a similar
way now under Strife as earlier under Love, but, in the intervals
between the movements produced by these, earlier, when Love came   10
to prevail over Strife, and now when Strife [prevails] over Love, the

universe is moved by some different motion, other than the ones by which Love and Strife move.

334a9-15 Another absurdity is involved in supposing that soul
15   is derived from the elements, or is one of them. [For how will the
alterations proper to soul occur, such as being musical, and then
again unmusical, or remembering or forgetting? For clearly, if
the soul is fire it will possess whatever affections belong to fire
qua fire, and if it is a mixture <of elements> the affections
appropriate to bodies. But none of these is appropriate to bodies.
These questions belong, however, to another study.[180]]

In generating everything from the four [elements], Empedocles generated soul from them as well, for, to quote:

'By earth, we see earth, by water, water,
By aether, shining aether; but by fire, blazing fire,
20   Love by love and strife by baneful strife.'[181]

So if soul is from the elements, it will have the same affections[182] as
the ones that the elements have; but soul has no bodily affection, such
as the ones undergone by earth, water, fire, air – 'cultured' and
'uncultured', 'memory' and 'forgetfulness', skills and sciences do not
15   occur in any of the elements; for these are neither bodily affections,
nor perceptible. Nor again do the properties of the elements occur in
the soul – rarity, density, heat, cold, lightness, heaviness or any of
what is seen to belong to bodies. And, in particular, if the elements,
according to Empedocles, are unchangeable, and the soul changes in
respect of knowledge and ignorance and virtue and vice, it would not
be made from the elements. [Aristotle] reasonably defers such discus-
30   sions to his work 'On the soul'.[183]

<2.7. FORMATION OF HOMOEOMERS>

334a15 But, as for the elements out of which bodies are composed.[184]

When he had completed[185] the arguments against Empedocles and
gone over all the branches of the division set out before,[186] refuting
269,1   the others and only leaving undisputed the branch that says that the
four [elements] are principles[187] *qua* changeable,[188] he returns again
to the exposition of them and says that as many as assume that they
are changeable, claim by implication that common matter underlies
them, and vice versa, as many as assume common matter, also hold
5   that they change into each other. For one [claim] implies the other –
to say that there is a common substrate implies that they are change-

able, and to say that they are changeable, implies the common matter. However, all those who assume that the elements are unchangeable and say that all other things come to be from them, as a house from stones and timber put together in a certain way, fall into incongruities, because they are not able to name the source from which the form of flesh or bone or each of the others are brought to completion. And this is a problem, he says, also for those who say that they are changeable.[189]

Having said this he first explains how those who assume that the elements are unchangeable are unable to preserve intact the coming to be of compounds. If the elements, he says, stay unchanged and being merely juxtaposed to each other in a given combination produce flesh (as stones and bricks and timber make the house), fire and water and the rest will not come to be from any part of flesh, just as all [the components] could not be separated out from any part of the house, for bricks and timber could not be separated out from stones. And in the same way, according to them, there will not be separation of all [the ingredients] out from flesh. But as it is, he says, we clearly see that water and earth and each of the others are separated out from any part[190] of flesh and bone, for burning a particular piece of flesh can turn it into fire or air, putrefaction can make it earth, and it is possible to dissolve it into water, if it is overcome by some liquid substance. So their assumption is false and militates against the evidence.

Perhaps they may counter this as follows: 'We do indeed say that all the elements are separated out of all flesh, because we say that flesh is a compound of them all, but we do not agree that all are separated out from each and every part of flesh. Although, according to the evidence, it appears as if they are all separated out from any part of it, this is not true. For in it there is something which is only fire and something which is only water, but it appears to perception that all [the elements] come from every part because each of the elements making up the compound is spread out very finely through the whole of flesh, so that sense perception cannot grasp them as separated out from each other, as is the case with drying powders assembled from several, e.g. four or six, ingredients.'[191] Such, perhaps, might then be the defence they would put forward. And if anyone were to say against them that they are destroying the nature of the homoeomers because they deny that every and any part of flesh is flesh (for 'homoeomerous' means having all parts similar to each other and to the whole),[192] their reply to him would be: 'We are not destroying the nature of the homoeomers as a general rule for we maintain that the four elements are homoeomerous, but we do not allow flesh and bone to be homoeomerous.'[193]

In this way, then, [Aristotle] proves that it is impossible to make flesh, bone, and each of the others from the elements if they are

10

15

20

25

30

35

270,1

5

unchangeable. But, he says, in the case of those who claim that they do change into each other, the argument also involves a problem: how will[194] there ever be the form of flesh or bone, or any other of the

10   homoeomers? For if they say that [the elements] are not preserved in the mixture, then either one of the contraries, say fire, will be destroyed and the whole will be water, or, if they are both destroyed, matter will remain, since they hold that this composite is in-between the simple bodies; it is potentially all of them and actually nothing, and it is fitting for them all to be named 'matter', for this is called

15   'in-between', and, although [being] potentially everything, is actually nothing.[195]

The However, Aristotle does produce a solution to the problem brought up against his own view. And his view is that the elements do change into each other, and he resolves [the problem] by stating what he had said earlier in the tract on mixture [*GC* 1.10, 328a23-31]. For al-though we do say that in a compound the pure form of fire is

20   destroyed, we deny that heat has been completely destroyed; for the compound is still hot, even though the fire would not be pure. For not everything that is hot is fire, but whereas pure fire is hot in the extreme, the compound is not extremely hot, but it is cold relatively to what is hot in the extreme, and hot relatively to what is cold in the extreme. And you can say the same about the cold, that extreme cold

25   is destroyed, and pure water is no longer in the compound except potentially, but cold is not completely destroyed, for cold relative to the extreme heat is still present. So when we say that the extremes of hot and cold have been destroyed, and a compound has come to be, cold relatively to what is hot in the extreme, and hot relatively to what is cold in the extreme, we are not saying that the extremes are

30   still preserved in actuality, nor will we be introducing matter.

The reasoning is the same in the case of moist and dry. For we say that in actuality it is dry and moist not in the extreme, but in some relation, [i.e.] dry relatively to what is moist in the extreme, moist relatively to what is dry in the extreme. And again, we say that the dry and moist in the extreme is dry and moist potentially and not in actuality, because extreme dry and moist are considered to be present

35   in the elements, but these are destroyed and not present in the
271,1 compound except potentially.[196] For simple [bodies] are in a composite potentially, not actually; but not in the first [sense] of 'potentially', in which we say that matter is potentially each of the contraries,[197] for matter is completely deprived and has nothing of the form of fire or

5   water, which it is said to be potentially, whereas a compound, even though not in a pure state, still does have an inhibited form of the fire,[198] and this fire as a whole is not pure, but, as I said, inhibited.

But perhaps it is in the second meaning of 'potentially' – the meaning in which someone is said to be 'potentially' a builder who has the knowledge of house-building in the sense of an acquired disposition,[199] but is not using it because of some impediment, either being asleep, or not having the needed matter at hand? Yet it does not seem 10 to be said in this sense, either, for we cannot say that the compound has the state and potentiality of pure fire, but does not put it to work, for it does not have the potentiality of fire. If it had, it would have actualised it in the presence of matter, but, as it is, it is not seen to be in action.

So, besides the usual ones, there is some further meaning of 'potentially', which Aristotle apparently mentions in the seventh 15 book of the *Physics*.[200] That there *is* another meaning of 'potentially' is clear from the following.[201] The potential in the sense of being suitable[202] and the potential in the sense of acquired disposition[203] are the extremes, and everything in-between these, for example, the change that takes place in the coming to be of a house, is different from the extremes. The house that is being built is not 'potentially' a house in the same way as the stones and timber are; the embryo that 20 is coming to be [a man] is not 'potentially' a man in the same way as the seed, the new-born child is not 'potentially' literate in the same way as the one at the due time of learning, nor the pupil in the same way as when he[204] is already being taught. And in this latter [state] itself there is a considerable breadth: some of it is closer to the form and some further from it.

[205]So this is clear, and we need to be aware, again, of the following 25 point which deserves careful attention. Perhaps someone will object that, if we say that the pure hot has not been destroyed *qua* hot, but has been destroyed *qua* pure hot, we can no longer say that fire also has been destroyed *qua* pure fire, but has not been destroyed *qua* fire without further qualification. For if fire *qua* fire is considered to be the extreme as being pure heat (for fire *qua* fire is not hot relatively 30 to one thing and cold to another, but hot in the extreme), if you say, then, that extreme heat has been destroyed *qua* extreme heat, and fire *qua* fire is extreme heat, clearly fire *qua* fire has been destroyed in the compound. And it will be true to say that fire *qua* fire has been destroyed once and for all, but that heat *qua* heat has not been 35 destroyed without qualification, but it has been destroyed *qua* extreme heat. And this is reasonable, for you cannot say that heat and 272,1 fire are the same, for it is not the case that if something is hot this is fire, but if something is hot in the extreme, this is fire, and if something is fire, it is hot in the extreme. But if fire *qua* fire has been destroyed once and for all, it is obvious that the compound will be fire potentially, according to the first meaning of 'potentially' (in which 5 we say also of matter that it is potentially fire), for a compound has nothing of fire *qua* fire. However, with respect to heat, this claim made above stays true, for when it has been destroyed *qua* extreme heat, but has not been destroyed *qua* heat without qualification, it is reasonable to say that the compound is potentially hot in the extreme,

10   not in the first meaning of 'potentially', but in accordance with the
     distinctions made above.[206]
         Let this be enough for this lengthy exposition, which does go
     beyond the proposed study, and we should return to the beginning.
     He proved that it is not necessary to bring in matter[207] when saying
     that neither of the extremes is preserved in the compound, because,
15   he says, once the extremes have destroyed excesses in the mixture,
     they produce an intermediate between the two extremes. Then, in
     case anyone should ask: 'If in the mixture an intermediate between
     the extremes is always produced, where does a great variety of
     compounds – flesh, bone, marrow, and the like – come from?', he pays
     due attention to this question and gives an explanation for the
     existence of differences in compounds from the difference in mixture.
20   Although each of the compounds partakes of all [the elements], it is
     not in the same proportion, but some partake more in heat, others
     more in cold. This is why, although all the compounds are potentially
     extremes, one has more heat potentially, another less, for what
     changes more easily is potentially hotter, and what changes more
     slowly, less so; what has a greater share of fire changes into fire more
25   easily, and what has a lesser share of fire more slowly. We should
     realise that, if we say the changing of the elements into each other
     comes about when they are not equal, the weaker ones, with their
     powers being overcome, changing into the nature of the stronger,
     with everything becoming fire or water, whereas compounds result
     when they are equal, we are not taking equality in a precise sense.
30   Similarly, when we say that the extremes in the compound produce
     some intermediate, we do not take this to be indivisible[208] and undi-
     vided (as a middle in a precise sense),[209] but as divided into many and
     having many differences other than the more and the less.

273,1   **334a16-18** For those who hold that they have a common [sub-
         strate][210] or change into each other, necessarily, if they accept
         one of these views, the other follows.[211]

     Whether someone assumes [the existence of] matter, the elements
     will always change in it, since [otherwise] the common substrate is
5   superfluous; and whether the elements change into each other, they
     will still have a common substrate, in which they effect change into
     each other. The battle of the contraries arises over something com-
     mon[212] to them both, which each of the contraries wants to master.

         334a18-21 Those, however, who do not make them come to be
         from each other, nor in such a way as to come from each, except
         in the way that bricks come from a wall.

10   Those, he says, who say that the elements do not have their coming

to be from each other ('from each other' in the sense of each coming from each), but are separated out from being inherent [in each other] in actuality, 'as bricks from a wall', cannot make flesh and bone from them, which is why he next charges them with incongruity.

334a21-32 The point we mention creates a difficulty also for those who <make>[213] [them come] from one another [, namely, 15 the problem of how something else over and above them comes to be from them. The sort of thing I mean is that water can come to be from fire, and fire from this (since they both have something in common, namely the substratum); but what is more, from them there comes to be flesh and marrow. How then can these come to be?

What will be the way of it according to those whose account is similar to that of Empedocles? It will have to be composition, the way in which a wall comes to be out of brick and stones. The elements out of which this mixture comes to be will be preserved, but will be put together alongside one another in small particles: this will be the way with flesh and each of the others. It follows that fire and water cannot come to be from any particle of flesh whatsoever.]

And, he says, those who say that the elements are changeable[214] and have fire and water coming to be from each other because of their common substrate, bone and nerve and the rest coming to be from both [fire and water] coming together, run into a problem as well: how should they explain flesh, and bone, and nerve, and each of the others 20 coming to be from simple [bodies] changing? Even if it be conceded, he says, that simple [bodies] come to be from each other – it is still not easy to explain how compounds [come to be] from simple [bodies] coming together. After saying this he first sets out the incongruities that follow for those who assume [the elements] to be unchangeable, and similarly sets out the objections brought against those who say that they do change.

334a32-b4 In the way that with wax, whilst from this part a 25 sphere might come to be and a pyramid from some other, [it would always be possible for it to happen the other way round. This does in fact occur in this way, i.e. from flesh both elements can come to be from any particle whatsoever. According to this account we have been discussing, however, it would not be possible: it would have to be in the way that stone and brick come from a wall, one from one place and one from another.

Equally a difficulty arises for those who posit a single matter

for the elements: how is something to come from both, e.g. from
cold and hot or from fire and earth?]

After explaining the incongruity that follows for those who say that
the elements produce flesh and bone by combining, while staying
unchanged themselves (namely, that they cannot produce fire and
earth and the others from any part of flesh taken at random[215]), from
274,1   the example of wax he makes clear the sense in which he holds that
all the elements come to be from any random part. Although we
accept that one part of wax produces a sphere and another a pyramid,
it was nonetheless possible for a sphere to come to be from the part
that had been shaped into a pyramid, even if it did not so come to be,
5   and for a pyramid from the part that had been shaped into a sphere,
in the same way, he says, the coming to be of both from any random
part happens in the case of flesh. Although water comes to be from
this part of flesh and fire from another one, it is still possible for fire
as well as water to come to be from either part of flesh; for what
changes into fire could also change into air, which they cannot adopt,
10   but which is apparently the case.

334b4-8 For if flesh is from both and is neither of them [, nor
again a composite in which the components are preserved, what
<account of the phenomenon> remains except <the view> that
that which comes out of these is their matter? For the destruction of the one produces either the other or their matter].

He now sets out the problem raised against those who say that the
elements are changeable.[216] If, he says, they claim that flesh is from
both [fire and water], yet identifiable with neither of its ingredients,
15   nor a combination of them as long as they are preserved and stay
unchanged, it remains for what comes to be from them to be nothing
else except matter, for when a contrary is destroyed, either its contrary will come to be, or matter. If, therefore, they say that neither
[any] one is preserved, nor both together, matter will result.

334b8-14 Is it then that since things can be hot and cold more
20   and less [, when one exists *simpliciter* in actuality, the other
exists in potentiality; when, however, it is not completely so, but
as it were hot-cold or cold-hot, because in being mixed things
destroy each other's excesses, then what will exist is neither
their matter nor any of the contraries existing *simpliciter* in
actuality, but something intermediate].

He now resolves the difficulty brought against his own view. What he
means to say is this: since heat and cold are spoken of as more or less
(when we mean 'hot' and 'cold' relatively to something else), but heat

is also spoken of as extreme, *simpliciter*, and without qualification, not in comparison with anything else, when something is actually hot 25 or cold *simpliciter*, it is potentially the contrary, and when it is hot not *simpliciter*, but relatively to something else (as cold relatively to the extremely hot, and hot relatively to the extremely cold, because the excesses of the extremes are inhibited in a mixture), then, he says, the object will be neither of the two contraries in actuality, but both potentially, and matter is not introduced; for when the excesses in the 30 extremes have been destroyed, some other intermediate form supervenes. And if someone asks in what sense we say that this mixed thing is potentially each of the contraries and 'intermediate' (for these are appellations[217] appropriate to matter), he should be aware that 275,1 although it is potentially each of the contrary extremes, yet it will no longer[218] be matter in a strict sense of prime and formless. For we do also say that fire is potentially water, not in the sense that fire is the matter simple and said in a strict sense, as those who raise the 5 problem intend, for fire is endowed with form. Moreover, earlier the senses in which matter is said to be potentially each of the contraries, and the compound is potentially the simple bodies, were distinguished,[219] and Aristotle draws this distinction in a general way in what follows.

334b14-18 Which, insofar as it is in potentiality more hot than cold, or vice versa, [is proportionately twice as hot in potentiality 10 as cold, or three times, or in some similar way. It is as a result of the contraries, or the elements, having been mixed that the other things will exist, and the elements from these latter, which in potentiality, in some way, are <the elements>].

After he had said that an intermediate between the extremes comes to be from mixture, and, since this intermediate is not undivided, but shows differences, he now adds this explanation of the cause. To the extent to which something, he says, is spoken of as potentially hot <rather> than cold and having the hot in excess, or being more cold 15 than hot, in the same proportion of excess [a thing] will be either two or three times as hot; for the excess is always in some proportion, either double, or half, or triple, or some such. Having said this as it were in parentheses he goes on to explain that compounds will arise from a mixture of simple and contrary [ingredients]. He said 'the other things' for the compounds, and 'the elements' again for the 20 simple [bodies], 'from them' is 'from the compounds', and 'being potentially' refers to the simple bodies. But having said, 'from contraries' he added 'or from the elements' because the elements, e.g. fire and water, are not contrary *per se*, but to the extent to which they are endowed with form, and they are endowed with form insofar as they are hot and cold or moist and dry, which are contraries *par excel-*

25   *lence.*[220] But without a substrate these do not exist, nor can they be
       mixed. That is why it is reasonable for him to add 'or of <the>[221]
       elements'; for these do mix. And perhaps it is possible to link 'or in
       some similar way' with '[the other things] will result from a mixing
       of the contraries'.[222]

       334b18-20 Not in the same way as matter but in the way we
30   have explained. And in this way what comes to be is a mixture,
       in that way it is matter.

       After he had said that the simple bodies come to be from compounds
276,1 which are potentially what the simple bodies are, he adds a qualifica-
       tion that compounds are not potentially simple bodies in the way that
       matter is. So what is the difference? It is that the compound is said
       to be potentially the simple [bodies] since it is endowed with form and
       is in actuality something different from simple bodies, whereas mat-
       ter is said to be the elements in potentiality in the sense that it does
5   not subsist by itself. So according to us and our argument, what comes
       to be from the simple elements, once the excess in each has been
       destroyed, is a *mixture*; whereas according to those who raise difficul-
       ties saying that the forms of the elements are completely destroyed
       in the compound, it is formless matter that results.[223] So although
       according to us *and* those who raise the problem, what is finally
10   produced is potentially simple bodies, this does not mean the same
       thing, because we say what comes to be is mixture, and they say it is
       matter.
           And perhaps someone will interpret the claim 'the compound is
       potentially the simple bodies not in the way in which matter is' more
       naturally by bringing in the difference of meaning which we men-
       tioned above, in the study [of the argument].[224] The difference is this,
15   that matter is said to be potentially the simple bodies while having
       no trace[225] of their form (which is the first meaning of 'in potentiality'),
       but this is not the case with the compound, for this *does* have
       something of the form of the simple bodies, even though they have
       been destroyed in their pure state (and this cannot be in accordance
       with the first meaning of 'potentially'). And the following point should
       be marked: if Aristotle says that it is not in the same meaning of
20   'potentially' that both matter and compound bodies are said to be
       simple bodies 'potentially', he does not think that in a compound fire
       and the other elements must be completely destroyed *qua* fire [etc.],
       but *qua* pure fire, so that pure fire is the same as the extreme hot, [226]
       while inhibited fire is the same as what is hot relatively to something
       else.[227] We said 'more natural'[228] about the interpretation that has
       just been given, because to say that a compound exists in actuality
25   and is self-subsistent, but not matter, is not to explain the difference
       with regard to the meaning of 'potentially' which Aristotle hints at

when he says that the compound and the matter are not to be taken
to be 'potentially' the simple bodies in the same sense. 'This is
mixture' and 'in that way it is matter' should be understood likewise
in accordance with the two interpretations we mentioned above.[229]   30

334b20-4 Since[230] the contraries are also acted upon as stated
in the definition in Book 1 [– for the actually hot is cold in
potentiality and the actually cold hot in potentiality, so that
unless they are equal they change into one another, and the
same holds in the case of other contraries].

It was his purpose to teach that sometimes the elements come to be
from each other in the [process of] change, at other times compounds
result, because, as long as one [element] prevails over another for the   277,1
most part, the lesser is overcome by the greater and changes, and the
whole becomes like [the greater]; but when the contraries are equal
then a compound results, each [contrary] acting and being acted upon
by the other, with the result that the excesses are destroyed and an
intermediate comes to be. This is the idea (*dianoia*), while the inter-   5
pretation of the text is as follows. Since, he says, the contraries are
naturally affected by each other, as has been explained before in the
[chapter] 'On Acting and Being Affected' [*GC* 1.7], because a contrary
is potentially its own contrary, as, for example, heat is potentially
cold, it is absolutely inevitable that, when one is more powerful than
the other, the weaker changes into it, and similarly with dry and   10
moist and the rest.

334b24-7 First, the elements change in this way; but flesh and
bones and suchlike come from these <elements>, [the hot becoming cold and the cold hot when they approach the mean].

What he says is this – that since they are naturally disposed to change
into each other, when they happen to be equally matched in their
acting upon each other, each makes the first impulse[231] of change as   15
into the contrary, but, since the powers are equal and neither prevails
over the other, an intermediate comes about, when the extreme
degree of each of the two is inhibited. And since this intermediate is
not something indivisible,[232] but is seen to cover a broad range,
therefore there is not one particular form of the intermediate, but
several compounds – flesh, bones and the like.

334b25-6 But flesh and bones, <and the like> come from   20
these.[233]

The intermediates, he says, come to be from these simple bodies,
when their extremes are inhibited by each other.

334b27 For here they are neither one thing nor the other [, and the mean is large and not an indivisible point. Similarly dry and wet and all the rest of this kind produce flesh and bone and the rest in the middle range].

In such a change, he says, neither of the [two] extremes comes to be,
25   but a mixture of both.

334b29-30 And all[234] the rest of this kind [produce flesh and bone and the rest in the middle range].

After saying that heat and cold and dryness and moisture in an intermediate state produce compounds, he added 'and the rest of this kind', because other powers, like sweetness and sourness, although
278,1   they do not happen to produce form,[235] yet also bring about an intermediate state in the compounds.

<2.8. EACH ELEMENT PRESENT IN EVERY HOMOEOMER>

334b31-2 All[236] the mixed bodies which are around the place of the middle body [are composed of all the simple bodies].

5   His purpose here is to prove that all natural composite bodies are composed of the four elements. Since in refuting those who say that bodies are composed of unchangeable elements he assumed that from each part of the compounds (e.g. flesh) each element is separated, it is reasonable for him now to set out to prove this very [claim], namely
10   that each compound is composed of the four elements. And he said 'which are around the place of a middle body' not for contrast, as though there are some mixed [bodies] not around the place of a middle body, the way some describe the concourse of the moist and dry exhalation, which, he says in the *Meteorology*,[237] rise being combined together (but these are not by nature mixed, nor do they result in
15   something one, but are adjacent to each other in juxtaposition), but this phrase is equivalent to: 'all the mixed bodies, which are *also* around the place of the middle body'. For it is a property of the mixed bodies to be around the place of the middle body. These, then, he says, are composed of all the elements, and in what follows he supplies his demonstrations.

334b32-5 Earth[238] exists in all of them, for a start, since each
20   element is mostly and in the great quantity in its own [place. Next, water, because the composite must be bounded]

First he proves that all compounds partake of earth. The outline of the argument is as follows. If each, he says, is most in excess in its own place, clearly the greatest quantity of earth will belong to the compounds that are in the place of earth (for the middle place is the place of earth). After this he gives a clear proof that they also must partake of water, from the fact that earth cannot keep together and be set within limits unless bounded by combination with water, as by some sort of glue.

> **334b35-35a4** And water alone of the simple bodies is easily bounded [; and because, moreover, earth cannot keep together without the moist, this being what holds it together: if the moist were taken out of it completely it would fall apart. For these reasons, then, earth and water exists in them].

He says that water alone of the rest is easily bounded, although air seems to be more easily bounded because it is also moister.[239] Therefore 'easily bounded' should be understood as standing for 'providing with boundaries', as in composition of earth, [earth] comes to be easily bounded only from a mixture with water.[240] Clay illustrates this, as it becomes easily bounded not by air, but by water. For water, being more fit for filling up than air, settles on earth and is unified with it, while air, because of its lightness and fine structure, easily escapes and slips away from mixture, and water, being both heavy and denser than air better combines with it and settles on it.

> **335a4-9** But also air and fire, since they are the contraries of earth and water [(earth is the contrary of air and water of fire, in the way in which it is possible for one substance to be the contrary of another). Since, therefore, comings to be are from contraries, and one member of each pair of contraries exists in these things, the other members must also exist in them; so that all the simple bodies are present in every composite body.]

Having shown that water and earth are present in composites, he now proves that fire and air must be present in them too. For if we say that compounds are mixed [bodies], and it is not any chance things that mix, but those that are naturally disposed to being affected by each other, and things affected are contraries, it is clear that since there are earth and water, the contraries of these must be there too. And air is contrary to earth, fire to water. So if dry and cold are in a compound through earth, air, which is moist and hot, must also be there so that a mixture of contraries could come about. In the same way if there is cold and moistness due to water, through fire both heat and dryness will be there likewise.[241] And after he said that fire and air are contraries to water and earth, he had to add: 'in the way in which it is possible for one substance to be the contrary of another', viz. not in respect of the substrate, but only in respect of the

20   specifying powers, i.e. the hot and the cold and the moist and the dry.
     For in respect of these the elements are contrary to each other, and
     in respect of the substrate they are united since it is common to all.
     But perhaps someone will say that heat and dryness are the form of fire;
     form is substance; and so it follows that form-substance has a contrary.
     How then did he say in the *Categories*[242] that no substance is contrary
25   to a substance? Or is it clear that in the *Categories* his argument was
     about composite substances?[243] You have a further clarification here of
     how he means that fire is contrary to water, as many times as he says
     that [they are so] not as a whole, but in respect of powers in them.[244]

> **335a9-14** There seems to be evidence of this in the nourishment
> of each thing.[245] [For everything is nourished by the same things
> as it is made of, and everything is nourished by a number of things.
> Even things which might seem to be nourished by just one thing,
> i.e. plants by water, are in fact nourished by more than one. For
> earth is mixed with the water – which is why farmers do their best
> to mix something with the water before irrigating.]

30   He now also deduces from nourishment that mixed bodies are [made]
     of the four [elements]. For since, he says, each thing is nourished from
     the same [kind of things] of which it consists, and nothing is nour-
     ished by anything simple, but by composites, it is clear that no one of
280,1 the mentioned mixed bodies is simple, but all consist of the four
     [elements]. As to what seems to be a conflicting fact in the case of
     plants, namely that they are nourished only by water, this he lays
     down and refutes saying that earth too is mixed in the water by which
     they are nourished. So if they consist of those [things] by which they
5   are nourished then it follows that they consist of earth and water. But
     if they consist of earth and water then necessarily also <of> contrar-
     ies, by the argument stated above. Consequently, they also partake
     of fire and air. These too, then, must be present in their nourishment.
     This is why farmers mix not just any earth that may chance, but
     manure, which partakes of fiery and airy substance; having mixed it,
10   he says, farmers use it in this way in watering.

> **335a14-21** Since[246] nourishment ranks as matter, whereas what
> is nourished is [the shape or form] taken together with[247] matter
> [, it immediately stands to reason that fire, alone of the simple
> bodies, should be nourished, though all of them come to be from
> one another. This is the view of the earlier thinkers too. For fire
> alone, or more than the others, ranks as form, since its nature
> is to be borne towards the boundary].

Now, as though for the sake of example and poetic manner of speech,
seeking the reason why, whereas all the elements change into one

another, some said of fire alone that it is nourished (for so the poet[248] 15
too said: 'all at once does fire eat them'), he says, then, that since
nourishment is the matter of that which is nourished, and the nourished is form taken together with and combined with matter (for this
[viz. form] is in fact what persists),[249] it is reasonable to say that fire
alone of the simple bodies is nourished, because of the simple bodies
it is form *par excellence*.[250] And he establishes that fire is form in the 20
following way. Since we see that fire in accordance with nature is
borne towards the boundary, and the boundary is the limit of something and circumference, and each [element] is in accordance with
nature borne to its proper place, it is clear that the boundary is the
proper place of fire, i.e. the limit and container of others. Since, then,
the form of each is in the limit – and he means 'form' not in the sense 25
of essential account, but in the sense of shape (for that is held to be
in the surface), – it follows that when fire is present in the limit, this
latter is its form. And it is in the boundary of the other elements and
in the limit which contains everything. Hence it is clear that it is the
form of the rest. Therefore it is reasonable to say that it alone of the
rest is nourished.

<2.9. CAUSES OF COMING-TO-BE AND PERISHING>

335a22 The claim that every body is composed of all simple   281,1
bodies has thus been dealt with.[251]

Having stated in the beginning what coming to be is, and in what
respect it differs from other kinds of change, having then devoted a
very long discussion in the middle to the change of the elements into
one another in general, and intending in what follows to speak about   5
coming to be in particular, and planning to expound more specific
changes of the elements in the treatise of *Meteorology*, he resumes the
discussion of coming to be in general, investigating how many principles
in general there are of things that come to be and pass away, and what
kinds [of principles] they are. For from these we shall also know the   10
principles of particular comings to be, because there are as many
principles of particular comings to be as there are principles of comings
to be in general. And so he says that the principles of things generable
and perishable are as many in number as those of things eternal, and
'the same in kind'. For matter is posited in both, and form too is
considered to be present in the former as well as in the latter, but in
generable things matter is considered as that which is potentially (as it 15
is in potentiality each of the contraries), whereas in the case of things
eternal it is not considered as that which is potentially, but is always in
actuality endowed with form, and it is not the case that sometimes it
acquires form, and sometimes becomes deprived of it, because there,
form is eternal and is always disposed in the same way, not having a

contrary, while here it is subject to coming to be and passing away,
20 because contrariety is held to be in it.[252]

And there also is, he says, the third, efficient, cause,[253] which in
things generable and perishable is the cause of coming to be, whereas
in things eternal, it is the efficient cause not of coming to be but of
permanence. Now, the principles of coming to be being this many, all,
he says, recognised the material and the formal, but as to the efficient
25 [cause], they dreamed of it, but no one articulated it. Some rendered
the Form as efficient cause, as Plato in the *Phaedo*.[254] He, after
reproaching others for adducing no notion of efficient cause (at which
point he commended[255] Anaxagoras for saying that the intellect is
efficient cause, although not even he[256] used it in the coming to be of
things generable),[257] says himself further on that Form by its pres-
30 ence produces that which is endowed with form.[258] But [Aristotle]
criticises him, saying that Form is not sufficient for production:[259] we
don't say that the image produces what comes to be in proportion with
it, but the craftsman,[260] and health does not heal the one who is ill
when there is no doctor. Further, he says,[261] if there are Ideas (for it
is these that Plato says to be Forms), why is it that when that which
partakes is present, it does not come to be directly?[262] For example, if
35 both the Form of health and the person afflicted with sickness are
282,1 present, why does not the afflicted person become healthy by changing from the state of illness directly, but instead there is, evidently,
the need of a doctor? In this way, then, he refutes those who say that
forms are productive.

Others, he says, made matter a cause, saying that it produces
because of its being changed.[263] Those who posited indivisible principles [i.e. atoms] were also of this view.[264] And he says that insofar as
5 they call it efficient cause because they link it with affections and
movement,[265] they give an account more in accordance with the study
of nature (for we call 'efficient cause' the starting point of movement),
and in this respect they deserve more approval than those who say
that immobile Forms [are the cause]. But insofar as they did not name
anything else as the cause of movement in matter, he thinks, they
10 deserve criticism. For matter obviously does not have the principle of
producing and moving, but rather of being moved and being acted
upon by another. Some others explained efficient causes in terms of
powers of bodies, heat and cold, but these are the instruments of the
efficient cause, not themselves efficient causes; for nature acts by
their means as instruments. And he proves that they act [in a
15 manner] inferior to that of instruments, since the instruments have
no effect upon matter when the art is not in charge, while the hot and
the cold, if not measured by nature or art, destroy the subject.[266] Having
established this, he expounds his own doctrine of efficient cause.

335a22-3 The claim that every body is composed of all simple
bodies[267]

By 'every' he refers to composites; for simple bodies are not composed
of simple [bodies], since then they would not have been simple.

335a24-8 Since[268] there are some things which are generable
and perishable [, and since coming to be does in fact occur in the
place around the middle body, we must say, concerning all
coming to be alike, how many principles there are of it, and what
they are. We shall in this way be able more easily to study
particular cases, namely when we have first obtained a grasp of
things which are universal].

He says 'some' not with reference to the sentence above: he does not
mean that some of the bodies composed of all the elements are
generable and perishable (for all the compounds of four elements are
generable and perishable). But since of all bodies, some are eternal and
some generable and perishable,[269] for that reason he says 'since there are
some [bodies] generable and perishable, which are joined together
around the middle of the whole, it should be investigated how many
principles there are of their coming to be and what they are'.

335a28-30 [The principles are equal in number] and identical in
kind to those which hold in the case of the eternal and primary
beings: one of them by way of matter [and one by way of form].

He says that the principles of both generable and eternal things are
of the same kind. For matter too, he says, is considered to be present
in both generable and eternal [things]; and he examines matter here
considered as the underlying substrate.[270] Therefore it is reasonable
that he says that they are of the same kind: for the underlying
substrate in a general sense[271] is seen to be present in both eternal
and generable things. For although in one case [matter] is superior,
and in the other inferior, they are of the same kind nonetheless, since
rational and irrational animal, too, which have[272] this difference[273] of
superiority and inferiority towards each other, still belong to the
same kind. The matter of eternal things is superior in the sense that
being always in actuality it is never in potentiality, whereas the
matter of generable things, since it is contraries in potentiality,
always is potentially the contrary of the form which is in it.

And perhaps someone might suspect that this difference is present
not because of the nature of matter, but because of the Forms.[274] For
since the form of the heavenly bodies does not have a contrary, but is
eternal and is always in the same state, for that reason its matter is
always in actuality; whereas that of the generable things, being
itself, too, in actuality and never staying formless, because of there

25

30

283,1

5

10

15 being a contrariety in form, always has [being] in potentiality, as a consequence.

However, we should recognise that the difference comes about not only through form, but also through matter itself. For both the matter of generable things would not have been able to receive a contrary while losing the one it had before, had it not been in possession of [being] in potentiality; and so, too, [the matter] of eternal things, had it had the potentiality to lose the form, would have lost it as the

20 potentiality proceeded into actuality. But it should be remembered, as we said in the beginning [283,1-2], that by the term 'matter' Aristotle refers here to the one taken in the sense of a substrate, and not to the one understood as 'being in potentiality'.[275] For if we take the matter he discusses here in the sense of [being] in potentiality, [the matter] of generable things will no longer be of the same kind as the one of eternal

25 things, since the latter does not involve [being] in potentiality.

335a31 [And the third principle must also exist,] for the two[276] are not adequate for making [things] come to be.[277]

He himself said elsewhere that when matter is suitable for receiving form, there is no need of any third party which would bind form to it, but it receives it of its own nature and spontaneously.[278] Why is it then

284,1 that here he apparently says that the two principles are not sufficient, but what is coming to be needs also an efficient cause? We reply to this that the fact that matter has become suitable is owed not to [matter] itself, but to the efficient cause. And for this there is the need of efficient cause, for making the matter suitable to work upon.[279] For

5 in this way the sculptor is said to bring about the form, namely by removing from matter that which impedes the form, not by imposing the form from outside. And the matter receives the suitability and acquires the form at the same time.

335a32 No more than in the case of the primary [beings].

'No more than in the case of the primary beings', he says, are form

10 and matter sufficient, but these [beings] need also an efficient cause, albeit not for coming to be, but for being and persistence.

335a32-5 The cause by way of matter of things which come to be is that which is capable of being and not being. [For some things of necessity are, i.e. the eternal things, and some things of necessity are not.]

The matter, i.e. the underlying substrate of things generable, he says,

15 is the being in potentiality, which can sometimes be and at other times not be. For since, he says, some things of necessity are, e.g.

eternal things, for which, he says, it is impossible not to be, and others of necessity are not, for which, he says, it is impossible to be, e.g. things which are never and in no way in existence except merely in concept, such as goat-stag,[280] and others, he says, are capable of both being and not being, such as the things that are generable and   20 perishable, it is likely, he says, that the underlying substrate of these last too is capable, both of being and not being this particular form.

335a35-b6 Of these the one class cannot not be [, since it is not possible for them to be otherwise, contrary to necessity; some things, however, are capable both of being and not being – which is that which comes to be and perishes. For this is at one time and at another is not. So coming to be and passing away belong necessarily to what is capable of being and not being. That is why it is the cause by way of matter of things that come to be].

Of these – he means just mentioned things, [i.e.] those that of necessity are and of necessity are not – 'the one class cannot not be', i.e. the eternal things, 'the other cannot be', [i.e.] the things which never   25 enter the process of coming to be, such as the centaur.[281] After this he also adds the cause, saying 'since it is not possible for them to be otherwise, contrary to necessity'; for the one class necessarily is, while the other necessarily is not. For this reason, then, the one class of these cannot be, while the other cannot not be. Hence, coming to be and perishing take place in that which is capable of both being and not being.   30

335b6 The cause by way of 'that for the sake of which' is the   285,1 shape or form.

Having discussed material cause, he now treats separately of the form, saying that form is the essential rational principle of each thing. He terms it 'that for the sake of which', explaining that formal cause concurs with the final cause, as he said in the *Physics*, too.[282] For indeed nature   5 has it as its goal and end to produce the form of each thing in matter, and that which results and which supervenes on matter, in fact, *is* form.

335b7-8 To these, however, must be added the third cause which every philosopher dreams of but none actually mentions.

He refers to the efficient cause, and alludes to both Anaxagoras and   10 Plato. For Anaxagoras, having declared the Intellect to be the efficient cause, makes no use of it in [his account of] the coming to be of things, but Plato, too, mentioned the efficient cause in the *Timaeus*,[283] and in the *Phaedo*[284] attached the efficient cause to the Forms, saying: 'But if someone tells me that the reason why[285] a given object is beautiful is that[286] it has a gorgeous colour or shape or any other such   15

attribute, I disregard all these explanations[287] – I find them all confusing – and I cling simply and straightforwardly, naively perhaps, to the explanation that the one thing that makes the object beautiful[288] is the presence in it or association with it (in whatever way the relation comes about) of that other Beauty. I do not go so far as to insist upon the precise detail.' Thus Plato turned out to be
20 unable to give the proximate efficient cause of things that come to be, but has had recourse to the Ideas.

> **335b9-16** But some thought that the nature of the Forms is an adequate cause for coming to be,[289] as Socrates in the *Phaedo*. [(He, you remember, after blaming everyone else for saying nothing to the point, adopts the hypothesis that, of things that are, some are Forms and some partake of the Forms, and that everything is said to be in virtue of the Form, to come to be in virtue of receiving a share of it and to perish in virtue of losing it; so if this is true, the Forms, he thinks, are necessarily the causes of both generation and corruption).]

25 He now addresses himself to Plato, who says that Forms are efficient causes and that they suffice by themselves to produce things that come to be. For he says that each thing has its being in accordance with Forms, and the fact of its having come to be in accordance with its participation of them, just as its perishing is in accordance with its loss of them. Thus
286,1 he said that coming to be and perishing belongs to things from Forms.
And some say in defence of Plato that Plato stated that creative Forms[290] are efficient causes, by participation in which things coming to be come to be and by the loss of which they perish. But if he posits
5 creative Forms, it is clear that he himself regards these as the efficient cause of the forms that are in generable things. For in my view, the one who says 'creative causes', immediately leads into the concept of efficient [causes]. Therefore someone might perhaps say that Aristotle reproaches Plato for this very reason,[291] namely, that he says that Forms themselves produce, assigning no causal rôle to the Maker who looks at the Forms and in accordance with likeness to
10 them produces things here.[292] And for that reason, arguing against him, [Aristotle] says that when there are health and knowledge, i.e. when there are the rational principles[293] of health and knowledge, and there are things receptive of health and knowledge, there still is a need of some other efficient cause, e.g. of a doctor and of someone knowledgeable. For if these do not act, then neither will the one who is ill become healthy, nor yet will the ignorant change to [the state of]
15 knowledge. Since if the Form were by itself sufficient to act, given that there is that which is receptive of it, why then is it not always the case that the one who is ill becomes healthy, or the one who is ignorant becomes knowledgeable?

335b16-23 For others, it is the matter itself;[294] for it is from[295] this that movement arises. [But neither party gives the correct account. For if the Forms are causes, why do they not always generate things continuously rather than sometimes doing so and sometimes not, since both the Forms and the things which partake in them are always there? Furthermore, in some cases we observe something else being the cause: it is the doctor who induces health, and the knowledgeable man knowledge, despite the existence of both health itself and knowledge and those who partake in it.]

Having explained in what way Plato says that Forms are efficient causes [335b12-16], he says in parentheses that others thought matter acts, being deceived by the change (*tropê*)[296] and movement that 20 are in it. After this he then turns to the refutations of Plato's doctrine,[297] and following that refutes also those who say that matter is the cause *qua* efficient.

335b23 And it is the same in all the other cases where something is performed in virtue of a capacity.

This is to say that the same argument as the one that we stated in 25 the case of medicine and knowledge applies in all cases where something is performed in accordance with acquired disposition.[298]

335b24-33 If, on the other hand, someone were to say[299] that it was matter which generated things on account of movement [, what he said would be more scientific than that just described. For that which alters a thing, or changes its shape, is more truly the cause of generation; and generally we are accustomed to describe as the producer, both in case of things which occur in nature and of those which result from skill, that thing, whatever it may be, which has to do with movement. Nevertheless, what these people have to say is also incorrect. For it is the property of matter to be acted upon and to be moved, whereas causing movement and acting belongs to another capacity. This is obviously the case with things which come to be through skill and those which come to be through nature: the water does not itself produce an animal out of itself, nor the wood a bed – it is skill which does this].

As many, he says, as posited matter as efficient principle, having in mind its movement and change (*tropê*), seem to have rendered the cause in a way more appropriate to the study of nature, because the more principal cause of generation is that from which there is the 287,1 beginning of movement (for this is how we usually define the efficient cause), except, he says, that they were unaware of the fact that matter does not have movement from itself. For neither does water from itself produce animals, nor does the timber produce bed, but 5 [these things] come to be by art and nature which are efficient causes. For the special property[300] of matter is not to move, but be moved.

> **335b34-5** [So these people are for this reason incorrect in their account,] and because they leave aside what is more strictly the cause; for they take away the essence and the form.

Either he reproaches them for leaving aside form as well as the efficient cause, or he is calling efficient cause form and shape, as 10 Alexander says, because that which is producing produces while being[301] in actuality, and that which is in actuality is such in accordance with form and shape. For each thing has its being in accordance with form.

But it is more plausible to say that he is referring to the final cause, which they destroy by making material cause responsible for coming to be and assuming that neither intellect nor nature preconceives the 15 end, but that the things that come to be do so incidentally.

> **336a1-6** Moreover, the capacities they attribute to the bodies, in virtue of which they make things come to be, are too instrumental [since they eliminate the cause in accordance with form. For since, according to them, the nature of the hot is to segregate and that of the cold to gather together, and that of each of the others is either to act or to be acted upon, they say that out of these and by their means everything else comes to be and is destroyed].

He has a further argument against those who posited matter as the cause of generation. He objects to them because they assumed that 20 all the powers are instrumental causes[302] of generation, and omitted the cause in accordance with form; and he clearly means 'form' here as efficient cause.[303] What kind of causes, then, did they assume? The hot and the cold; for they say that all else comes to be because the hot dissociates and the cold gathers together. And we agree that each of the things that come to be by nature has these as underlying the 25 moving [cause]. For that which, using these as an instrument, is the cause of coming to be and passing away, is different. And Alexander says that those around Parmenides have been of this view.[304]

> **336a6-12** In fact, however, it is evident that even fire itself is moved and acted upon. [Again, what they do is rather like someone assigning the responsibility for things' coming to be to

the saw and the various tools: for, necessarily, it is only if someone is sawing that something is being divided, and it is only if someone is planing that something is being made smooth; and it is the same in the other cases. So, however much fire acts and causes movement, the question how it causes movement remains something which they do not go on to consider, nor that it is worse than the tools.]

Even fire itself, he says, which they say to be by far the most active,[305] evidently is altered and acted upon, whereas the efficient cause in a strict sense is not acted upon. And indeed we would not say that 30 nature is acted upon, insofar as it is efficient cause, but if at all, [that] its underlying substrate [is acted upon], while [nature] itself always 288,1 imparts motion. Fire, however, not only moves but also is acted upon, and furthermore, even when it moves, it does so not as an agent, but in the rank of instrument, as a saw. For although what comes to be does so as a result of its sawing, nonetheless it is not [the saw] itself that acts. Fire, too, is this way, or rather it is even inferior to the 5 instruments, not being ruled by art, for the reason which we mentioned.[306] But if someone inquires why [Aristotle] does not posit an instrumental cause of natural [things], since in general he recognises such powers as satisfying the definition of instrumental cause, he should know that [Aristotle] subsumes them under matter; for such things are proximate matter.

<2.10. EFFICIENT CAUSE OF COMING-TO-BE AND PERISHING>

336a13-15 We have spoken in general about the causes be- 10 fore,[307] and have now dealt with [matter and form].[308]

Having stated the way in which others erred in the account of efficient cause, some making matter [the efficient] cause, some form, and having proved that neither of these, neither matter nor form, satisfies the definition of efficient cause, he now says that we have 15 already distinguished the [the kinds of] causes in general before, in the *Physics* [*Phys.* 2.3], where we have also produced an account of efficient cause, and that in the present treatise we have already discussed matter and form. But at this point he explains the efficient [cause], and says what has also already been said by him in the *Physics* [*Phys.* 8], that the circular movement of the heavens is the efficient cause of things that come to be and perish. For it causes the 20 change of seasons, and together with the seasons the elements change and the generation of fruit takes place. For we see that when the sun approaches us the plants sprout, and the fruits are born, as well as many animals; but as it moves away, the contrary [processes] follow. And it is well said that the life flowing from heavens to things 25

here is that very nature in accordance with which things that are born are born.[309] From this, he says, it is clear that we rightly said in the *Physics* that change in respect of place is prior to all transformations including coming to be itself; for [locomotion] is the cause of coming to be, not coming to be of [locomotion]. For since that which is coming to be *is* not yet insofar as it is coming to be, but that which
30 changes in respect of place moves while it already exists, it is reasonable to say that what is, is the cause of what is not, and not that what is not, i.e. what is coming to be, is a cause of what already is and moves in respect of place. [*Phys.* 8.1, 250b12-15]

Having said this, he next raises a problem as to how we say that circular motion is the cause of coming to be and perishing. Since these
35 two changes are contrary to each other, what can possibly be their
289,1 cause? For one and the same thing cannot be the cause of contrary changes. For the efficient [causes] of contraries, I mean the ones that produce [them] by nature, must be contrary [to each other]. Consequently, if change in respect of place is the cause of coming to be and perishing, then the motions of efficient causes must themselves, too, be contrary, either by virtue of their direction[310] or, at any rate, by
5 virtue of unevenness.[311] By virtue of direction, so that there are two contrary motions, one producing coming to be, another, perishing. By virtue of unevenness, so that there is, indeed, one local motion, however, since that which moves is not always disposed towards us in a similar way, but sometimes draws near and sometimes moves away, it produces coming to be, when it approaches, and perishing when it withdraws.[312] Now, we should realise that as a matter of fact both turn out to be the case. For there are indeed two motions, one
10 from east to west, as [that] of the fixed stars, and another in the opposite direction from west to east, as that of the planets. Because [this latter] occurs on an inclined circle, it makes the motion of the sun uneven in its relation towards us, in that the sun sometimes becomes closer [to us] and sometimes farther away. Now, coming to be and perishing have both [the property] of being uninterrupted and
15 [that of] being contrary to each other: being continuous and uninterrupted comes to them and to things generable and perishable from the perpetual motion of the heavenly bodies, and their being contrary from the unevenness that is due to the inclined circle. For this reason the two motions, the fixed one and the wandering one, should be alleged as causes of continuous change in respect of coming to be and perishing. In fact, motion along an inclined circle alone is the cause
20 of each of the two [viz. coming to be and perishing]. For because this movement is everlasting, the [process of] change in things that occupy this [viz. sublunary] region is not interrupted; and because this movement is uneven in relation to us, the [respective] changes of coming to be and perishing are contrary.

But there would not have been such an orderly arrangement of the universe, had there not been the movement of fixed stars: for it is from there that night and day always follow each other in turn in orderly manner. And [supposing] for consideration that this [motion][313] did not exist, if the sun moved only in an inclined circle, the whole of a winter would be one night-time, if it so happened, and summer, one daytime, and generally speaking, the whole year would be one daytime-and-night-time.[314] 25

Once these things have been stated in this way, if someone inquires why it is that we say that the departure of the sun produces perishing, while its approach produces coming to be, although in summer, too, there is not only coming to be but also perishing, and likewise in winter not only do certain things pass away but some also 30 come to be, and, speaking generally, the coming to be of one thing is the perishing of another – if someone asks why [Aristotle] claims that coming to be is at one time, and perishing at another, he should realise that it is the coming to be of a superior substance that Aristotle calls 'coming to be' throughout, and that of an inferior one [he calls] 'perishing', and common usage has it similarly.[315] Since, 290,1 then, by and large, when the sun approaches the comings to be of superior [substances] follow, that is, of fruits and animals, and of the superior elements, fire and air,[316] and all the other things which are not easy to go through in an account;[317] and when it withdraws all these things decrease, for this reason we mark off coming to be by the 5 approach of the sun and perishing by its departure. For the sun is precisely[318] that which holds the ruling position in relation to coming to be, since it is because of it that there are summer, and winter, and other turns [of weather].[319]

336a15-18 Next, since it has been proved that change by way of local motion is eternal [, generation also, these things being so, must take place continuously; for the locomotion will produce the generation perpetually by bringing near and then removing the generating body].

The causes in general, including the efficient cause, have already 10 been discussed before (he means, in the *Physics* [2.3]); and it must also be stated now that the circular motion, which it is eternal and both brings close and moves away the generating [body], is the efficient cause of perpetual coming to be. By the 'generating [body]' he means the sun.

336a18-23 At the same time it is clear that what was said earlier too was well said [namely calling locomotion and not generation the first of changes. For it is much more reasonable to suppose that what is, is the cause of coming to be for what is not, than that what is not, is the cause of being for what is. Now that which is changing its place is, but that which is coming to be is not. That is why locomotion is in fact prior to generation].

15   He now proves that it was reasonable to say in the *Physics* [8.1] that change in respect of place, and of this [kind of change], the kind that is in a circle, is the first of all [kinds of] transformation. For since it has been proven to be the cause of coming to be and perishing, it is reasonable that it is prior to all [the kinds of change]. And that it is the cause of coming to be and of the things that come to be, he proves in the following way. What moves in respect of place, already is; what

20   is coming to be is not yet; therefore, it is reasonable that what is, is the cause of what is not, not vice versa, what is not [being the cause] of what is.

336a23-b2 Since it has been assumed, and indeed proved, that things are subject to continuous coming to be and perishing[320] [– and we hold that locomotion is the cause of coming to be – it is obvious that, if the locomotion is one, it will not be possible for both <coming to be and perishing> to occur, on account of their being contraries (for it is the nature of that which is the same and remains in the same state always to produce the same effects, so either there will always be coming to be or perishing); but the movements must be more than one, and contraries, in virtue of direction or unevenness, since contraries have contraries as their causes.

For this reason it is not the primary locomotion which is the cause of coming to be and perishing, but that in the inclined circle. For in this latter there is both continuity and being moved with two movements; for, if there is always to be continuous coming to be and perishing, there has always to be, on the one hand, something being moved so that these changes may not fail, and, on the other hand, two movements, to prevent there being only one of the two results].

Since, he says, the coming to be and perishing to which things are
25   subject have been 'proven to be continuous', and this has been proven through the eternity of circular motion. Such is the structure of the text.[321] And he is investigating how we say that locomotion is the cause of contrary transformations. For, he says, given that there are two transformations, coming to be and perishing, it is not possible to assume one movement as the cause of both. We must either say (i) that there are two movements, in accordance with the two contrary
291,1 local motions, or (ii) that the local motion is one, yet differentiated because of the unevenness of its movement, and the unevenness in relation to us occurs because the movement of the planets is on an

inclined circle, and therefore that which moves produces at different times a different relation to us, sometimes approaching, and at other times withdrawing, which, he says, is indeed the case.[322] For the 5 locomotion of the fixed stars could not be the cause of coming to be and perishing, since it is one and the same, and since it produces no difference in relation to us; but the locomotion along an inclined circle, since it has both the eternal and the uneven [as its attributes], is the cause of contrary transformations, i.e. coming to be and perishing, by virtue of [its] unevenness, and the cause of continuity of 10 coming to be and perishing by virtue of [its] eternity. But we should realise that the fixed [locomotion], even if it does not produce coming to be and perishing, nonetheless is the one that imposes such an orderly arrangement of day and night [as we now have]. If this were not the case, but [locomotion] were on an inclined circle alone, so that the whole year would be one day-and-night, the present arrangement of comings to be would not have been preserved,[323] as those parts of the earth that are uninhabitable make clear. These are the [parts] 15 under the poles of the universe,[324] in which the motion of the heavens is millstone-like.[325]

336b2-5 So the locomotion of the whole is the cause of the continuity [whilst the inclination is the cause of the approach and retreat. For this results in its coming to be further at one time and nearer at another].

By 'the locomotion of the whole' he does not mean the movement of the fixed [sphere], as Alexander interpreted the phrase (for he set up the cause of the continuity of coming to be and perishing higher than 20 the inclined circle),[326] but what he says is this. Having shown that locomotion along an inclined circle is the cause by virtue of which [the processes of] coming to be and perishing are continuous, because it has [as its attributes] both continuity, which is the cause of perpetual coming to be, and unevenness, which is the source of contrary transformations, he now explains how the locomotion of the planets has each of these [attributes]. And he says that continuity belongs to this 25 [locomotion][327] because the entire sphere of the sun moves eternally, and [its] 'approaching' and 'moving away', as he says, which is its unevenness, is due to the obliquity of the inclined circle; for it is because of this [obliquity] that it comes about that the sun sometimes approaches and sometimes withdraws.

336b5-7 And since the distance is unequal the movement will be uneven. [So if it generates by approaching and being near, 30 this same thing destroys by retreating and coming to be further away]

As to the way in which the motion of the inclined circle is uneven, he explains that [it is] because it makes the sun closer to us or distant from us. So it is not itself uneven, but the relation of the sun towards us is uneven. For the apparent unevenness of its motion follows from its bringing the generating [body] closer to us and moving it away from us.

336b8-9 And if it generates by repeatedly approaching, it also destroys by repeatedly retreating.

By 'generation'[328] he means here not the passage from not being to being, but growth and progress up to the culminating point. So, too, by 'destruction' he means the way from the culminating point to complete destruction, i.e. diminution and decay. He says, then, that for some things one revolution of the sun suffices for the completion of form, e.g., the annual fruits and the transformation of the elements,[329] whereas for others, he says, there is need of more revolutions, as is the case with many animals. By 'revolution' he means the approaching and the retreat of the sun.[330] If, then, it happens[331] to take many approachings for a thing to reach the complete form, then, he says, it takes many retreats for it to decay.

And he accounts for coming to be by approaching, and for perishing by retreat, although he said that both coming to be and perishing take many revolutions to be completed, so that clearly in the case of coming to be there is not just approach of the sun but also retreat, and that in the case of perishing the sun not only moves away but also draws near.[332] Against this it should be said that although in either of the two dispositions both the approach and the retreat of the sun is understood [to be involved], it was perhaps reasonable for him to assign coming to be to the approach of the sun, and perishing to its retreat, because nature when strengthened benefits more from the approach of the sun, and gives birth and grows, whereas when weakened, it is more affected by departure than by approach, as is the case with effluence and addition. For in both growth and diminution there is both effluence and addition of nourishment, but when a body is still strengthened and growing, the addition is greater than the effluence, while when a body is decaying the addition is smaller than the effluence. Someone might perhaps reasonably reply to this that when a body is growing and proceeding towards completion, it is not possible for the approaching [of the sun] to produce a greater effect, and that the reason why there arises no co-perception[333] of the effect of its retreat, is that the retreat itself also contributes no less to the growth and permanence of things.[334] At any rate, the processes of concoction in winter are finer and the activities are vigorous;[335] and if the sun were in fact to be close all the time, so that there were to be summer all the time, it could not in general sustain the bodies of animals and plants, but they would perish very easily, as is clearly illustrated by the hot zone which always has the sun close by and is uninhabitable.[336] So much, therefore, should be said, namely, that he defined growth by the approaching of the sun and diminution by its retreat, not allocating each to each in a precise sense, but since, as we 5 have said before, although each of the two [viz. approach and retreat] produces both coming to be and perishing, nevertheless the approach of the sun [produces] coming to be to a greater extent, and the retreat [produces] perishing to a greater extent.

336b9 And the perishing and the coming to be that are by nature[337] take place in equal time.[338] 10

Since he has said that if something should retain its coming to be over the time of many revolutions, its perishing too will persist through many revolutions, and that the time of coming to be is equal to that of perishing, i.e., of growth and diminution (for this is how we chose to understand [these terms] from the beginning),[339] it is necessary for him to add the phrase 'that are by nature', so that you do not take the 15 perishing that happens by chance to be of the same time length as the coming to be, but rather the one which happens in accordance with natural laws due to the decay of the animal that has made its way to the end.[340] For if some forced perishing occurred, it would no longer be the case that it arrived at the end in the time equal in length to that which was taken by its coming to be. And one should call 'forced' not only the cases of perishing that happen because of some external event, such as cuts, falls, burns, etc., but also those that occur through 20 wrong and disorderly nourishment.[341]

What, however, remains problematic, even when these things have been further specified in this way, is the following: if a human life perchance continues up until one hundred and twenty years, its prime in most cases goes on only up to forty years at the maximum, so that on this reckoning perishing takes a much longer time than 25 coming to be, and is not at all equal in time-interval.[342] For many have continued living until [the age of] a hundred and twenty years, but no one had the [process of] growth, nor advancement towards a more perfect state up to [the age] of sixty years.

But if we take 'coming to be' not as the process leading to a complete form, but in the strict sense of coming to be and perishing, it will be true indeed that both happen in an equal time-interval (for 30 obviously the coming to be of one thing is the perishing of another, since it takes a thing to come to be as long as it takes another thing 294,1 to perish), but [in this case] we no longer take the coming to be and perishing to have the same thing [as their subject], as Aristotle apparently means.[343] But not even the claim that if something comes to be over several revolutions, it also passes away over several is in

agreement with this interpretation: indeed, it is not at all easy to conceive of coming to be said in a strict sense as happening over
5 several revolutions. For if someone should say that he calls gestation coming to be, meaning by this latter coming to be in a strict sense, viz. the one proceeding from not being to being, and if we assume that a certain animal, say, an elephant, is gestated over several revolutions, in this way, too, it is unintelligible to say that over the time over
10 which something is gestated it also passes away; for what kind of perishing should one think of as taking the same time as gestation, is not [an] easy [question].

336b10-15 This is why the times and the lives of all sorts of things have a number which defines them. [All things have order, and every time and life is measured by a period,[344] though not the same for all, but a smaller for some and a longer for others. The period, i.e. the measure, is a year for some, more for others, less for others.]

Since there is order in things that come to be and the [specific] form
15 of each particular thing[345] is measured by nature, each particular thing happens to arrive at its complete form in a defined period of time.[346] And since the time-interval from coming to be up to the complete form and culminating point is equal to the time-interval passing from the culminating point to natural perishing,[347] it is clear that the whole lifespan of each particular [living thing] is defined in accordance with number, so that species will be distinguished from
20 each other by number.[348] For the lifespan of man is different from that of horse, and so with each of the others, but nevertheless the time-interval for each species is defined: a certain lifespan of the human species which it cannot overstep has been defined, but the time-interval of particular individuals is no longer defined, since many die sooner than the prescribed time. Consequently, for a species there is
25 a defined time-interval which none of the individuals can overstep, and the lifespan of each particular individual is not the same, but differs in each case, since many perish sooner than the time, while no one oversteps it.

336b15-19 There are things obvious even to perception, which are in agreement with this reasoning of ours [for we see that while the sun is approaching there is generation, but while it is retreating, diminution, and each of these in equal time. For the times of the perishing and the coming to be that are by nature[349] are equal].

30 Having said from the start that the time for coming to be and for perishing that are by nature is equal, he now supplies evidence for

this claim from comings to be and perishings that happen with each revolution of the sun. For as we have said previously, we see that 295,1 when the sun approaches, coming to be follows, and when it withdraws, perishing, but the approaching of the sun is equal in time to its departure. He has also aptly added 'by nature' here, after mentioning perishing. For in the case of animals, as well as in the case of the annual fruits, it is also possible to conceive of perishing that is forced. 5

336b20-5 Often, however, it happens that things perish in a shorter time because of the mingling of things with one another.[350] [For, matter being irregular and not everywhere the same, the comings to be of things are necessarily irregular, some faster, some slower. So it comes about as a result of the coming to be of these things that the perishing occurs of others.][351]

This should be understood not in relation to the immediately preceding, but in relation to what was said earlier.[352] For having said that life-spans and time-intervals are prescribed for each species, he says 10 here that it often happens that [things] die in a shorter time-interval than prescribed. And his task now is to investigate the cause of this very [fact], why it is that some individuals die prematurely, without fulfilling their natural cycle. So, he says that this happens because of mingling (*sunkrasin*) or collision (*sunkrousin*)[353] with one another; for it is written in two ways.[354]

(i) If it were 'mingling' (*sunkrasin*),[355] he would be blaming the lack 15 of measure and bad mixture of the elements; for it is often the case that matter, because of its unsuitability or its inappropriateness, does not receive the orderly arrangement from above in a perfect manner,[356] and as a result the animal gets dissolved quicker because of the weakness of its frame, since the material mixture is in many cases not durable enough to receive for long the life that is being dispensed.[357]

(ii) But if it has 'collision' (*sunkrousin*), he is illustrating the 20 coincidence of causes with each other, i.e. of the material and the efficient cause, both proximate and first.[358] For father is the proximate efficient cause and the heavenly bodies the remote and first cause.[359] And matter, and such-and-such a choice, and way of life are a cause of such-and-such a frame of a body.[360] If then there happens to be such-and-such a seed from the father, and such-and-such a seed 25 and blood from the mother[361] ([for] they say[362] that blood stands for matter, and seed for the efficient cause), and the mother's way of life during gestation happens to be such or such, or the environment is in fact very poorly mixed,[363] so that one of these [factors] prevents the movement of heavenly bodies from manifesting its most perfect activity over what is being born and from bestowing [on it] the appropriate 30 orderly arrangement, then perishing follows before the prescribed

time, because such-and-such matter and other causes get interwoven
296,1   with such-and-such movement of heavenly bodies, where matter is
the cause of irregularity, as has been said previously.[364] [It is] as if
something disorderly[365] and inappropriate happened with a chair or
drawing board because of the unsuitability of matter, through no
fault of the craftsman.

(iii) But the [reading] 'collision' could also be taken as referring
5   only to the heavenly bodies.[366] For since not only the sun, but also
other planets, and indeed the fixed stars (even if not to the same
extent) do, at any rate, act upon [the processes of] coming to be, he
says that such-and-such concurrence of their aspects – which he calls
collision[367] – is a cause of different fixed length of life for different
[beings].[368] For frequently because of such-and-such combination of
10   these [viz. heavenly bodies] with each other the body which gets
shaped[369] by them turns out to be easy to dissolve, and its lifetime
short.

336b25-9 As we have said, coming to be and perishing will
always be continuous and, owing to the cause we have mentioned, will never fail. This happens with good reason [for we say
that nature in all cases desires what is better, and that being is
better than not being]

15   Having stated the causes,[370] both material and efficient, of there
always being coming to be, and having said that the fact that the
coming to be of one thing is the perishing of another is a material
cause of perpetual coming to be, and that the eternal movements of
heavenly bodies is an efficient cause (for it is because they move
eternally that coming to be is never interrupted), he now gives the
final cause due to which there is always coming to be; and he says
that the fact that everything from its own nature desires the good is
20   a cause. For the good is the principle of all things, and everything
desires its proper principle; but it is being rather than not being that
is good for each thing; hence, everything of its own nature desires
being. So, while everything desires being and that which is better,
those things that are closer to the first principle were able to partake
of eternity and of being always the same in number, as [did] the
25   heavenly bodies – albeit with deficiency (namely, with extension and
change of place),[371] – whereas all those that are farther away, not
being able to remain[372] the same in number, because they are distant
from the first principle (which is the source of being for all [things]),
share in the eternity in species, so that each thing, because it desires
but is not able to be eternally, being very distant from the first
principle, gives birth to another like itself, and in this way cheats[373]
30   its perishing.[374] And it acquired this eternity in species, in which it
has shared, by imitating the circular movement of the heavenly

bodies: for things that are generated return to the same [point] from which they began by means of a cycle. For in order for man to be generated by man, a cycle is accomplished: first there is the seed, and from this the embryo, after that a child and an adolescent and a man, and again the seed and the embryo. So it is clear that the succession of the species, while being in a straight line, has eternity by imitating locomotion in a circle.

297,1

336b29-32 It has been said elsewhere how many ways there are in which 'being' is used[375] [and this cannot exist in all things since some are too far removed from the principle. Accordingly god has filled up the whole in the only way that remained by making coming to be perpetual.]

5

'Being' is said in two ways, either in species or in number. For each thing is said to be either in virtue of preserving its species or its number. Thus, the heavenly bodies are said to be in virtue of remaining the same in number,[376] while things generable and perishable have eternal being in species. These, then, are the meanings of being which he says have been distinguished elsewhere.[377] He inserts this short saying parenthetically; consequently, we should silence it and put together the whole statement: 'Since the nature of each thing desires the better, and being is better than not [being], and being in number cannot be present in all things because of the fact that they are distant from the [first] principle, for that reason', he says, 'god has filled up the whole in the way that remained, by making coming to be perpetual'.[378]

10

15

And from this it is clear that Aristotle thinks the first principle to be the cause of all things eternal as well. For, supposing that god has in fact produced[379] things that are eternal and totally unchangeable, and also things that are eternal but bodily in their substance, and possessed of dimension,[380] and have change in place, he added 'god filled up the whole in the way that remained'. For in order that the arrangement of the universe should be complete, there remained another way of creation, by the succession of things which have eternal species, though they are generable and perishable in number. So, by the progression of these he filled the whole universal order created by him, making coming to be uninterrupted and unbroken.

20

336b32-37a1 This was the way to connect being together as much as possible, since to come to be continually and coming to be are the nearest things there are to being.[381] [The cause of this, as has frequently been said, is circular locomotion, since this alone is continuous.]

25

For this, he says, would be the way for the being and subsistence of

things to have a sequence[382] or ordered progression of existence, since
298,1 after the things eternal which persist[383] in number, there are things
eternal in species but generable and perishable in number. For
coming to be is close in its essence[384] to being (understand being
everywhere in the strict sense, i.e., as being always the same), and
reproduction is close to eternity. He thus compared each one with the
5 other, coming to be with being and eternal coming to be with eternity,
which he signified by 'coming to be continually'. So things that are
and are eternal are closest, in terms of their respective essences, to
things that are generable and are properly allotted perpetual coming
to be in that they retain their progression one after another.

337a1-4 [That is why even the other things which change into
each other] in respect of their affections and capacities,[385] [as do
the simple bodies, are imitating circular locomotion]

10 Either (i) he says the same thing pleonastically,[386] or (ii) by 'capacities'
he means their tendencies[387] in accordance with which they have
their movements, while by 'affections' heat and coldness and the rest
of the qualities.[388] Or, alternatively, (iii) he means by 'capacities' the
hot and the cold, by 'affections' the moist and the dry.[389]

337a7-12 At the same time from this something which some
people have found puzzling[390] becomes clear [namely, why, when
each of the bodies is moving to its proper place, the bodies have
not in an infinite time separated out. The cause of this in fact is
their change into one another. If each remained in its own place
and was not changed by its neighbour, they would by now have
separated out].

15 From what has been previously said about the elements, that changing into each other, they circle back to the same [state], because the
coming to be proceeds in a sort of circle, he by deduction finds a means
to the solution of a certain problem that has been raised. The problem
is, how, if each of the simple bodies strives to reach its proper place,
the elements have not been separated over a long time when each has
20 reached its proper place, so that there never is either water or earth
above, or fire below. And he resolves the problem on the basis of the
previous arguments.[391] For if, he says, the elements were unchangeable, it would have been reasonable for those who say so to believe
that this is an impasse. But since the elements continually change
into each other, even if this fire is separated from the place below,
another will come to be of necessity, and there will always be fire
25 below, as well as earth and water above, with no place separated
out for each: for this would have been the case had they been
unchangeable.

337a12 Now, they transform, because of the double locomotion [and because they transform, none of them can remain in any of the places assigned].

By 'double locomotion' he means either the one in an inclined circle, by virtue of its approach and withdrawal, or at any rate [he says] 'double', because they[392] perform one motion following the fixed [sphere] from east to west, and the other, proper one, in the opposite direction, from west to east.[393]

299,1

337a15-17 [It is clear, then, from what has been said] that there is such a thing as coming to be and perishing, and owing to what cause, and what the generable and perishable is.

5

Thus, he has proven that there is coming to be and perishing, and we stated earlier how he has proven it. And it has been shown what the cause of coming to be and perishing is, from the fact that matter is potentially the contraries. For when matter is fire in actuality, it is water in potentiality, and when it comes to be water in actuality, fire perishes. As for 'and what the generable and perishable is', [it has been shown that it is] what is capable of both being and not being.

10

337a17-20 [But] since[394] there must be something that causes motion,[395] if there is going to be motion [as has been said before in other works, and if <there is motion> always, that there must always be something <to move it>, and if it is continuous, <the mover> must be one and the same thing, immovable, ungenerated, and unalterable]

It was his practice in other works, not to remain at the level of natural causes, but to raise himself to the transcendent causes (in the *Physics*, at any rate, after he discussed natural change,[396] he later, in the eighth book, raised himself to a certain cause which is transcendent to all natural change, in that it is both immobile and eternal, when he said: 'So, on this principle the heaven and the world depends', and likewise in *On the Soul*, when from the arguments about the soul he soars up to the intellect). In a similar way here too, having said that the circular movement of the heavens[397] is the efficient cause of perpetual coming to be, he now proves that there also is some transcendent cause of circular motion eternally imparting motion, which is immobile, eternal, unalterable, and one in number. For if, he says, there is something that performs an eternal and continuous motion, there is necessarily, too, what eternally causes motion without being moved, being one and the same in number, causing a continuous motion. And if, he says, things performing such a movement, viz. [that is] eternal and continuous, are many, it is necessary

15

20

25

that the movers be many as well, since there is one eternal mover for each movement. And these many [movers], if they are co-ordinated and not dependent upon each other, must depend on one principle from which they also have their order. So it is clear that there is one principle of motion of all things, which is eternal and immobile.[398]

30   'Since there must be something that causes motion, if there is going to be motion, as has been said before in other works'. The whole

300,1   argument would be completely stated as follows. Since, if there is eternal and continuous motion, there must be something which eternally causes motion, one and the same in number; but there is eternal continuous motion; therefore, there is that which causes motion eternally, one in number, immobile and unalterable. Such is the

5   whole argument; but it seems to have been stated elliptically by Aristotle, because the additional assumption and the conclusion have been omitted, while the mode is hypothetical.[399] For he has said that if there is eternal motion, there must also be the eternal mover (for it was proved that everything which moves is moved by a mover), but he has not stipulated by an additional assumption that there is eternal motion at all. As to the fact that [the mover] will also be

10   immobile, he took it as previously demonstrated (for it has been proved that the primary mover is also immobile). Similarly, it has also been proved in the eighth [book] of the *Physics* that since motion is continuous, [the mover] is one and the same in number: for if the movers were different in succession, the motion could not be continuous. And with 'has been said before in other works' he must be

15   referring to what has been proved in the *Physics*.

337a20-2 And if the circular motions are more than one,[400] [there must be] more than one [moving cause], but all these [moving causes must be[401]] in some way under a single principle.

If, he says, circular movements are more than one, then the moving causes, too, will be more than one, but even if they are more than one, they must all be under one [moving cause]. And he added 'in some

20   way' because 'under' in a strict sense is said of things embracing in respect of place.[402]

337a22-4 Because time is continuous, motion must be continuous [given that it is impossible there should be time without motion]

Having posited in the beginning virtually,[403] although not explicitly,

25   that there is continuous motion, and having proven the consequence from this, that the mover which causes that motion is eternal, immobile, and one in number, he now deems worthy of an argument the additional assumption that was posited virtually, that there is con-

tinuous motion, and proves that from time. For since time is continuous, motion too must be continuous: for time is the measure of motion,
and clearly, of continuous motion. But only circular motion is of this   30
sort. Time, hence, is the measure of circular motion.

337a24-5 [Time, then, is the number of a particular continuous   301,1
motion, of circular movement therefore,] as was determined in
our account in the beginning.

By 'account in the beginning' he means the *Physics*; for it begins and
precedes the study of nature.

337a25-30 Is the movement continuous in virtue of the continuity of the thing that moves or the continuity of that in respect of
which it moves [e.g. its place or some affection of it? Obviously,   5
in virtue of that of the thing that moves.[404] (For how could an
affection be continuous otherwise than in virtue of the continuity of the thing to which it belongs? If, however, it is also in
virtue of that in respect of which, this belongs only to place, since
it has a certain magnitude).]

Having assumed that there is continuous motion whose measure is
time, and that this is [the motion] of the body moving in a circle, he
now investigates the source from which the movement[405] gets its
continuity, whether it is because the thing that moves is continuous
or because that in respect of which movement occurs is continuous.
That 'in respect of which' and 'in accordance with which' there is
movement, is affection and place.[406] Now, 'affection' would not be said   10
to be continuous except accidentally, by virtue of the fact that the
thing in which it is observed is continuous. For we say that the white
is continuous because the body in which it is observed is continuous;
'continuous' is the property of quantity and is assumed to exist in
respect of it. But if someone says that a growing thing grows by the
addition of magnitude, and therefore it is reasonable to say that
growth is continuous,[407] we reply that Aristotle now means by 'con-   15
tinuous' that of which it is always possible to assume the next,[408]
whereas of growth it is not always possible to assume the next; for a
growing thing does not grow *ad infinitum*.[409] So the affection would
not be continuous.[410] If, therefore, continuity belongs to any of those
things in respect of which there is movement, it will belong to place
alone. For place is a kind of a magnitude.[411] And continuity belongs
not to all of it, but only to the circle: for in this it is always possible to   20
get something that is next, because there is neither beginning nor
limit. So, since continuity belongs to a circle *qua* place, do we say that
motion has continuity on account of its place? Pursuing this inquiry
no further, but leaving it aside, he produces an account of what

moves, by saying that 'of this, only that which moves in a circle is
25   continuous', and next renders it as the cause of continuous motion.
And this is reasonable. For even if place does have continuity, [it does
so] not from itself, but from the body which is in it. For place,
according to Aristotle, does not have subsistence on its own, but
co-exists with the body of which it is the place. For it is a certain
relation of the container towards the contained. So it is because the
30   body is continuous that the place too is continuous. Therefore it is
reasonable that he explains the cause of continuity of the movement
by that which is moved.

302,1   **337a30-3 Of this, only that which is in a circle is continuous [so
as to be always continuous with itself. This, then, is what
produces continuous movement, the body which travels in a
circle, and its movement produces time.]**

'Of this', he says, i.e. of the magnitude.[412] But we should take note that
after he said first 'obviously in virtue of that of the thing moved',[413]
i.e. because that which moves is continuous, the motion too is continuous, and after he spoke parenthetically about place, he added 'of this,
5   only that which is in a circle is continuous', referring no longer to
place, but to the body which moves. For the body which is circular[414]
is continuous with itself, i.e. it is connected with itself and has no
continuity with anything else.
    From this continuous magnitude, he says, motion, too, has conti-
nuity, and from motion, time. Consequently, magnitude is the cause
10   of the continuity for motion, and motion [is the cause of the continu-
ity] for time.[415]

<2.11 NECESSITY IN THE SPHERE OF COMING-TO-BE AND PERISHING>

**337a34-b1 Since in the case of things which are moved continu-
ously by way of coming to be or of alteration, or of change in
general, we see that which is successively and comes to be this
after this [without any intermission].**

Having proved in what precedes that continuity belongs to coming to
15   be, [now],[416] since things that move continuously by way of coming to
be have succession and the coming to be of the second after the first,
he investigates whether things that come to be have necessity, so that
the second follows from the first[417] by necessity, or whether nothing
comes to be by necessity, but all things are contingent, i.e. capable of
coming to be and not coming to be. It is clear, indeed, he says, that
20   some of them have an outcome that is contingent; it is, however, to be
investigated whether not all [of them] are such. And he proves in two

ways that not everything has its following upon the antecedents [as] contingent,[418] but some things have it of necessity (in which case it is impossible that the consequent should not follow from the antecedents): (i) from the usage of terms and (ii) from the subject matter itself.[419]

(i) From usage, because of things that are not yet, but are capable   25
of being in a future time, we normally use [the expressions] 'is going to be' (*mellei*)[420] and 'will be' (*estai*), applying 'will be' to the things that follow[421] of necessity (for if '[it] will be' is true, at some point there necessarily has to be what we referred to as 'being in future'), whereas '[it] is going to be' [refers] to the things that are capable also of not having come to be: for when '[it] is going to be' is true, it is still possible that that of which we spoke as going to be will not come about. And if it has not come about, someone who said it was going to   30
be did not speak falsely. For '[it] is going to be' is equivalent to 'it can', and 'being able' and 'being possible' are judged not by outcome, but by unimpeded disposition.[422] For wood has the ability to be burned, even if in fact it never *is* burned, and a virgin has the ability to have   303,1
intercourse with a man, even if in fact she never does.[423] In this way, then, if we were to say that after spring there will be summer, then there must be summer at some point; and if we say, when a seed has been cast down, that an ear of corn is going to grow, i.e. is capable of growing, then even though the assertion is true, it can fail to grow,   5
because the outcome was contingent.[424] In this way what has been proposed is supported by evidence from usage.

(ii) [The argument] from difference of [respective] subject matters is as follows. Since some of the things have their being of necessity, and it is impossible for them not to be, while others are capable both of being and not being,[425] it will be the same way with things that are coming to be: namely, some of them will come to be necessarily, others contingently. For, if something has its being of necessity, it also has   10
its coming to be of necessity. For instance, the sun when it is in Aries, has its being [there] of necessity; for clearly it was not possible for it not to be there and when it was not yet [there], it necessarily would come to be there, and it could not fail to come to be there. Similarly, what has its being contingently also has its coming to be contingently, for it is capable of both being and not being. For instance, if it is   15
possible for a house, or for a literate person, or for a carpenter to be, then the coming to be of these entities is also possible; for it was possible for each of these neither to be nor come to be, as well. And if some particular ear of corn has its being not of necessity, but was also able not to be, it is clear that its coming to be did not follow upon the casting down of seed into the earth with necessity, but it could also   20
not follow.

Is it the case, then, he says, that these things have no necessity at all, i.e. the ones that are capable of being and not being? Or is there

necessity in these too in some way, to the extent to which we say,
'since there is the second, the first preceded of necessity'? For if fruits
have come to be, the seed must necessarily have been cast down
25   before. This he calls the necessity *ex hypothesi*. For one should know
that necessity is of two kinds, one called necessity *simpliciter*, as
when we say that the second follows from the first with necessity,
another *ex hypothesi*, as in 'if the second has come about, then of
necessity the first had existed', and everything that is and is coming
30   to be shares in the necessity *ex hypothesi*, (for everything commonly
partakes of it, and necessities [of this kind] are seen to be and are in
everything),[426] whereas it is no longer the case that everything shares
in the necessity *simpliciter*, for it is not the case that each one is of
necessity, but many are capable of both being and not being. Hence,
it is clear, that where there is necessity *ex hypothesi*, necessity
simpliciter is not always there; but where there is necessity *simplici-*
35   *ter*, there necessity *ex hypothesi* will also be present, so that the
304,1   [following two sentences] will convert: (i) when there is the second,
the first is there of necessity, and (ii) when there is the first, the
second follows of necessity.[427] However it is not by virtue of the first,
he says, [viz. that the second follows] but by itself. For when the
second follows upon the first of necessity, it follows not by virtue of
the first, but by virtue of its own nature, because it is by its nature
5   such that it is impossible for it not to come to be. This is why it was
reasonable that he termed it *simpliciter*, because it has necessity
from itself and is necessary by nature,[428] whereas the other one has
necessity by hypothesis, not by nature, but is said to have necessity
after the fact: for having assumed that the second has come about, we
10   say that the first pre-existed of necessity.[429]

After he explained this in this way, he then goes on to prove that
necessity *simpliciter* belongs only to the things that move in a circle,
and not to the ones that move in a straight line. And that it is
impossible for necessity *simpliciter* to belong to the things that move
in a straight line, he establishes from division.[430] That, he says, which
moves in a straight line, moves either (i) in an infinite or (ii) in a finite
15   straight line. But necessity *simpliciter* will belong neither to [the
things] that move in an infinite straight line, nor [to those that move]
in a finite [one].

(i) To [things] that move in an infinite straight line necessity
simpliciter will not belong because we say that necessity *simpliciter*
is where the second follows upon the first of necessity,[431] but in the
case of infinity, there is no prior and posterior,[432] for it is without a
20   beginning and without a limit.[433] For (a) it is not possible to assume
necessity *simpliciter* in the case of past events, so as to say that
because of the first that which came to be second followed: (aa) for it
is totally impossible to assume the beginning and the first of infinity.[434] (ab) But if it is not possible to assume the first, the second will

not be there either. (ac) Hence, nor will there be necessity *ex hypothesi*.[435] (ad) For it is generally impossible that anything could have come to be in the infinity. (ae) For each of the things assumed as having [so] come to be has an infinite distance from the beginning, such that it would have been impossible for this thing to traverse it and end up at the point at which it would have come to be.[436] This, then, is the case with past events.[437] In a similar way, (b) in the case of future [events] necessity *simpliciter* is impossible in infinity: for there is no 'posterior' in infinity.[438] Hence it will not be possible to say that if this came to be, that which is posterior will follow. Thus, it is clear from this that necessity *simpliciter* does not belong to things that move along a straight line in infinity.

(ii) That neither [does it belong to] things that move in a finite straight line,[439] he proves in the following way.[440] The coming to be of necessity *simpliciter* is that for which it is impossible not to come to be; but that for which it is impossible not to come to be, is always coming to be; but coming to be always is impossible in a finite straight line. For since 'to come to be always' is understood in two ways, either (a) in the sense that coming to be is continuous and always one, or (b) in the sense of coming to be over and over again[441] (as when we say that the sun comes to be in Aries, and always comes to be in Aries, not because it comes to be in Aries all the time and continuously, but because [it does so] over and over again, hence always), if you assume the necessary coming to be in a finite straight line in the sense [(a)] that coming to be is continuous and one, it is impossible. 'For it will follow', he says, 'that something is always the case which is capable of not always being the case'.[442] For that which moves in a finite straight line stops movement and will move no longer when the line has been completed. Thus, those who say that it always moves of necessity assume as always moving of necessity that which cannot move always. If, on the other hand, someone assumes 'moving always' in the sense [(b)] of moving over and over again, he will be introducing some sort of an eternal turning back, which belongs only to a circular recurrence: for in a straight line there is no turning back that comes about eternally. This is clear, first of all, from manifest facts, because there is no such thing that eternally performs turning back on a straight line. Further, what moves eternally is eternal, and the eternal [thing], because it has eternal power, will not sometimes move and sometimes not, but [will] always [move] continuously. But movement in a straight line, if it turns backwards, does not remain continuous, but is interrupted by a pause in the middle.[443] Therefore it is impossible [for anything] to move continuously in a finite straight line. And besides, none of the things moving in a straight line are eternal, but all are generable and perishable. If, then, it has been proven that necessity *simpliciter* belongs neither to things moving in an infinite nor in a finite straight line, it is clear that it will not belong to things moving in a straight line in general.

Then [it will belong to things moving] in a circle. For local motion in a circle alone has necessity *simpliciter*, since circular movement alone is eternal, being one and continuous movement. As to the parts of this[444] movement, they are different in number, but the same in
25 species. For movement from Aries into Taurus is not the same in number with that from Taurus into Gemini, but [it is] the same in species [with the latter], and the revolutions of the periodic return [of the zodiac][445] are the same in species, but different in number. Hence coming to be of necessity and eternally, again and again, belongs to recurrence alone, as when we say that the sun comes to be in Aries of
30 necessity, because it never fails to come to be in Aries during the annual revolution. So, it is proven from what has been said that necessity, whether taken in the sense of continuous and unbroken movement, or understood in the sense of [being] over and over again in recurrence, it will [in either case] belong only to things moving in a circle.

306,1   **337a34-5 Since in the case of things that move continuously by way of generation or of alteration, or of change in general.[446]**

Since coming to be is not movement in an unqualified sense, but there is a certain movement in the process of coming to be (for coming to be is not without movement),[447] it was reasonable for him to say 'in
5 things that are moved by way of generation'.

337b3-7 That some are, is immediately obvious, for[448] the difference between 'it will be' and 'it is going to be'[449] [is a direct consequence of this; for that of which it is true to say that it will be is something of which it must be true to say some time that it is, but that of which it is now true to say that it is going to be – there is nothing to prevent that not coming to be: a person who is going to take a walk may not take a walk].

Having inquired whether in things that come to be continuously there is necessity, or whether there is none, all things having [their] coming
10 to be as contingent, he takes it as agreed upon that some things do have [their] coming to be as contingent. As to [the point] that not all things [are such], but there are some that come to be of necessity, he sets it out subsequently, through the usage of 'it will be' and 'it is going to be'.[450]

337b7-13 And[451] more generally, since[452] some things that are, are capable also of not being [there will also, clearly, be things

coming to be that are like that, i.e. their coming to be will not take place of necessity.

Are they all, then, like this? Or not, some being such that it is necessary *simpliciter* for them to come to be, and just as in the case of being there are some incapable of not being and some capable of it, so in the case of coming to be? For example, it is necessary, after all, that there should come to be solstices and impossible that it should not be possible].

The second proof of the proposition that some [things] have their coming to be as contingent, and some as necessary, is taken from the nature of things.[453] For since some things are capable of both being and not being, while others have being of necessity, and it is impossible for them not to be, in the same way, he says, [they] will be disposed in relation to coming to be. For things capable of both being and not being will also have their coming to be [as] contingent. But since not all things are such, but there are things which have being of necessity, the coming to be of these things is also necessary. Such, for instance, is the case of the seasons: summer and winter have their coming to be as necessary, for it is impossible for these not to be.[454]

337b14-16 Granted that the coming to be of something earlier is necessary if a later thing is to be, e.g. if a house, then foundations, and if foundations, then clay: does it follow that if there have to come to be foundations a house must necessarily come to be?

What he says is something like this. Is it the case that where there is hypothetical necessity [*kata hupothesin*] necessity *simpliciter* will also be observed? E.g. if when a house is coming to be, the foundations must have come to be, and before those, clay: does it[455] also hold *vice versa*, that if the foundations have come to be, the house must come to be? Or is *this* no longer necessary, since after all it is not natural for the second to follow upon the first out of necessity *simpliciter*; but when the second is such as to exist of necessity, in that case [the sentence] will be convertible, and as when there is the second, of necessity there will be the first, so too when there is the first, of necessity there will be the second, which is necessary *simpliciter*.[456]

337b16-18[457] Or not any more, unless it is necessary *simpliciter* that the latter itself comes to be? [In this case, if foundations have come to be, it is also necessary that the house come to be.]

That is to say, the house does not always follow upon the foundations, if the house itself does not have being of necessity. Therefore, if not of necessity, neither is it necessary for the house to be when the foundations have come to be.[458]

337b18-20[459] For such was the relationship of the earlier thing
10   to the later, namely, that if there is to be the latter, necessarily
      there will be the former, earlier thing.

The logical agreement, he says, of the earlier with the later was of some such kind that if there is to be the later, the earlier, too, necessarily has to be. If, then, the agreement of the second with the first is the same, namely when there is the first, there always is the second, in this case conversion makes no difference.

337b20-1 If, accordingly, it is necessary for the later one to come
20   to be, it is necessary also for the earlier one, and if the earlier
      one comes to be, it is [then][460] necessary for the later one to do
      so.

That is to say, where the later has necessity by itself, there the conversion is equivalent, and not only the earlier follows upon the later, but the later, too, follows upon the earlier.

25   **337b21-2** And if the earlier, the later, then, is also necessary.[461]

It should be read in a transposed order 'and then if the earlier, the later is also necessary'.

308,1   **337b22-3** But not because of the earlier one, but because it was
         assumed that it was necessary that it will be.

In the case of necessity *simpliciter*, he says, the second follows upon the first out of necessity, but not because of the first, he says, but because of its proper nature, since [the second] itself is one of the
5   things that come to be out of necessity, i.e. eternal things.[462] For that [thing] has from itself necessary coming to be which has eternal coming to be. And we should realise that using this very claim as agreed upon, i.e. 'that which of necessity follows upon the first has necessary coming to be because of itself and not because of another [thing]', he goes on to demonstrate that on a straight finite line it is
10   impossible to assume necessity *simpliciter* in the process of coming to be, because it is impossible to think of eternal coming to be in a finite straight line. For necessity leads to the eternal: for that which has the necessity of coming to be from itself and not because of another [thing] is such.

But it will seem that many facts are in conflict with Aristotle's arguments. For we see that many among natural things, generable

and perishable, of those that necessarily follow upon certain things   15
that have preceded them, have the necessity of coming to be not
because of themselves but because of the things that have preceded
them, e.g. upon starvation emaciation follows of necessity, not because it by itself has necessary coming to be, but because of the
starvation that has preceded [it]. For emaciation does not come to be
out of necessity by itself, but when starvation has preceded. In the
same way, too, when much has been eaten, beyond the capacity to   20
digest, slow digestion will follow, not because of itself,[463] and after a
blow upon a fleshy part a weal will follow, not because of itself, but
because of the blow, and after water has been poured over the earth
mud will follow out of necessity, not because of itself. And there are
many other [cases] where the second follows upon the first of necessity, not because of itself, but because of the first. And neither is this   25
always convertible: for it is not the case that if [there is] slow
digestion, then always too much has been eaten, but this happens to
come about also because of worries, insomnia, and other causes; and
upon killing death follows of necessity, however it is not the case that
if there is death, killing has also preceded.[464]

337b25-32 If, then, it proceeds to infinity downwards,[465] it will
not be necessary *simpliciter* for this to have come to be [, but   30
neither *ex hypothesi*;[466] for there will always have to be some
further thing in front of it on account of which it is necessary for
it to come to be; so, given that the infinite has no starting
point,[467] there will be no first member on account of which it will
be necessary for it to come to be. Nor, on the other hand, will it
be true, in the case of a finite series, to say of that that it is
necessary *simpliciter* for it to come to be – a house for example,
when the foundations come to be.]

Having posited the twofold meaning of 'of necessity', [viz.] on the one
hand, as that which has necessity *simpliciter*, on the other hand *ex
hypothesi* and in a contingent way, and having proved that in the case   309,1
of things that are out of necessity the logical agreement is convertible
(for both when what is later has come to be, necessarily what is earlier
must have come to be, and when what is earlier has come to be, what
is later must follow as well), while in the case of things that are
contingent the agreement is no longer convertible (for in this case, if   5
there is what is later, what is earlier necessarily has to have been,
but if there is what is earlier, it is no longer necessary for what is later
to come to be), he now intends to teach that necessity *simpliciter* is
only in things moving in a circle, and that it will not belong to any of
the things [moving] in a straight line. For whether the straight line
is posited as infinite or finite, necessity *simpliciter* will not follow.   10
    And he now proves, so far, that if an infinite straight line is posited,

and, further, certain things are moving or changing along it, necessity *simpliciter* cannot belong to them. For if (a) necessity *simpliciter* is this: when upon that which is first, when it [already] exists, what is posterior of necessity follows, having necessity due to its own nature, and [if] (b) it is not possible to assume the first and the posterior in the infinite, it is manifest that (c) in this case there will be no necessity *simpliciter*. (d) But neither [will there be necessity] *ex hypothesi*, as he says,[468] which was: 'if what is posterior, then of necessity also what is prior'. If therefore there is no prior and posterior in an infinite straight line, then not just necessity *simpliciter* is not there in it, but neither is there necessity *ex hypothesi*, for the same reason.[469]

But we should realise that the argument like this apparently is not well formed to reach its goal.[470] For if (i) someone wanted to eliminate an infinite straight line and said that nothing can come to be in an infinite straight line, since everything that comes to be comes to be for the sake of some end, but every infinite thing is[471] without an end, he would say something that is both true and irrefutable (for there can be no infinite straight line at all). But if (ii) he assumes an infinite straight line, and since the infinite is without a beginning and with-out a limit, he says that on it, it is impossible for the second to follow upon the first of necessity, his argument will not be plausible. (iii) For although there is no beginning and no end, there still is succession and the coming to be of this after this. In this way, at any rate, Aristotle while saying that time has neither beginning nor end still says that succession and the first and the second are observed in it.[472] So, as far as Aristotle's claims are concerned, necessity will not be eliminated.[473]

(i) Someone might perhaps also raise the following problem with regard to what has been said: if coming to be is infinite and in a straight line, the succession will possess necessity *simpliciter*, for it is necessary that man should always come to be from man, and it is not possible that man should not have come to be from man.[474] (ii) The following should be replied to him: the succession in accordance with kind, by which man comes to be from man, comes about in a circle, because there is the recurrence of the same into the same, which is a proper attribute[475] of a circle: for first there is the man, then in this way the seed, and then the embryo, and child, and again man, and again seed. (iii) But if someone says that in the case of a straight line too there is the turning back[476] from the same into the same,[477] he should realise that in the case of turning back[478] on a straight line, the last point in which the moving thing has arrived is the first point in which it arrives when it runs back from the limit in the process of turning back,[479] just as on a ladder, when you revert from the ground, you turn back to the last step first.[480] (iv) In the case of circular movement, a thing after making a circle arrives at the point from which it has recently departed, e.g. Pisces, as to its final point. For

the sun having departed from Pisces, starting upon a new circle, does not relapse into Pisces in a continuous way, but is carried first to Taurus, and, last of all, to Pisces. (v) So, if the succession of kinds has been proven to come about in a circle, it is not difficult [to see] how necessity belongs to it, because it is in a circle. For it has been said previously that only in the movement in a circle is there necessity.   20
(vi) At any rate the succession which comes about not in a circle but in a straight line – and [the succession] of individuals is of this kind, in which from Tantalus [comes to be] Pelops, and from him Atreus – this one no longer has necessity. For it is not the case that if [there is] Tantalus, there is Pelops under any circumstances, nor if there is Sophroniscus is there, by the same token, necessarily Socrates.[481]

337b32-5 For when they come to be, if it is not necessary for that   25
always to come to be [, it will follow that something is always the case which is capable of not always being the case. But 'always' must belong to the coming to be, if its coming to be is necessary]

Having proved that it is impossible to assume necessity *simpliciter* in an infinite straight line, he now shows that neither is it possible [to do so] in a finite line. For if what comes to be of necessity is the same as what always comes to be of necessity, but what comes to be in a straight finite line does not come to be always, 'it will follow', he says, 'that something always comes to be the case which is capable of not   30
always being the case', which is incongruous.

337b35-38a3 For 'necessarily' and 'always' go together [(since what necessarily is, cannot not be), so that if it is necessarily, it is eternal, and if it is eternal, it is necessarily. If, therefore, the coming to be is necessary, the coming to be of this thing is eternal, and if eternal, necessary].

i.e. what comes to be of necessity is the same as what always comes to be.

For 'together' signifies 'the same'. Since, then, what comes to be in   311,1
a finite straight line does not exist always (for it has a limit at which it no longer exists), if someone says that in the case of this [(i.e. finite straight line) there is] necessity, which is the same as 'always', he will fall prey to the incongruity mentioned above: for he will say of something that is capable of not being that it exists always. If, then, coming to be is of necessity, it will also be always; but if always, then   5
it is impossible for it to be in a straight line.

338a4-9 So if the coming to be of something is necessary *simpliciter*, it is bound to make a circle and turn back. [For the

coming to be is bound to be either finite or not, and if not, in a
straight line or in a circle. Of these, if it is to be eternal, it cannot
be in a straight line on account of there being no sort of starting
point (neither of members of the series going downwards, taken
as it were from the future, nor upwards, as it were from the
past)]

Now, briefly summing up what was said before he draws the conclusion. For since, he says, it is necessary for coming to be either to have
10   limit or not, and it has not (for how would it be eternal having limit?),
it will be either in a straight line or in a circle. But it has been proven
that it cannot subsist in a straight line (for necessity cannot exist[482]
either in the case of a finite or an infinite [straight line], because there
is no 'what is earlier' and 'what is later', either in the case of past nor
in the case of future [events], as in each case movement must come to
15   be through the infinity).[483] Consequently it remains that necessary
and eternal coming to be and movement pertain to circular movement
alone.

      338a9-13 But it has to have a starting point; nor be eternal
      while being finite.[484] [That is why it has to be in a circle. So there
      is bound to be conversion; i.e. if *this* comes to be necessarily, then
      [so does] the prior, and again, if *that*, then the posterior comes
      to be necessarily]

Necessary coming to be, he says, both always is and has a starting
20   point. For we call eternal not the [coming to be] that is one in number
and continuous, but the one that is the same over an infinity.[485] If,
then, one cannot assume a beginning in the case of an infinite line,
nor [apply] 'always' in the case of the finite,[486] then necessary coming
to be is not at all possible in a straight line. Therefore only the coming
to be [that proceeds] in a circle will have necessity, in which case the
conversion also necessarily takes place. For if there is the first, there
25   always is the second; and if the second, then also the first, as has
already been proven.

      338a13-15 This, moreover, always takes place continuously,
      since it makes no difference[487] whether we say that [it proceeds]
      through two or more[488] stages. [So that which is necessary
      simpliciter exists in movement and generation in a circle]

Having shown that necessity belongs only to circular movement,
because it exists in things that are eternal and have a starting point,
of which [two attributes] 'eternal' does not belong to those that move
312,1   in a straight finite line, and 'having a starting point' does not apply
to an infinite straight line, so that it remains that movement in a

circle alone has necessity, and for it alone does the conversion necessarily hold; having said this, since he considered conversion with respect to two things,[489] he adds by way of explanation that consecutively, the second is always necessarily followed by the third, and this 5 latter by the fourth. 'For it makes no difference', he says, 'whether [it proceeds] through two or more stages', for maintaining conversion and the necessity of consequence.

338a15-17 And if it is in a circle, it is necessary for each one to come to be and to have come to be; and if necessary, the coming to be of these things is in a circle.

Now, concluding the whole argument, he says that if something is 10 coming to be in a circle, this has necessary coming to be, and if something comes to be necessarily, it comes to be in a circle.

338a17-38b5 This is reasonable, because[490] on quite other grounds movement in a circle, i.e. that of the heavens, has been shown to be eternal [– namely, that those things come to be and will be of necessity which are the movements that belong to this and which are because of it. If that which moves in a circle causes something to move continually, the movement of these things must also be in a circle. For example, the locomotion above it being in a circle, the sun moves in this way, and since it moves in that way, the seasons because of it come to be in a circle and return upon themselves, and since these come to be in this way, the things affected by them do so in their turn].

Having shown that necessity is a property of circular movement 15 alone, he says that it is 'reasonable' that this follows, since it is in accord with what has been demonstrated elsewhere. And it has been demonstrated in the eighth book of *Physics* [8.9] that movement in a circle alone is eternal. If therefore necessity *simpliciter* belongs to things eternal, as was proven earlier, it is reasonable that it belongs to circular movement alone. For, the circular movement of the heav- 20 enly bodies alone is eternal, but through it other [movements] are also eternal, as many as are brought to completion by it. For since the movement of the fixed stars is eternal, for this reason so is the movement of the planets, hence, of the sun, too; and because the movement of the sun in an inclined circle comes about eternally, for this reason the recurrence of the seasons is eternal as well, i.e. summer and winter and the rest.[491] And because the seasons come 25 back in a circle, for this reason the coming to be and perishing of animals and plants and the rest both comes about in a circle and acquires eternity.[492] For coming to be and passing away are due to the change of seasons.

313,1 **338b5-18** Why then is it that some things are apparently[493] like this, e.g. water[494] and air coming to be in a circle, and if there is a cloud,[495] then it must also[496] rain, and if it will rain, there must be cloud, too, but human beings and animals do not turn back on themselves [in such a way that the same ones come to be again (since there was no necessity, given that your father came to be, that you should have come to be, only that he should have, given that you did), and it seems that this coming to be is in a straight line (*eis euthu*). Why is there this difference? This again[497] is where the investigation begins: do all things come back on themselves in the same way, or not, but rather some in number and some only in form? It is obvious that those whose substance, i.e. what is moved, is imperishable will be the same in number, since movement follows the thing moved, but those whose substance is, on the contrary, perishable, must come back on themselves in form, not number].

5 He now sets out a certain problem: why is it that with air and water and other elements the coming to be in a circle is both necessary and convertible (for, he says, if there is a cloud, there will be water, and if water has come to be, cloud had previously existed)[498], but in the case of individuals, he says, this no longer holds. For if there is Socrates, Sophroniscus had previously existed, but if there is Sophroniscus, the

10 coming to be of Socrates will not necessarily follow. And he resolves the problem saying that the coming to be of the individuals is 'straight' (*eis euthu*), i.e. in a straight line. For Sophroniscus does not turn back, as would have been the case if the coming to be of individuals were in a circle.[499] If therefore the coming to be of individuals is not in a circle, it is plausible that it has neither necessity

15 nor conversion. Why, then, is it that water and air *do* turn back? – Because their recurrence is not in number, but in species. For it is not the case that air is preserved the same in number in recurrence and in the change into air from water, except that in the case of animals, too, the coming to be is proven to be turning back in a way and making a circle, as we have shown previously. But perhaps someone might

20 raise a problem, why is it that in the case of some things turning back comes about while they remain the same in number, whereas with others [it takes place] as they perish in number and are preserved only in respect of species. And for this reason he makes an addition,[500] saying 'this is[501] where the investigation begins: do all things return on themselves in the same way?', as he investigates the very [question] stated above. For if they owe their turning back to circular

25 movement, why is it that among the things that move in a circle, some perform a turning back while remaining the same in number, whereas others preserve the succession in species while perishing numerically? And he says that this is in agreement with what is said

in many places, that as many things as are incorruptible and move in a circle turn back while remaining the same in number (for the sun, being the same in number, moves in the same way over and over again), while as many things as those whose substance is perishable do not remain the same in number, but preserve species in recur-   30
rence: this is the case with animals, and plants and the transformation of the elements.

338b18-19 But if these too are the same in number, still they   314,1
are not things whose substance comes to be, the sort, namely, that is capable of not being.

Having proved that the coming to be of the elements is accomplished when each of them perishes numerically, but remains the same in kind, he now says that if someone said that these themselves, i.e. the   5
elements, remain the same in number *** of whom Empedocles was one,[502] it is to be replied that such a one will be saying in effect that the elements are not generable, not assuming, as we do, the substance to be generable and of a kind that is capable also of not being.[503]

Someone might, as Alexander says, raise a difficulty against Aristotle. For if matter always persists as the same, and the efficient   10
cause is always the same, what would be the reason for there not coming to be again, over some longer period of time, the same things from the same matter, produced by the same [causes]? Some indeed say that this happens during the rebirth and the Big Year, in which there happens the restoration of all things as the same. This being the case, there could also be the rebirth and recurrence in number of   15
particular individuals whose substance is perishable.[504] To this it should be replied that even if it is granted that Socrates is re-born,[505] the Socrates who came to be later will not be one and the same in number with the Socrates who had come to be earlier. For that which is one and the same in number cannot have intervals: for one in number comes about not on account of being from the same things, but on account of persisting as the same, when being earlier and later.   20
Therefore the sun is the same in number, but Socrates, as he said,[506] is not the same in number; for the indivisible form does not persist, even though matter persists.

Appendix: Textual Questions

1. Notes on the text of Philoponus' commentary printed by Vitelli

These include departures from Vitelli's text and the instances where Vitelli's textual suggestions are supported by V. Details are to be found in the notes to the translation.

246,6 For *puria panta* read *pur hapanta* with V a

247,24 For *antikampsei* read *anakampsei* following (T) GV a and Vitelli's suggestion in the apparatus

248,3 For *antikuklêsei* read *anakuklêsei*, following Vitelli's suggestion in the apparatus

255,14 For *tis* read *ti* following RV

255,26 For *autên* read *auton* with GT

256,21 Read and punctuate with V: *hupothesin. ei gar to P eis X metaballei*

259,27 Vitelli's reading *tropon* (following the Aldine) is supported by V

263,2 Read *poiêseie* with T^2 as suggested by Vitelli in apparatus

263,28 Read *ê allo hoper etukhen* with V

263,29 Read *ou gar dê pur ge phêsin ê gê* with V

264,25-6 Retain *kai* deleted by Vitelli

265,12 Read *ê psektê hôs* adopting Vitelli's suggestion made in the apparatus

265,15 Read *hupothesei autou* as in V

267,5 Read *hê men gê* with F, as recorded by Vitelli in the apparatus

268,2 Read *kai proteron, poteron ton auton ê allôs kai allôs*;

268,5 Read *to tou kosmou kinêtikon* with R V

269,20 Vitelli's addition of *merous* (based on the Aldine reading) is supported by V

270,9 Read *estai* instead of *hama* of the MSS, following V, which supports Vitelli's suggestion in the apparatus

272,31 For *atopon* read *atomon*

275,2 Perhaps for *oukhi dê* read *ouk êdê*

276,22 Adopt the reading of V, which after *pur* adds: *hôs einai tôi men akrôi thermôi tauton to eilikrines pur*

277,26 Read *kai panta alla ta toiauta* with Philoponus' MSS

279,16 Transpose Vitelli's comma from after *hudôr* to after *hugrotês*

280,29 Read *haplôn* as suggested by Vitelli in the apparatus instead of *allôn* of the MSS

281,27 Read *apedexato* with Va (Z) and following Vitelli's suggestion in the apparatus

281,28 Delete *hoti* as Vitelli suggests in the apparatus

286,7 Read *dia touto auto* with Z V instead of Vitelli's *dia touto autôi*

286,17 For *au tên* read *autên*

287,10 Read *energeiâi on poiei* with V which supports Vitelli's conjecture

290,25 Read: *dia tên kuklôi kinêsin aidion ousan*

292,12 Read *tukhoi ti*

296,27 Read *meinai* with V instead of Vitelli's *einai*

298,1 Perhaps read with V a *aidia diamenonta*

303,2–5 Read: *houtô toinun ei men phaiêmen hoti meta to ear estai theros kai anankê einai pote to theros kai ean legomen tou spermatos katablêthentos, hoti mellei phunai stakhus kai dunaton phunai, alêthous ousês ktl.*

305,24 Read *tautês* with V for Vitelli's *autês*

307,15.16 Transpose from line 15 following Vitelli's suggestion in his apparatus

307,9.14 Transpose from line 9 following Vitelli's suggestion in the apparatus.

309,23 For *einai* read *estin* following Vitelli's suggestion in the apparatus

310,9.10.12 Read *anakampsis* as Vitelli suggests in the apparatus

310,10 Read *anakampseôs* as Vitelli suggests in his apparatus

310,12 Read *anakampton* as Vitelli suggess in his apparatus

312,3 Read *tên antisrophên; epeidê tên antistrophên peri duo tina etheôrêsen* on the basis of Vitelli's suggestion in the apparatus backed by V a

313,5-10 Replace full stop after *antistrephei* (313,7) with left parenthesis, insert right parenthesis at 313,8 after *proüpêrkhen*

2. Notes on Philoponus' text of Aristotle

This is the list of Philoponus' quotations from Aristotle whose readings differ from the text of Aristotle printed by Joachim.

238,30 (332a4). *ei gar esti ti tôn phusikôn sômatôn hulê*. Aristotle's text omits 'some' (*ti*), giving the sense: 'if the matter of natural bodies is, as some believe, water, air and such'

239,19 (332a10). *hama einai* Philoponus, *einai hama* Aristotle

240,23 (332a15). *huparxei ara touto tôi aeri*. Joachim's text of Aristotle differs in word order (*huparxei ara tôi aeri touto* following

MSS EL, whereas HJ have it as in Philoponus' text). Vitelli prints *touto* following R (in agreement with V), where GTZ have *toutô*

241,1 (332a17-18). *ara* printed by Vitelli following R, where GTZV have *ara par'amphotera*, which is the reading of Aristotle MSS F¹HJL. Joachim prints *ar'* with EF²

241,13 (332a23). *enantiôseôs* Philoponus, *enantiotêtos* Aristotle

243,27-8 (332a30). *anankê metaballein* and *eirêtai* Philoponus, *metaballein anankê* and *dedeiktai* Aristotle

245,12 (332b8). *ta panta* (so too in the comment, 245,16) Philoponus, *panta* Aristotle (cf. Philoponus at 245,19)

245,12 (supplied section of the lemma) (332b9). 'Everything comes from fire or earth', *ek puros ê gês einai panta* printed by Joachim after EL (transpositions *ê ek gês einai* HJ, *einai kai gês* F). Philoponus' text apparently had 'from fire or air', *ê ex aeros einai*, cf. 246,4-5

246,29 (332b10). Vitelli prints *hoion* which is the reading of all Philoponus' MSS (and Aristotle's MSS HJ as reported by Joachim); Joachim prints *hôsper* which is the reading of his EFL (and the Aldine of Philoponus)

252,7 (332b33). *ei gar palin to pur eph' ho to* P Philoponus; the second *to* omitted in Aristotle

252,7 (332b33). Vitelli prints *metaballei* following R and reports the readings: *metabalei* Z; *eis allo metaballei* GT; V has *metaballei eis allo*. Joachim prints *eis allo metabalei* following JH and reports the variant *metaballei* in EFL (no omissions of *eis allo* recorded)

255,29 (333a13). Vitelli prints *ginontai* following RZ (+V) (where GT have *ginetai*); Joachim prints *ginetai* reporting no other readings

255,30 (333a15). Vitelli prints *katôthen* and reports *katô* in GT; Joachim's Aristotle text has *katô*

255,29 (333a13). Vitelli's MSS GT add *pasas* ('all the contrarieties'), as in Joachim's Aristotle text (where the omission of *pasas* in MS H is reported, and a variant *gar hapasas* in FJ²)

262,10 (333a32). *kai tôi einai ison thermon ktl.* *tò* MSS. GRTZ (and Aristotle codd. JL, in Joachim); *tôi* Vitelli, following Bekker's Aristotle text (= Joachim)

263,14 (333b9-10). *all'oukh.* This reading (333b9) coincides with Joachim's MSS FHJ; Joachim prints *ou gar* following EL

263,15 (333b10). *katha* printed by Vitelli (*kathaper* Z; *kathôs* a); Joachim prints *kath'ha* and reports *katha* EHL *kathaper* F

264,29 (333b21). *proteron* where Aristotle's text has *protera*

265,18 (333b23). Vitelli prints *eiê* after RZ; the text of Aristotle (333b23) and the Aldine have *ên*

266,1 (333b26). *phainontai* Philoponus and Joachim's EL; Joachim prints *phainetai*

273,1 (334a17). *einai to koinon* Vitelli following his MSS, *ti einai*

koinon Joachim 334a17 with EL (*einai ti* FJ, *einai ti ê* H), cf. 273,6
at n. 212

273,2 (334a18).Vitelli prints *sumbainein* following the text of Aristotle. In the apparatus, he reports the reading *sumbainei* for all his
main MSS, GRTZ, suggesting that Philoponus might have had the
reading *anankêi* (iota subscript is often omitted in the MSS). V has
sumbainein, supporting Vitelli's reading

276,31 (334b20). *epeidê* in Philoponus, except V, which has *epei de*, as
Aristotle's text (except *epei dê* E reported by Joachim)

277,26 (334b30). *kai talla <panta> ta toiauta* Philoponus MSS;
<panta> deleted by Vitelli. Aristotle: *ta toiauta* (= '[and] such')
Joachim with F²EL; *talla ta toiauta* (= '[and] the rest of this kind')
F¹HJ (accepted by Vitelli)

278,3 (334b31). *panta* Philoponus MSS and Joachim's J, *hapanta*
Aristotle's text (except J) and the Aldine edition of Philoponus

278,19 (334b32). *gê* S V and Aristotle (except MS H); *gês* RZ (Aristotle
MS H); *tê* (*sic*) GT

279,29 (335a10). *hê trophê hê hekastôn* printed by Vitelli (following
RTZ, *hê²* om. GV); *hê trophê hekastou* Joachim with E¹H (*hekastôn*
E²FJL)

280,11 (335a14). *epeidê estin* Philoponus MSS, except V which seems
to have *epei d' estin* as in Aristotle

280,12 (335a15). *to suneilêmmenon* (in agreement with *to eidos* at
a16) Philoponus; *suneilêmmenê* (in agreement with *hê morphê* at
a16) Joachim following E (*hê suneilêmmenê* J, *suneilêmmenon* FL,
apparently H). The words *hê morphê kai to eidos* are not present in
Philoponus' lemma

282,19-20 (335a22-3). Where other MSS have a truncated lemma, V
adds *eirêtai* after *haplôn*, completing Aristotle's sentence

282,22 (335a24). *epeidê* Vitelli's text (*epei de* V), *epei d'* Aristotle

283,26 (335a31). *hai duo* R; *hai* omitted in the rest of the MSS (as in
Joachim's EL); Vitelli draws attention to 284,1, where all the MSS
have *tas duo arkhas*

283,26 (335a31). Philoponus: *gennêsai* ZV (printed by Vitelli); *gennêsai* R; *pros to gennêsai* GT; Aristotle: *pros to gennêsai*

285,23 (335b9). *genesthai* Philoponus (cf. 285, 27), *ginesthai* Aristotle

286,17 (335b16). Reading *autên*. Vitelli writes *au tên* (the reading of
Aristotle MS H and Philoponus MS V (as it seems)) and reports
autên GRTZ, *autên tên* a; Joachim prints *autên tên*

286,17 (335b17). 'From'. Vitelli prints *hupo*, reporting *apo* in (G) and
the Aldine, which is the reading of Aristotle

286,27 (335b24). 'Were to say'. Vitelli prints *phêsei tis* (MSS: *phusei
tis* R: *phêseié tis* V), Joachim prints *tis phêseie* following F (*phêsêe*
E; *phêsei* H; *phêsin* J; *phêsi* L)

288,10 (336a13). Vitelli prints *to proteron*, where Aristotle manu-

scripts have *te*, except H which omits it. V has *te*; and *to* is not
supported by Philoponus' comment under the lemma (288,15)

290,23 (336a23-5). *genesis kai phthora.* Vitelli reports the reading *kai
genesis kai* in GT, which coincides with the Aristotle manuscripts
EL (336a24-5) (Joachim)

293,9 (336b9-10). *kai en isôi khronôi hê phthora kai hê genesis*, where
Joachim prints *kai hê phthora* following Aristotle manuscripts
except HJ

295,7 (336b20-1). The readings of this lemma in Philoponus manuscripts are as follows: *sunkrasin* SV: *sunkrisin* GRT: *sunkrousin* Z.
In the text of Aristotle, all the manuscripts collated by Joachim
(EJFHL) read *sunkrasin*. Dr Marwan Rashed has kindly informed
me that the reading *sunkrousin* occurs in Leid. Voss. Q 3, Paris
suppl. gr. 314 (perhaps dependent on the eleventh-century anno-
tator of E), Matr. 4563 (in ras. *krasin* M^1), all of which instances,
he suspects, depend on Philoponus' commentary

297,5 (336b29). *legetai* Philoponus, *legomen* Aristotle

299,11 (337a17). Philoponus MSS have *epeidê* (except V which has
epeidê d') where Aristotle MSS have *epei'd*. *epeidê*-sentence lacks
a conjunction and does not avoid hiatus

299,11 (337a17). *anankê einai ti kinoun* in all Vitelli's MSS (*to kinoun*
V: *ti to kinoun* a); Joachim printed *anankê einai ti to kinoun* (his
MSS: *to* om. EFJ *kinoun* om. E supra lin. add. J), translated by
Williams as 'something must be the mover'. The difference between the two readings can be treated as negligible in the present
context, although strictly speaking they rest on different metaphysical assumptions: on Vitelli's reading, the being of a mover is
not tied to any specific ontological class, while in Joachim's text,
the article *to* of *to kinoun* could be interpreted (although it does not
have to be) as an operator of a definite description. Since Aristotle's
actual position endorses both the derivative status of 'the mover' in
the proof for the existence of the first immobile mover in the *Physics*,
and the distinct ontological status of this entity in the *Metaphysics*,
neither of the readings will *ultimately* present doctrinal difficulties,
but I translate the lemma as it has been received in most Philoponus
manuscripts. I am grateful to Alan Lacey for querying this point

300,16 (337a20-1). *ei pleious hai kuklôi kinêseis.* Vitelli seems to be
following his R which has this text; GTZV have *ei pleious men hai*.
Joachim prints *ei pleious hai en kuklôi kinêseis* following his (and
Bekker's) EFJ, where Bekker follows HL which have *ei pleious eien
hai kuklôi ktl*. Note *eien* in Philoponus' comment (300,18 below),
which may or may not be a mere coincidence

300,16-17 (337a21-2). *pasas de pôs einai tautas hupo mian arkhên.*
Joachim prints *anankê* after *tautas*, apparently following all of his
manuscripts except EL. Vitelli notes *anankê* at 300,19, in Philoponus' comment

302,3 (337a27-8). Vitelli prints *dêlon dê tôi to kinoumenon* (and reports the reading *de* in GTa), where Aristotle's text has *dêlon dê hoti tôi ktl.*

306,6-7 (337b3-4). *hoti men gar enia dêlon kai euthus to gar estai kai to mellon*: *kai*[1] om. GT; *gar*[2] is omitted in all Aristotle's manuscripts and in Philoponus' V which has the same interpunction as in Joachim and Mugler: *hoti men gar enia, dêlon, kai euthus to estai*, 'that some are is obvious, and the difference between "it will be" and "it is going to be" is a direct consequence of this' (Williams trans.). *to mellon*, in all MSS of Aristotle (337b4) and Philoponus. Joachim conjectures *to mellei* on the basis of Philoponus, 306,12 and 302,25; see at nn. 449, 450

306,13 (337b7). *te* Philoponus, *d'* Aristotle MSS

306,13 (337b8). 'Since', *epeidê* Philoponus, *epei* Aristotle (except MS F)

307,20: '<Then>', [*toinun*] is absent in Philoponus at this point, but added by Vitelli on the basis of Aristotle and Philoponus at 307,25 which I print as a lemma (see n. 461)

308,30-1 (337b26-7, in the supplied part of lemma). Joachim at 337b26-7 prints *all' ex hupotheseôs* (= 'but *ex hypothesi*'), following EJ and Alexander *Quaest.* 2.22 (cf. also *Quaest.* 3.5, 89,1-2, discussions in Bruns 1892, 19-25; Sharples 1979, 36-7; Sharples 1994), and reports the reading 'but neither *ex hypothesi*' (*all' oud' ex hupotheseôs*) (HL and Philoponus, 'neither' (*oud'*) added above line also in F[1]). Marwan Rashed in his forthcoming edition agrees, reporting *all'* EWF[1]J[1] Alexander *all'oud* LHV Philoponus (comm.) *all'ouk* M. Bruns 1892 has argued that the quotation of Aristotle's text without negation in the title of Alexander's *Quaest.* 2.22 was added by a later editor of the collection, while Alexander's argument is based on the reading *all'oud*, the way Philoponus has it. This argument has been rightly questioned by Sharples 1994. Averroes' *Middle Commentary* notably takes the text to be without negation. On the other hand, had Alexander had the reading 'but *ex hypothesi*' and Ammonius 'but neither *ex hypothesi*', one could expect Philoponus to register this discrepancy (as he sometimes does provide us with textual information, e.g. at 295,12-296,10 above). This raises some further questions about Philoponus' use of Alexander's commentary.

311,17 (338a9-10). *anankê d'einai arkhên, mête peperasmenês ousês, kai aïdion einai*. Joachim prints: *anankê d'einai arkhên ...* † *mête peperasmenês ousês*† *aidion einai*, reporting: *arkhê* E[1]: *mête*] *mê* L *peperasmenês ousês*] *peperas ousês* E. post *ousês* add. *kai* FHL. Joachim suspects that some words dropped out after *arkhên*, and suggests writing something like *epi peras ekhousês*, or *epi peperasmenês eutheias*, following Philoponus' commentary, 312,1 (cf. n. 486). Mugler writes *anankê d'einai arkhên mê peperasmenês ousês, kai aidion einai*, but unfortunately supplies no apparatus to this place. Averroes' *Middle Commentary* paraphrases this text as follows: 'But if it is rectilinear, one of the two things must be the case: either it will not be eternal, or it will not have a beginning (*mabdâ' = arkhê*). For the straight line, if it has the beginning and the last point, must be finite (*mutanâhiyah = peperasmenê*) or not permanent; and if we assume that it is infinite at both ends, it will not have a beginning, for those things that are infinite have neither beginning nor end' (131,21-132,3 'Alawî, Kurland trans. lightly modified)

311,26 (338a13). 'Makes no difference', *ouden gar diapherei*. Vitelli prints this following RZ, where GTa have *ouden gar touto diapherei* (= 'it makes no difference *to this*'), which is also in Joachim's Aristotle (except for the MS E, which omits *gar touto*)

311,27 (338a14). 'Two or more', *pleionôn* is in all Philoponus MSS (cf. also 312,6); *pollôn* in all Joachim's Aristotle MSS and the Aldine Philoponus

312,13 (338a18). 'Because', *epeidê* Philoponus *epei* Aristotle

313,1 (338b5). *phainontai* Vitelli with MSS except GT and Aldine which have *phainetai* as in Aristotle (where Joachim reports *phainontai* in J)

313,1 (338b6). 'Water', *hudôr* in all Philoponus MSS and in Joachim's L (for 338b6); *hudata* in the Aldine edition of Philoponus and in Joachim's Aristotle (MSS, except L, and printed text)

313,2 (338b7). 'If there is a cloud', *ei men nephos*. After *nephos* Joachim's Aristotle (338b7) and the Aldine Philoponus have *estai*

313,2 (338b7). 'It must also rain', *dei kai husai*. Joachim prints *dei husai* following EL, while his MSS FHJ have *kai* as in our text

313,23 (338b11-12). 'This is where the investigation begins', *arkhê de tês skepseôs hautê* in all MSS, where Aristotle's text has *palin hautê*; but because this is a quotation in a context, we cannot be certain whether Philoponus' text of Aristotle had this omission, cf. text at n. 497

3. Philoponus' readings from Plato's *Phaedo*
(different from those printed in E.A. Duke, W.F. Hicken,
W.S.M. Nicoll, D.B. Robinson, J.C.G. Strachan (eds)
Platonis opera tomus I, Oxford, 1995 (= OCT))

285,14 (100D1). *di' ho ti* Philoponus, *di' hoti* OCT

285,14 (100D1). *ê hoti* Philoponus (in agreement with MS families Delta and T and Papyrus 3 in OCT), *ê* printed by OCT (= Beta)

285,15-16 (100D2). *talla* Philoponus (*ta alla* V), *ta men alla* OCT (all MSS)

285,17 (100D5). *autokalon* Philoponus R for *auto kalon* of Philoponus and OCT

Notes

1. 237,7-8. 'A study', *theôria*, is an exegetical term for the exposition of the main points of Aristotle's argument in a given section of the text (normally, a chapter), contrasted with *lexis*, line-by-line reading of the text.

2. 237,10. *GC* 2.1, 329a10-12. 'For it is not possible for this body to exist without a perceptible contrariety – for this infinite (*apeiron*) which some say is the principle must necessarily be either light or heavy, or cold, or hot'. Anaximander is not mentioned by name by Aristotle in this treatise.

3. 237,11. Aristotle's attribution of this theory at 329a13 is 'as it is written in the *Timaeus*'. There is a tradition among Neoplatonic commentators to attribute the doctrines expounded in the *Timaeus* to the dialogue character Timaeus as opposed to Plato, cf. Themistius *in An.* 10,23 and 12,28 (where Timaeus is explicitly distinguished from Plato). In this commentary, *Timaios* without an article refers for the most part to Plato's dialogue; but at this point, as at 228,13, Philoponus seems to be referring to the character of the dialogue who expounds its doctrines (cf. Vitelli's *Index Nominum*, s.v. *Platôn*, and C.J.F. Williams's note ad 228,13 in Williams 1999b). I am grateful to the anonymous reader for raising this issue, and to Dr Anna Somfai for a helpful discussion of it.

4. 237,8-15. This statement of Aristotle's goal in this chapter is a good illustration of non-sceptical use of *diaphônia* (cf. Mansfeld 1988).

5. 237,15-20. This description of Aristotle's aim (*skopos*) is not alternative, but complementary to the diairetic one, characterising it in terms of its own content rather than its position in the *diairesis*.

6. 237,15 (see also 238,29). Philoponus' 'logical' *diairesis* of possible views of matter (= 'corporeal principles of things': 237,22.23) referred to later in the commentary (see diagram on p. 28).

7. 237,25. Neither of these thinkers is mentioned by Aristotle in this treatise (cf. 11,9-12). On classifications of Presocratic theories in the commentaries, cf. Rashed 2001, 43-7.

8. 237,26. Read *metablêton* with MSS, where Vitelli prints *metablêtikon*. Vitelli changed *metablêton* to *metablêtikon* also at 269,1.11; 273,16; 274,12 below; this change does not seem warranted by anything particular in the text, so I retain the manuscript reading (V agrees with others in *metablêton* at all these places). The meaning does not seem affected by the choice of reading (*metablêtikon* differs from *metablêton* in that it adds to the common meaning 'changeable' the meaning 'able to produce change' (see LSJ, s.v.), but this latter meaning seems relatively irrelevant in this chapter).

9. 238,7. Philoponus' sequence of transformations (fire, air, water, earth) corresponds to the one found in Stoic cosmogony. The Stoics, however, do not claim that fire is the corporeal principle *qua* matter: in their cosmogony, matter, the passive principle, corresponds to earth and water. Here we might be dealing with the interpretation of Stoic cosmogony by either Philoponus, or his source who in this case could be Alexander (cf. n. ad 246,1 below). Cf. Hahm 1977, Mansfeld 1983, White 2003, 133-8. An explicit reference to the Stoic doctrine is made in the fragments from Alexander's commentary preserved in Jâbir b. Hayyân translated by Gannagé, cf. 244,29-255,8 with n. below. In Philoponus' diairesis, the Stoic position corresponds to branch 4 (see diagram on p. 28).

10. 238,7-8. In the commentary on *GC* 2.1, Philoponus cites Parmenides for the doctrine of two elements (earth and fire) and the tragedian Ion of Chios for three (earth, fire, air); see 207,15-20 in Williams 1999b, 117.

11. 238,13. cf. *GC* 1.1, 315a4-5; 2.6, 333a16-20 *et passim*.

12. 238,15. Plato, *Tim.* 54B6-D1, cf. Aristotle, *Cael.* 306a2, discussion in Cornford 1935, 216-17.

13. 237,22-238,16. Averroes in the *Middle Commentary* on *GC* 2.1 mentions *two* distinct divisions which, he says, agree with one another: 'Some people maintain that these four bodies have a substrate and matter (*maudû'an wa hayûlâ*) which exists in actuality. And some of them assume it [, i.e. matter, to be] one of them, either air, or fire, and some assume this matter to be some intermediate thing between these bodies, but at the same time something that exists in actuality. And some say that [the four elements] have no substrate prior (*aqdamu*) to them. And their difference (*ikhtilâf*) over this is like their difference over their number: for those who say that the elements (*al-ustuqussât*) are only two of these match with those who say that they are only fire and earth; and those who say that they are three match with those who say that they are fire, earth, and air; and those who say that they are the four themselves match with Empedocles who believed that the elements are these four, and that coming to be and perishing happen (*ya'ridu*) to things because of the combination and dissociation of these, and not* because of their alteration' (88,16-89,4 'Alawî; Kurland, 68-9, trans. modified). Kurland argues for secluding *lâ* ('not', missing in both Hebrew and Latin versions) in the Arabic MS, but a good case can be made for retaining it, if 'alteration' (*istihâl*) is taken to refer to the mutual transformation of elements: the absence of such transformation is a characteristic feature of Empedocles' theory (see diagram on p. 28).

14. 238,21-5 (cf. 238,25-9). Explanations why branches 3 and II-c of the *diairesis* are absent in the actual text of Aristotle. Ultimately, the explanation is Aristotle's parsimonious style: 3 does not appear in the text because it is obviously untenable; II-c is refuted by the same arguments as are used in *GC* 2.1, 329a10-12. Cf. 239,1-7 at n. 17 below.

15. 238,30. 'Some' omitted in Aristotle's text, see Appendix. Philoponus takes 'the natural bodies' to refer to the elements.

16. 239,4. *gumnazein*, literally 'practise', 'exercise', used in the commentary several times (239,4; 244,22; 248,7; 250,9; 253,18) as a technical exegetical term, in the meaning of 'expounding', 'studying', 'presenting' an argument. Note that in the 'character classification' of Plato's dialogues reported in D.L. 3.49, *gumnastikos* is a subspecies of the 'investigating' (*zêtêtikos*) kind (contrasted with 'debating' (*agônistikos*)). For a recent discussion with bibliography, see Opsomer 1998, 27-33.

17. 239,1-7. cf. 238,25-9 and n. 14 above.

18. 239,14-15. *touto gar esti to antidiairoumenon*. This remark seems to be incorporated in the *Middle Commentary* of Averroes ad loc. (102,17-20 'Alawi; cf. Kurland 81 n. 1): 'This one [element] either persists while changing into it, or it does not persist nor is sustained (*lâ yabqâ wa lâ yathbutu*). And if it does not persist and ceases [to be], then it is not an element. For it is characteristic of the element [that] it should persist, since it is a part of a thing of which it is an element'. The last sentence summarises the solution of the problem discussed under the 'fourth branch' (246,19 below).

19. 239,15-16. cf. 238,20-1 above and 244,16ff. below.

20. 239,19. '[To exist] at the same time', see Appendix.

21. 239,24. Aristotle distinguishes four kinds of change (*metabolê*), in respect of the four main categories: substance (coming to be and perishing, whereby substances come to be); quality (alteration); quantity (growth and diminution) and place (local motion). Characteristics of 'unqualified' substantial change, i.e. coming to be and perishing, are discussed by Aristotle in *GC* 1.3; characteristics of alteration in *GC* 1.4. On alteration, see Williams 1999a, 26 and n. 31.

22. 239,26-7. 'That contraries are present in the same [substratum].' Note that this difficulty may raise a further problem for the view according to which elements are substances. Substance, according to Aristotle's preliminary definition in the *Categories* 5, 4a10-21, can receive contraries, while the elements cannot, according to this argument. For a similar argument, cf. 241,16-26 below; Williams 1982, ad 332a4.

23. 240,18-21. The point that air in truth is hot and not cold was particularly relevant in the Peripatetic-Stoic debates over this issue. One of the treatises from the *Mantissa*, a school collection attributed to Alexander, is devoted entirely to the argument that air is naturally hot (*Mant.* 8, 126,24-127,26).

24. 240,23-4. 'Will accordingly belong to the air', see Appendix.

25. 240,25. As a procedure, on methodological grounds. See 240,25-6 with n. 27 below.

26. 240,26. *genomenon* is printed by Vitelli following the Aldine edition, giving the sense 'it (fire) has become air', whereas other MSS have *genomenos* (V apparently *ginomenos*), giving the sense 'when air has come to be'.

27. 240,25-6. Aristotle's proof at 332a8-15 consists of two parts: (i) *Assuming*: (a) air is the principle; (b) it only undergoes alteration changing into fire (i.e. it persists *qua* air); (c) it undergoes alteration in respect of hot/cold; (d) fire is hot, and air cold, to begin with; *it will follow* (e) that the result of this alteration will be legitimately described as 'hot air'. (ii) *Assuming*: (a); (b') fire, when changing into air also undergoes only alteration, i.e. it persists *qua* fire; (c') fire undergoes alteration in respect of hot/cold; (d') = (d); (e') since in the process of this alteration fire, while becoming air, will lose its property of hotness, the description 'hot air' given to it earlier will no longer be valid.

Philoponus seems to contest the assumption (b'), pointing out that it may be in conflict with the assumption (a), according to which the principle is the only element that undergoes 'alterations', while others can be described as coming to be and perishing.

28. 240,27-8. i.e. the statement that when air comes to be fire it will acquire heat to become 'hot air'. Philoponus here seems to continue his defence of the theory of one elemental principle, showing how the model set up by Aristotle for the sake of refutation can be salvaged. Assuming that (a); not-(b') (fire does undergo perishing when transforming into air); (c'') it does so by losing the property of dryness, and becoming 'moist', like air; (d'') = (d') = (d) (thesis about the elemental qualities); (e''): the description of fire as 'hot air' can stand, on the principles quite close to those of Aristotle's own theory. The only difference between Philoponus and Aristotle at this point is their respective treatment of the alteration: Aristotle assumes that this kind of change should be symmetrical for any pair of elements; while Philoponus points out that because of the assumption of one elemental principle (out of four), this symmetry cannot hold.

29. 241,1. 'Therefore', see Appendix.

30. 241,11. Aristotle does not mention Anaximander at this point (cf. 241,27 and n. 36 below). On the 'or' (repeated by Philoponus from Aristotle's text) see Williams 1982 ad loc.

31. 241,13. 'With a contrariety', see Appendix.

32. 241,14-16. The following refutations of Anaximander's view all show in three different ways that Anaximander's 'intermediate body' must have contrary constituent qualities, and is, thus, impossible. The three arguments may or may not come from different sources: the practice of listing several different solutions to the same problem (or reconstructions of the same convoluted statement, as in this case) is characteristic of the commentaries and 'school treatises' of Alexander. There is, I think, something remarkable about the way the arguments are introduced. Whereas in Alexander, different solutions are usually listed without any evaluative epithets, in the order of increasing plausibility, the last one being the one that wins the author's support, in this case we have the penultimate solution marked as *ameinon*, whereas the last one is described as *suntomôteron*, which might suggest several hands at work. Alexander's influence is present in (ii), see 241,27 with n. below.

33. 241,23. 'Retain' (*apotithemetha*), cf. at 242,28 below.

34. 241,16-26. (i) According to Aristotle's theory of change, if this body undergoes change in which it acquires a quality A, it must be characterised by ¬A (the privation of A) prior to the process of change; if it is to persist in the process of change (as it should, being the principle of other elements), it must keep ¬A as well as acquire A. So, A&¬A. Cf. 239,26-7 and n. 22 above.

35. 241,26. *ameinon de touton ton tropon kataskeuazein to parakeimenon*. cf. n. 32 above and 242,7 below.

36. 241,27. On the 'middle body', cf. *Phys.* 3.4, 203a16; 3.5, 205a27; *Cael.* 3.5, 303b10, *GC* 2.5, 332a21, *Metaph.* 1.8, 189a14. The description 'denser than fire but thinner than air' comes not from the *GC*, but from *Phys.* 1.4, 187a12-22, where Aristotle distinguishes two ways in which the 'physicists' speak of the principle: '(i) Some of them posit being to be one underlying body – either (ia) one of the three or (ib) something else which is denser than fire but thinner than air – and generate the rest making them many ... by means of Density and Rarity ... (ii) Others say that things come out from the One, in which the contraries are present. And this is how Anaximander speaks, and also those who say that what exists is one and many, like Empedocles and Anaxagoras'. In *Phys.* 3.3, 204b22-9, Aristotle seems to indicate that Anaximander's rationale for introducing the apeiron was to ensure that it does not have any of the contrary qualities that characterise the four elements.

In ancient commentaries, there was an influential tendency, started most probably by Alexander (cf. Frohn-Villeneuve 1980, 40), followed by both Philoponus and Simplicius, to downplay the differences between (i) and (ii), and identify the middle body of (ib) with Anaximander's *apeiron*. On the other hand, Porphyry, according to Simplicius, emphasised a difference between (i) and (ii) and followed Nicolaus of Damascus in attributing the 'middle body' of (ib) to Diogenes of Apollonia (see Simplic. *in Phys.* 149,11-18). Simplicius, while on the whole siding with Alexander, points out that Theophrastus in *Placit.* does not mention anyone except Anaximenes for the theory of rarefaction and concentration. Philoponus in his later *Physics* commentary devotes an elaborate comment to this passage, arguing that both (ib) should be taken as referring to Anaximander, and pointing out that the opposite view is due to the fact that the text is not carefully written and needs some restructuring (90,15-91,6 Vitelli). Averroes' *Middle Commentary* includes this description in its first formulation of the notion of 'intermediate body' (103,21-104,1 'Alawî).

Modern scholars seem to be divided on the issue, too. While some commentators (Diels, Ross) stress the difference between (i) and (ii), so that Anaximander is taken to belong to (ii) but not (i); others (Joachim, Kirk (with qualifications), Kahn) tend to take the 'middle body' to be attributed by Aristotle to Anaximander (for references and discussions, see Frohn-Villeneuve 1980, 39-43). For a most recent analysis of the passage, see Horstschäfer 1998, 125-31, who suggests that Aristotle does not include Anaximander in group (i), but the 'middle body' listed under (i) for the sake of completeness may have Anaximander's theory as its source (cf. 241,11 and n. 30 above).

37. 241,26-242,7. (ii) The argument is based on an 'interpolated' concept of the infinite (*apeiron*) (see previous note), hardly representing Anaximander's theory. The assumption of the refutation is that the density and looseness of texture (*puknotês* and *manotês*) are completely independent from all other tangible qualities of the elements. This does not square very well with Aristotle's own treatment of these qualities elsewhere (cf. *Phys.* 7.7, 260b7-10) or with the treatment of them earlier in this commentary as direct effects of the hot and the cold (225,25-31, see Williams 1999b, 137 and n. 301). However, dropping the 'independence' assumption would undermine the refutation: if being thinner involved being more liquid, and being denser being more solid, then the criticised theory might still have an answer to this objection.

38. 242,7-13. (iii) The argument differs from (i) in that while there the main assumption was that the intermediate body as such persists through any single process of change retaining all its qualities, including the one that is to be replaced in the process of change, here the main point is that because the intermediate body should be able to enter all the elemental transformations, it must contain all the elemental qualities, and thus have contraries in the same substratum. For the wording ('in a third way, more briefly') cf. 241,26 and n. 35 above.

39. 242,13-14. Averroes' *Middle Commentary* seems to contain the elements of all three arguments, but presents them as one argument: 'For this body would be both air and fire at the same time, or air and water, and two contraries would exist in it at the same time, in accordance with what has been explained for the case when the substrate is [taken to be] one of the elements. And it will follow that the thing will simultaneously be both existent and non-existent, since one of the contraries present in each pair of these [viz. the elements] is a privation, for cold is the privation of hot, and dry is the privation of moist. And this follows because since some intermediate body is assumed to be between the two contrary extremes, and the intermediate body is assumed to differ [from them] only in terms of 'the more and the less' and not in that it possesses a nature different from theirs – as, for example, it is assumed in accordance with this view that it differs from them in fineness and coarseness – then the intermediate must be of the [same] nature with the two extremes, and both contraries will be present in it simultaneously, which is absurd. That is what he [i.e. Aristotle] meant when he said that if there is a substrate between air and fire, it must be air and fire simultaneously, for if it differs from fire only in that it is coarser than fire, then it is coarse fire, and if it differs from air in that it is finer than it, then it is fine air, while being already [i.e. from the previous hypothesis] coarse fire, so that it will be coarse fire and fine air, which is absurd' (104,1-13 'Alawî, Kurland trans. lightly modified).

40. 242,18-19. cf. *GC* 1.3, 318b14-18 with Philoponus' commentary ad loc., 56,25-57,7 (Williams 1999a, 83).

41. 242,19-22. cf. *Phys.* 3.1, 201a3-6; *Metaph.* 11.9, at 1065b9-11.

42. 242,26-7. Does this reflect the tradition according to which Anaximander's *apeiron* does not have any elemental qualities? (Cf. Theophrastus ap. Simplic. *in Phys.* 24,16-18 = 226A FHSG, part).

43. 242,27-8. The reference is to the three arguments above. For 'be assumed' (*hupotithesthai*) at 242,28, Vitelli in his apparatus suggests 'retain', 'reserve' (*apotithesthai*) perhaps thinking of 241,23 above.

44. cf. *GC* 1.3, 318b6; 2.3, 330b14, with *Phys.* 1.5, 188a20-2.

45. 243,18. Note that Philoponus in his paraphrase supplies the predicate ('the principle') absent in Aristotle's sentence at 332a26-7, making *panta* into a modifier of the subject, and changing the meaning of Aristotle's sentence. Cf. 257,26 and n. 112 below.

46. 243,20. *asômatos kai aneideos*. Not Aristotle's terms, but cf. Alexander's description of prime matter in *de Anima* 3,26-4,4f., and the discussion in de Haas 1997, 21-6.

47. 243,23. See 238,13 and n. 11 above.

48. 243,24. See 238,14-15 and n. 12 above.

49. 243,27. 'Should change', see Appendix.

50. 243,29-244,2. Aristotle discusses this in the previous chapter, 2.4, 331a22-6ff. He does not use the terms 'association' (*koinônia*) and 'kinship' (*sungeneia*) in his description of relations among the elements. His technical term is *sumbolê* rendered by Williams 1982 as 'counterpart'. Cf. Philoponus' commentary ad loc., 233,1-15, Williams 1999b, 144-5 (and Alexander ap. Jâbir b. Ḥayyân, Gannagé 2005 (forthcoming), sec. 50).

51. 244,6-7. 'Two are incapable of being composed (*asustatoi*), while the remaining four when composed (*sunistamenai*) give form to the four elements.' *asustatoi* can mean both 'incapable of being composed' and 'incapable of subsisting', without any violation against the sense in this context. I keep the first of these two translations, because of the way 'when composed' (*sunistamenai*) is used in the next (*de-*) clause, where the meaning of composition seems to be intended.

52. Aristotle's text expounded here is 332b1-5, which follows immediately after the text of the next lemma. One need not assume any transposition made by Philoponus in this case: he probably discusses it here because it contains the point already previously made by Aristotle (while the point that matter does not add a new constituent for the pairs is relatively new).

53. 244,15. *aneideos*: cf. 243,20 and n. 46 above.

54. 244,22. See 237,29-238,7 with n. 9 above, and the Introduction, pp. 3-4.

55. 244,25. cf. *GC* 2.1 with Philoponus' remarks ad 329a29 on the nature of the first and second principle (matter and contrarieties, respectively), 211,11-212,2 (Williams 1999b, 121-2).

56. 244,25-9. Lack of persistence and lack of the efficient cause are supplied by the commentator as two main points of objection to the hypothesis of one changeable element as principle. Aristotle's infinite regress arguments in the rest of the chapter are treated here as a response to a possible defence of this hypothesis by a theory similar to that of the Stoics.

57. 244,30. 'They might say' (*eipoien an*). This reading, conjectured by Vitelli on the basis of a later correction in one MS (T), seems to be supported by V.

58. 244,29-245,8. This is a paraphrase of the Stoic theory. It is not clear whether some historical school version of Zeno's theory (according to which fire rather than *pneuma* is the first principle) is specifically targeted here, or whether it is taken for the sake of example (since the same arguments will presumably apply to the case of *pneuma* as well). This theory apparently meets both points of the objection of 244,25-9: the theory of fire as *proximate* matter leaves room for the passive substrate (see 238,7 with n. 9 above), and fire as active principle is taken to be the efficient cause that produces the elements (for *poiein* as the function of fire, see 245,20.24.26.33). Reference to the Stoics (*ahl al-riwâq*) is explicitly made in the Arabic fragments of Alexander's commentary; cf. Gannagé 2005 (forthcoming), section 94. Cf. also 237,29-238,7 above.

59. 245,11. 'Everything', see Appendix.

60. 245,11. Not a part of the lemma; Philoponus' text apparently had 'from fire or from air', cf. 246, 4-5 below, and the Appendix.

61. 245,22. In the Stoic theory, each element is associated with just one elemental quality: fire is hot, air cold, water moist, and earth dry. Notably, this defence seems to make use of Aristotle's theory of mixture, according to which elemental qualities in mixture mutually destroy their excesses, and are actually present in a reduced state, while potentially remaining pure qualities (*GC* 1.10, cf. Alexander *Mixt.* 15; *Quaest.* 2.20, 64,24-32; on the Stoic theory of mixture in general, see Lewis 1988, Sorabji 1988a, 79-105; 1988b, specifically on parallels and disanalogies with Aristotle, and on Alexander's criticisms, Todd 1976). The 'Stoic' defence (we do not know whether this argument has a historical source or whether it is a dialectical construct) is supposed to be that the reduced states of heat (perhaps in conjunction with 'inert' properties of matter) produce three other elemental qualities.

62. 245,32. Aristotle does explain in *GC* 2.3, 331a3-6 that of the two constitutive qualities each element possesses only one is 'dominant', while another is present as it were in a 'recessive' mode: so fire is more hot than dry, and air more moist than hot (see Philoponus' commentary ad loc., 230,8-231,13, Williams 1999b, 141-2, with a discussion of an objection to the Aristotelian theory which coincides with the Stoic position). On these lines, one might say that if fire (hot + dry) were to change into air (hot + moist) without changing its dominant quality (hot), but changing only in respect of its 'recessive' (in the Stoic theory, 'inert', or passive) characteristic, which it does not possess in the extreme, the argument from 'extremes' probably would not work so convincingly?

63. 246,1. In this paragraph, Philoponus develops a new possible defence of the Stoic view on the basis of the Aristotelian text that says that the elements come to be 'from' fire undergoing change. The argument is that if one assumes that all the elements contain something of the nature of fire, it is possible for fire to retain *some* of its nature throughout all changes, and thus be the principle of the elements *qua* matter. This objection will be refuted in the next paragraph.

64. 246,4-5. 'From air' (*ex aeros*) as printed by Vitelli after RZ (so too V); these words are omitted in GT. The Aldine, rather curiously, has 'from fire or fire' (cf., perhaps, 246,2.6); the text of Aristotle has 'from earth' (see Appendix (332b9)).

65. 246,6. Reading with V a *pur hapanta* instead of Vitelli's conjectured *puria panta*, where his MSS have *puri hapanta*. Vitelli's conjecture is not implausible: the word *purios* does occur in Philoponus; palaeographically, *puria panta* could easily become *puri hapanta*. But the point that everything has fiery nature would introduce a whole new idea which does not seem reflected in the rest of the argument: thus, at 246,1.9-10.12.16 – i.e. in all the places where the expression comes up – it is *pur panta einai*. Further, the way the sentence goes: *ek puros metaballontos ta panta ginesthai pur panta hupotithemetha dia to ek toutou metaballontos ginesthai panta pur* is a more natural reference for *toutou* than *puros*. Finally, having *puria* instead of *pur* would perhaps trivialise somewhat the point made in the last part of the sentence; and of the two readings, *puri* and *pur*, the latter seems to be a good *lectio difficilior*.

66. 246,10. 'Three-dimensional' (*trikhêi diastata*). The Greek has the plural: three-dimensionality seems to be treated here as a property of all generable things taken severally, yet the property which they possess 'in accordance with their substrate', i.e. ultimately, a common property of the substrate. In conjunction with the 'traditional' theory of prime matter, this brings us close to a view of prime matter as three-dimensional substrate. On Philoponus' relation to Stoic corporealism, see de Haas 1997, 104-19.

67. 246, 29. 'As', see Appendix.

68. 246,34. *idion*, 'special characteristic', corresponds to the 'property' of Aristotle's *Topics*, cf. *Top*. 1.5, 102a18-31; cf. also 287,5; 310,7.

69. 247,10-16. Transformations of water into earth and fire into air are mentioned by Aristotle among the examples of 'fast' elemental changes which take place between the two elements that have common counterparts (*sumbola*, in the case of fire/air, it is heat; in the case of water/earth it is coldness: *GC* 2.4, 331a25-b3). Other examples cited by Aristotle include transformations from air into water (common counterpart moist) and earth into fire (common counterpart dryness). Aristotle does not explicitly mention the reverse processes, as our commentator does in the case of fire and air, but they can be implied in his theory of quantitative prevalence of one element over another.

70. 247,16. *exôthen*, i.e. from the viewpoint of Aristotelian theory of elemental transformations, not necessarily shared by the 'air' theorists. It is interesting that Philoponus explicitly distinguishes this kind of criticism from the 'immanent' criticism of the arguments.

71. 247,24. Reading *anakampsei* instead of *antikampsei* following (T) GV a and Vitelli's suggestion in the apparatus. Vitelli prints *antikampsei*, the reading of all MSS except T G V (and the Aldine) which have *anakampsei*, and suggests in the apparatus that the latter must be the right reading. *antikamptein* is not in LSJ, and, apart from this commentary, there are only seven occurrences in the whole TLG corpus to date, all of them of a later (Byzantine) date.

72. 248,3. Reading *anakuklêsei* instead of *antikuklêsei*, following Vitelli in his apparatus. The compound root *antikukl-* has a single occurrence in the TLG corpus to date. Unfortunately, V has a lacuna at 248,2-5 (*all'ouk ... metabolê*).

73. 248,7. 'Brought this up', *aneballeto*. For this meaning cf. Philoponus *in An. Pr*. 81,32.

74. 248,20-1. 'The extremes, and the ones that are contrary [to one another], and those next to one another in order (*ta ephexês allêlôn keimena*).' This enumeration seems to contain the elements of two different classifications: 'the extremes' (*ta akra*) is supposed to refer to the 'extreme' elements, namely earth and fire, a corresponding opposite term would be 'the intermediate ones' (*ta mesa*), encompassing air and water; 'contrary' (*ta enantia*) probably refers to the elements which are opposed to each other in the 'square of elements', e.g. fire and water, air and earth (for this usage and classification in Aristotle, see *GC* 2.3, 330b30-31a3). Cf. also Alexander's problem with Aristotle's argument and exegetical solution (249,18-24 at n. 77 below), according to which *enantia* in this proof is used as a synonym of *eskhata* (= *akra*). I am grateful to the anonymous reader for drawing my attention to this sentence.

75. 249,3. Alternatively, if we suppose that air has not preserved its whiteness in the process but turned black, water will be black and moist. Step (a) has ruled out the possibility of water = fire, so fire must be dry. Thus, the arbitrariness that might be suggested by step (b) is in fact restricted by the assumptions of Aristotle's theory of elements.

76. 249,22. 'From the terms set down' (*ek tôn paratethentôn*), by setting down concrete terms which illustrate the contraries in Aristotle's theory of elements. On Alexander's use of this term in his logical works (including the commentaries on Aristotle) see Barnes et al. 1991, 25, 30; Mueller and Gould, 1999a, 1999b, 'Greek-English Index' s.v. *paratithenai*; Moraux 2001, 63.

77. 249,18-24. Alexander's point is that Aristotle's proof does not show that the extremes – fire and earth – change into each other, but rather that the elements that are 'contrary' (fire and water, air and earth) do so change (cf. 248,20-1 with n. 74 above). He regards the point that is established by Aristotle in this argument as more general, from which a more specific point about mutual transformation of earth and fire follows. Philoponus apparently agrees with this analysis.

78. 249,24-6. Fire is black and dry in the argument 248,21-249,6 above; earth black and moist in the argument 249,6-18 above. This sentence gives an example of a proof 'from the terms set down' (*ek tôn paratethentôn*): the general point is illustrated by the concrete cases (and it is clear that the general point will not be affected by a different set of concrete properties).

79. 250,3. 332b14, C.J.F. Williams trans., cf. 248,7 at n. 73 above.

80. 250,21-3. cf. *GC* 333a1 (below): *estô dê tôi men P to K, tôi de X to F.* Philoponus explains that K stands for *kalon* ('fine'), and F for *faulon* ('bad'). C.J.F. Williams in his translation of Aristotle adopts letters K and Y, which I replace, respectively, by G for 'good' and B for 'bad' throughout, including the lemmata.

81. 250,30-3. This is a paraphrase of *GC* 333a7-8. Cf. 254,8-14 at n. 98 below. This point is picked up by Philoponus or his source later on, in the commentary on *GC* 2.11, see 304,16-32, especially 304,25-8 at n.436 below.

82. 250,33-4. 'It will also follow, he says, that all are the same' (*hepsetai de, phêsi, kai to panta ta auta einai*). *GC* 333a13: 'everything will come to be one' (*ginetai de kai panta hen*) (see Appendix ad loc.)

83. 251,8. The term that I render as 'rational' (*rhêtos*) is to be taken not in the modern technical sense of 'rational number', but more likely as synonymous with *arithmêtos*, meaning 'countable'. For a discussion of the term *rhêtos* in Euclid and pre-Euclidean sources, see Fowler 1999, 161-95.

84. 251,10-16. The assumption of this objection is that each element will still be constituted by a *pair* of qualities as in Aristotle's system. Note that the formula (2^n), although correctly illustrated, is not stated.

85. 251,22. The conclusion that the number of contrarieties is infinite will follow either from a correct view that more than one element corresponds to one contrariety or from an incorrect view that one element corresponds to one contrariety; so the assumption that elemental transformations are in an infinite straight line will be refuted, whether the refutation is carried out on Aristotelian terms or in an *ad hominem* fashion. In order to distinguish between the two kinds of infinity, our author would seem to need the concept of ordinal number, which was not available until the works of Georg Cantor.

86. 251,27. Vitelli prints *taûta* ('these') following the MSS, but suggests *tautà* ('the same') in the apparatus. The two words are easily confused by scribes, and the difference in this case is rather minor.

87. 251,28. 'I should say' (*phêmi toinun*), perhaps an indication of Philoponus' own contribution. This whole discussion is missing in Averroes' *Middle Commentary*.

88. 252,7. 'If the next move of F', see Appendix.

89. 252,7. 'Is to change', see Appendix.

90. 252,15. For the notation, see 250, 21-3 with n. 80 above.

91. 252,17. i.e. the assumption is that change is linear, not cyclical.

92. 252,23. i.e. the premiss that Aristotle attributes to the advocates of linear order of elemental transformations, as a part of his *ad hominem* refutation of their view.

93. 252,28-253,1. cf. 251,10-16 and n. 84 above.

94. 252,28-253,2. i.e. adopting Aristotle's own assumptions in his theory of elements. The conclusion to be anticipated upon this change of premises is that elemental transformations follow not a linear but a cyclical pattern.

95. 253,11. 'Particularly if, he says, they change into each other.' Aristotle nowhere says exactly this. His phrase at 333a2 is 'for they change into each other'; Philoponus comments on it in the next section. Whether we are dealing with an instance of *phêsin* referring not to Aristotle but to a secondary source (see Introduction, p. 2 and n. 22), or whether there is some undetected problem with Philoponus' text at this point, is hard to say.

96. 253,16. cf. 252,22-8 above.

97. 253,21-4. The assumptions of the proof (linear change; and the fact that F changes into X in respect of B/G) are consistent with the view that not all of the elements change into each other.

98. 254,8-14. cf. 250,30-3 and n. 82 above and 2.11, 304,25-8 n. 448 below. 'Subsist', *hupostêsetai*, seems to be a technical term for 'exist in actuality', here and below, 255,13.15.

99. 255,5. 'That' (*touto*). The exact grammatical reference is somewhat vague because of a parenthetical clause; it can be either an extreme or an intermediate element; in each case, the doctrinal point is clear.

100. 255,14. Read *ti* (to be understood as referring to a *stoikheion*) following the MSS RV where Vitelli prints *tis*.

101. 255,16-17. This involves an additional assumption that two elements constituted, each, by an infinite number of contrarieties, differ in respect of exactly one of them. 'Observed', *theôreitai*, refers to the fastest type of change, cf. *GC* 2.4, 331a23-b4.

102. 255,26. For the purposes of translation read *ei oun eis auton* [sc. *ton aera*] *phthasai tên metabolên tên eis aera adunaton* (following Vitelli's GT), where Vitelli prints *eis autên* following R (*autên* R: *auton* GT: *auton dunaton* Z: *auton ton eskhaton horon* a: *auto* V). The meaning is a bit obscure, as witness all the desperate *lectiones variae*, and much depends on how we understand 'the change into air' (*tên metabolên tên eis aera*). I take it to refer back to 255,23, 'we have shown that some intermediates do not change into anything', in conjunction with 255,24: 'let us suppose now the intermediate to be air'. Philoponus here invokes the assumption made earlier in Aristotle's argument (as he reconstructs it), that 'linear' change into the intermediates is not possible (cf. 255,2-7); air being the intermediate, the whole gives a satisfactory sense to the antecedent of the conditional.

103. 255,29. 'Come to be', see Appendix.

104. 255,30. 'Lower', see Appendix.

105. 255,30. 'The contrarieties', see Appendix.

106. 256,20-1. Reading and punctuating with V: *hupothesin. ei gar to P eis X metaballei*. Vitelli prints the text of his MSS: *kai touto dêlon ek tôn par'autou proeirêmenôn exêgoumenou tên hupothesin † ei ge ktl.*, placing an obelus sign after *hupothesin* and reporting *eite* G (?): *eite gar* a. Admittedly, *gar* rather than *ge* in V a may be an influence of Aristotle's text cited in the next note.

107. 256,21-2. The reference is to 332b32: 'If the next move of F, i.e. fire, is to change into something else (and not turn back), e.g. into X, there will be a contrariety between fire and X other than those mentioned.'

108. 256,31. Step (a) of this argument is already familiar from the earlier discussion of the addition of one contrariety per element (251,1-252,6 above).

Step (b), however, seems to show some differences with the author's attitude towards infinite sets earlier in the commentary. Whereas previously our commentator or his source apparently endorsed the thesis that all infinite sets have the power set of the same size (cf. 251,22 and n. 85 above), in this argument he is no longer content with that and draws a clear, albeit non-technical, distinction between the infinite set of qualities possessed by each element and the infinite set of contrarieties possessed by all the elements together.

109. 257,8-13. An ingenious, if a little sketchy, reconstruction of Aristotle's reasoning is based on treating 'changes into' as an asymmetric relation. The two assumptions attributed to the proponents of linear change are: (i) F changes into X; (ii) X does not change into F. From this, our author concludes (iii) X does not have a contrariety with F (conclusion explicated in (iv)). (v) follows from the fact that X has no contrariety with F. The author seems to assume that relation 'has contrariety with' is also asymmetric, so that while F may have contrariety with X, X does not have contrariety with F, and therefore may be considered as 'the same as' F. 'Is the same as' thus also may lose its symmetry in this interpretation (although this is never explicitly stated).

110. 257,13-20. This is to explain why those who treat elemental transformation as linear are not entitled to a view of relations between the elements as symmetric.

111. 257,21-2. 333a19-20 = DK 31B17 v. 27, not a part of the lemma, but cf. 258,4 at n. 115 below.

112. 257,26. 'Whether all the four are elements.' The Greek phrase (*ei ta tessara stoikheia esti panta*) can be construed in several ways: (1) taking 'the four' (*ta tessara*) as subject, 'elements' (*stoikheia*) as predicate, 'all' (*panta*) as modifying the predicate, giving the sense: 'if the four are all the elements [there are]'; (2) taking 'the four' (*ta tessara*) as subject, 'elements' (*stoikheia*) as predicate, 'all' (*panta*) modifying 'the four' (*ta tessara*): 'if all the four are elements'; (3) taking 'the four elements' (*ta tessara stoikheia*) as subject, 'all' (*panta*) as predicate: 'if the four elements are everything'. Reading (2) should be chosen, (a) because it is required by the logic of the preceding sentence (it has been shown that neither one, nor several of the elements can be the principles of the rest; so it remains to see if all the four of them are elements), (b) because it is supported by the statement of the 'true opinion' below, at 257,31 (see next note), and (c) because it is supported by Philoponus' construal of 332a26 (cf. 243,18 and n. in 2.5 above). Will Rasmussen points out to me that the wording of 332a26 may lend an indirect support to (2), because it says only that there is nothing perceptible *prior* to the four elements, thus not precluding the possibility of there being something perceptible alongside them. This might allow a conclusion that all four (and possibly some others?) are elements, but not that the four are all the elements there are.

113. 257,31. This sentence supports the view of Philoponus' interpretation of Aristotle's phrase proposed in the previous note.

114. 258,1. 'Nor movement in accordance with nature' (*oute kinêsin tên kata phusin*). This probably refers, in the first instance, to the 'natural motions' of the elements.

115. 258,4. cf. 257,21-2 and n. 111 above.

116. 258,8. The Aldine adds here 'will be in accordance with quantity': *kata tên posotêta estai, ê kata tên dunamin*.

117. 258,19-20. See 258,33-259,3 with n.120 below.

118. 258,22-7. Two different bodies are said to be 'equal' because they are produced from the same amount of prime matter.

119. 258,29. Pint, *xestiaion*, cf. Philoponus *in Meteor.* 24,24.

120. 258,33-259,3. Aristotle in *Meteor.* 1.3 argues that the intervals between the heavenly bodies are filled with the 'first substance' called by the ancients aether, which is different from fire and earth. He begins his argument by refuting the hypotheses that the filling element is fire or air. The argument against air as the heavenly space-filler is that if such were the case, 'air would far exceed its due proportion in relation to its fellow elements' (340a4-5, Lee trans.). The refutation is based on the evidence of ordinary phenomena of change such as in the case of evaporation: the quantity of vapour being formed, although greater than that of the water from which it is formed, still is not excessively disproportionate to it. Aristotle claims that what is true of small quantities (parts of the totalities of the elements) should be true of the whole totalities as well. Therefore, because the size of the heavenly cosmos is so much greater than the size of the earth, it is impossible that it could be filled by air. The metric for 'quantity' in Aristotle is understandably vague. Philoponus in our passage seems to be providing it with a more technical meaning: the basis of comparison is matter which can extend and contract itself, so the assumed metric seems to be spatial. Cf. Philoponus *in Meteor.* 23,24-36 (with the example of 'parts' taken from physiology), Alexander *in Meteor.* 9,13-25.

121. 259,4. 'Unless because they have equal the matter which can receive the amount of each of the two things compared', i.e. (assuming one litre of water equals ten litres of air) one litre of water has matter that can receive ten litres of air (so that air-receiving matter of water is equal in amount to the matter of air), and vice versa, ten litres of air have just enough matter to receive one litre of water.

122. 259,7-8. cf. Aristotle, *Meteor.* 1.3, 340a13, with Lee's note ad loc.

123. 258,8-18. In other words, on this construal the elements do change into each other (cf. n. 133 ad 262,7 below on the kind of change).

124. 259,22. *to trikhêi diastaton.* cf. n. 120 ad 258,33-259,3 above. For discussion of this concept in Philoponus see Wildberg 1988, 204-19; de Haas 1997 (who does not discuss this passage). It is perhaps worth noting that this passage carries no specific marks by which Philoponus registers his own contribution; so the idea of matter as three-dimensional substrate of change in principle could be found in some of his sources.

125. 259,27. Reading *tropon* with V a and Vitelli. Vitelli's addition of *tropon* (following a) is supported by V.

126. 260,6. 'Incoherent', *apoklêrôtikon.* For this meaning, cf. Philoponus *in Meteor.* 82,35.

127. 260,1-11. The only way the argument (iib'') could work would be to assume that there are no contraries among the qualities that different elements have. This assumption is criticised in the commentary as unnatural and anti-teleological.

128. 260,14. 'Masses', *onkous,* not in the modern (e.g. Newtonian) sense, but just as a common way of referring to a part of a bodily aggregate (Williams 1999a translates *onkos* as 'bulk', which gives good sense in the context (*in GC* 117,33); here I agree with the suggestion made to me by an anonymous reader, because the present context (theory of change) is slightly more technical and abstract).

129. 260,15-16. cf. 258,33-259,3 and n. 120 above (Aristotle, *Meteor.* 1.3, 340a11).

130. 260,18. *to hupekkauma.* See n. 120 ad 258,33-259,3 above.

131. 260,27. On the character of change, cf. n. 133 ad 262,7 below.

132. 262,3. 'In respect of an equal quantity' (*kata poson ison*), the elements whose quantities are commensurate, i.e. reducible to a basic 'equal' quantity that serves as a mathematical base of comparison. So the difference between one pint of water and ten pints of air can be expressed by means of an arithmetical operation over one pint, which is a basic 'equal quantity' in this case.

133. 262,7. 'Change', *metabolê*. In Aristotle's classification of changes (see n. 21 ad 239,24 above) this would be a 'mixed' case: what is being changed is a quality, but it is not an alteration, since the quality is changed in respect of its intensity, not its nature; it is not a quantitative change because it is not growth and diminution.

134. 262,10. 'Being [said to be] equal', see Appendix.

135. 262,15-16. 'For the same which is greater will have such a proportion because it is of the same kind' (*to gar auto pleon tôi homogenes einai toiouton hexei ton logon*), a controversial sentence obelised by Williams in his translation of Aristotle ('For the same thing, when it becomes more, will have such a proportion in virtue of its being homogeneous'). Joachim's paraphrase: 'For the same thing, if it be greater in amount, will, since it belongs to the same kind as the thing of less amount with which it is being compared, have its *ratio* correspondingly increased'. Migliori: 'An identical body, to the extent that it is greater, will have a definition on the basis of homogeneity'. Philoponus' explanation is not the worst among these. He takes the sentence to explain the inappropriateness of comparison by measurement for the Empedoclean elements: 'For it is the same power, taken in a larger quantity, by virtue of its being of a similar kind, that will have such an account', i.e. an account in terms of an equal quantity represented by different amounts of bodily substance.

136. 262,24-5. On change, see n. 133 ad 262,7 above.

137. 263,2. Reading *poiêseie* with T^2 as suggested by Vitelli in his apparatus. Vitelli prints *poiêsei* (*poiêsei* RZ: *poiêsê* GT^1: *poiêseie* T^2: *poiêsoi* a) and suggests reading *poiêseie* following the correction made in T.

138. 263,2. Literally, 'grown' (*êuxêtai to hudôr*). For Aristotle's non-technical use of *auxanein* as referring to increase in a generic, not biological sense, see Bonitz, *Index*, s.v.

139. 263,5. 'In the first part', *en tôi prôtôi logôi*. *logos* here refers presumably to the first book of the treatise (cf. *GC* 1.5, 321b10ff.).

140. 263,7. 'The alterative power', *hê alloiôtikê dunamis*. Aristotle does describe the process of alteration (see n. 133 ad 262,7) as a constituent part of the process of growth (321b35-22a15), but does not use the concept of 'alterative power'. The whole analysis of the process of growth in terms of alteration, addition, and assimilation seems to be of Galenic provenance (for the functions of *alloiôsis*, *prosthesis,* and *exomoiôsis,* cf. Galen, *Nat. Fac.* 1.5-12 *passim*). Cf. Philoponus' use of this concept at 97,36; 102,4; 123,5; 191,28. On Philoponus' use of Galen, see Todd 1977.

141. 263,7. *to auxanomenon.* By 'growing thing' we can understand both 'growing organism' as a whole and any of its parts (cf. Aristotle's principle that each part of a growing thing undergoes growth, *GC* 1.5, 321a2-5; 18-20, and his examples of 'shank' (321a30) and anomoiomers (*GC* 1.5, *passim*) and Philoponus' discussion ad loc.).

142. 263,10-11. 'For nothing comes to be when things come to be as it may chance, as he says, but only when they do so by a certain formula' (333b9-11, not a part of Philoponus' lemma, but see 263,14-15 at n. 145). The sentence is ambiguous, allowing for two different interpretations of the scope of 'as he says': (a) including 'when things come to be as it may chance', leaving out 'nothing comes to be' , which are then to be understood as the words of Aristotle's assessment of Empedocles' claim; (b) including the whole sentence, which then will have to be taken to be contrasted by Aristotle with the Empedoclean theory of growth presented above. In this case 'as he says' can be rendered as 'according to what he says'. Philoponus (263,14-15 at n. 145) and Mugler accept the interpretation (a), while Williams, Forster, and Joachim give the interpretation (b). I am grateful to Edward Hussey for discussion of this passage.

143. 263,11-12. For the tripartite division of things coming to be by nature, by choice (that includes art), and by chance, cf. Alexander *Fat.* 4,167,16-168,25; *Mant.* 163,25-6; 168,16; 177,24; 181,21; 185,9-10; Philoponus *in Phys.* 2.8, 269-89 (passim); *in GC* 7,7-9.

144. 263,15 (*GC* 333b10). 'As', *katha.* See n. 142 ad 333b9-11 and the Appendix.

145. 263,14-15. This is Philoponus' interpretation of the text at 333b9-11, see n. 142.

146. 263,16. I render *logos* as 'formula', assuming that it picks up *GC* 333b11 (cf. 'proportion' Williams, 'raison' Mugler).

147. 263,21. DK 31B8, part (full fragment: 'I shall tell you something else. There is no growth of any of all mortal things // nor any end in destructive death, // but only mixture and interchange of what is mixed // exist, and growth is the name given to them by men', Inwood trans.). For different interpretations of *phusis* here, see Frohn-Villeneuve 1980, 138-9.

148. 263,23. 'Structural differentiation', *diorganôsis.* cf. Philoponus *in Phys.* 787,7; *Aet.* 129,1; 284,3; 487,8; *Opif.* 280,12; *in An.* 26,7; Iamblichus *VP* 37,23-38,7; Proclus *in Parm.* 792,34; Simplicius *in Cael.* 389,19.

149. 263,24. cf. Aristotle's discussion of the distinction between homoeomerous and anhomoeomerous parts in *Meteor.* 4.12.

150. 263,29. 'Cause', *aition.* keeping, with Williams, the traditional translation, on the understanding that in many contexts, as here, it refers to an explanation by more than one causal factor.

151. 263,27. 'Sinew', *neuron.* In a paraphrase of Aristotle, this can be translated as 'sinew', but in Philoponus' own vocabulary this could already mean 'nerve' (as it does in the more specialised contexts in *in An.*). In this commentary, only the 'old' Aristotelian meaning seems to be in use (11,26; 13,22; 111,28; 264,1; 273,18.20). Generally, in the late Aristotelian commentaries the term is often invoked as a mere example of a *tissue*, without any reference to it as a specific *organ*.

152. 263,28. Read with V *ê allo hoper etukhen*.

153. 263,29. Vitelli prints *ou gar dê ge, phêsin, hê gê* (unless it is a typographical error); I am reading *ou gar dê pur phêsin ê gê* following V.

154. 263,30-264,3. cf. Aristotle, *DA* 1.5, 410a4 quoting fr. DK 31B96, and particularly Philoponus' discussion of the quotation in his commentary, where Empedocles' ratios are interpreted in terms of Pythagorean 'harmonic numbers' (*in An.* 176,28-178,17).

155. 264,18. For the idea of there being counternatural things (*para phusin*) in nature, cf. 266,29-31 at n. 169 below, and Alexander *Fat.* 170,1-8; 193,16-18; Philoponus *in Phys.* 200,20ff.

156. 264,20. Empedocles has nothing to say about this mixture's being nature (cf. also n. 142).

157. 264,25-6. *tên mixin kai monon epainei* MSS; Vitelli deleted *kai*, but it should stay: *kai monon* is Philoponus' regular adverbial construction; cf. *in GC* 251,29; 257,6; 260,8; *in An. Pr.* 187,17; *in Meteor.* 8,1; 11,31; 20,28; 69,9; 83,32; 92,33; 111,13; *Aet.* 481,14; 529,20; *Opif.* 16,4; 61,15; 91,11; 271,22; 294,25).

158. 264,29. 'Prior', see Appendix.

159. 265,12. The text has *hôs psektê*. Vitelli suggests in the apparatus *ê psektê hôs*, which I adopt.

160. 265,15. Reading with V *hupothesei autou*. The assumption is that the elements undergo change when they form the Sphere being brought together by Love. This sentence may imply that the commentator is not familiar with Empedocles' poem, at least at the time of writing the commentary. Averroes in his *Middle Commentary* says that the absurdity is that both the elements and Love are prior to the Deity (viz. the Sphere) (90, sec. 41 Kurland; 111,14-20 'Alawi).

161. 265,18-19. 'Love is defined', see Appendix.

162. 265,23-4. cf. *An. Post.* 1.2, 71b16-25; 72a14-24; 1.10, 76b23.32.35; 77a3.25.

163. 265,28. The subject of 'says' (*phêsin*) here is not clear. It has been suggested to me by an anonymous reader that it could be Empedocles. But 'unless' (*ei mê*) seems to me a signal of a paraphrase (of 333b23-4), and this supports a natural understanding of asyndetic (without connectives) construction of *phêsin* as introducing quotation (direct speech), so I believe Vitelli's punctuation (commas around *phêsin*) is correct: the subject is not Empedocles. Whether he is Aristotle, or we have here a rare reference to Ammonius, is hard to say – see next note.

164. 265,28-9. The commentator apparently understands the words 'this type of movement' (and 'this [other one]') in the second half of the second sentence of our lemma ('unless to be caused by Love is defined as to be moved with this type of movement, and to be caused by Strife [as to be moved] by this [other one]') as referring to specific kinds of movements corresponding to the operation of Love and Strife respectively. He interprets these movements as two kinds of self-motion, presumably, because they cannot be reduced to anything beyond the first principles or separated from their operation. This interpretation seems to depend on the interpretation of the demonstrative pronoun *toiadi*, Philoponus takes *toia* as referring specifically to Love and Strife ('*such* kind of movement'), while modern translators take it in a more indefinite sense as a variable ('such-and-such' a movement). This ambiguity is similar to the case of *hode hêde tode*, more famous because of the key technical expression *tode ti* (see LSJ s.v. and Smith 1921). Whoever came up with this interpretation, Philoponus rejects it in the following sentence.

165. See Appendix.

166. 266,4-5. 'As I too have come here now', (*hôs kai egô deur'eimî*), what seems to be a 'platonising' reading of fr. DK 31 B 115, v. 13 (*tôn kai egô nun eimí* Hippolytus and Diels). Diels notes this reading as occurring in Philoponus *in An.* 73,31; Asclepius *in Metaph.* 197,17 (and *eîmi* also in Plutarch *de Exil.* 607C (cf. De Lacy & Einarson ad loc.) and Plotinus 4.8.1, 20 (*genomenos hêkein* 'has come here', Armstrong)). For further references and discussion of Empedocles in Platonic tradition, see Burkert 1975, Mansfeld 1985 (Philoponus' text not discussed). For a recent overview of the tradition of Empedocles in late antiquity, see Primavesi 2002, cf. De Smet 1998, 157 (fr. 1 (a,c)).

167. 266,21. cf. Aristotle's criticism of Empedocles' censuring of Strife in *Metaph.* 2.4, 1000a24-9.

168. 266,30. 'There will be' (*estai*), as Vitelli prints following R, or 'there is' (*esti*), as in the MSS GTV and the Aldine; in the latter case, the meaning could be: 'but since there is [movement] contrary to nature, therefore there certainly is movement in accordance with nature.'

169. 266,29-31. cf. 264,18 and n.155 above.

170. 267,5. The text has *hê men ênekhthê*; Vitelli records in the apparatus the reading *hê men <gê>* in F, which I adopt for the purposes of translation.

171. 267,6. Note that the 'aether' (*aithêr*) of Aristotle's text is replaced by 'fire' (*pur*). Cf. next note.

172. 267,8-9. *GC* 334a2 = DK 31B53, cf. *Phys.* 2.4, 196a22-3, where the subject is 'air' (*aêr*) not 'aether' (*aithêr*).

173. 267,10-11. *GC* 334a5 = DK 31B54 (for 'roots' (*rhizai*), cf. 31B6, v. 1).

174. 267,18-19. *GC* 334a5-7, cf. his account of Empedocles' doctrine in *GC* 1.1, 315a14.

175. 267,23. In Vitelli's text (which follows most MSS) the participles 'causing to disintegrate (*diakrinousa*)' and 'bringing together' (*sunkrinousa*) are in feminine, thus referring to movements (*kinêseis*, feminine) as the subjects of corresponding activities. V and the Aldine have the first one in neuter (*diakrinon*), referring to Strife, and suggesting that the second one refers to Love (*Philia*, feminine) instead of movement.

176. 267,28. cf. discussions of this passage by Joachim and Williams both of whom agree with Philoponus.

177. 268,1-2. Vitelli following the MSS prints *pôs homoiôs ekhein ton kosmon legei nun te kai proteron, ê allon kai allon*, and suggests that something like <*ei ton auton*> is missing after *proteron*. After *proteron*, the Aldine adds *proteron ton auton*, which must be an error or a misprint for *poteron*. So I read *proteron, poteron ton auton*. Cf. Bagolini's translation: *quaerit autem Alexander quomodo similiter se habere mundum dicit nunc et prius, utrum eundem, an alium et alium*. It should be noted that the MSS text is not completely unfeasible as it stands, especially if we assume that it is a paraphrase of the text of Alexander's commentary, where *ê* could be the beginning of a solution to the problem. (The whole could be rendered then as 'how does he say that the world is in a similar way now and earlier; is it *qua* being different each time'.)

178. 268,1-14. viz. at the time of separation and at the time of unification. Does this question imply that Alexander is unfamiliar with Empedocles' poem? Cf. Frohn-Villeneuve 1980, 124-36. Alexander discusses two possible solutions to the question, marked as (i) and (ii) in the text.

179. 268,7. *pou*, literally, 'somewhere', taking it to refer to the co-presence of the proper movement of the universe in parallel with the elemental movements and movements of the Sphere; whereas the second exegesis (after 'or') suggests the consecutive co-presence, where the universe is moved with its proper movements in the intervals between the clear states of 'elements' (after *Neikos*) and 'Sphere' (after *Philia*)?

180. 268,14-15. 'These questions belong, however, to another study.' This sentence can be regarded syntactically as a part of Aristotle's sentence at 334a15 (so Migliori in his translation). Joachim prints it at the beginning of the following chapter, and Williams follows. Mugler in his edition, in agreement with Philoponus, splits the sentence into two, printing the *men*-part (this sentence) as the last sentence of Chapter 6, and the *de*-part as the opening sentence of Chapter 7.

181. 268,18-20 (DK 31B109 (Inwood trans.)). (This fragment is quoted by Aristotle in *Metaph.* 2.4, 1000b5 and *DA* 1.2, 404b8, both of which could be Philoponus' indirect sources.)

182. 268,21. 'Affections' translates *pathê*; 'properties', another standard technical meaning of this term, would also suit here, except that the sense of 'being affected' emphasised by the commentator would have been lost.

183. 268,30. This refers to Aristotle's mention of 'another study' at 334a15.

184. 268,31. The discussion under this lemma covers the whole of 2.7; it is referred to as *theôria* at 276,14 (cf. n. 1 above and n. 224 below). There is a German translation of 268,31-271,24 in Böhm 1967, 287-90.

185. 268,32. 'When he had completed', *sumplêrôsas*. This technical term of exegesis as used by the Neoplatonic commentators is discussed by Luna 2001, 106, 215-17, who lists at 217 the occurrences of this term in Hermeias *in Phaedr.*, Simplicius *in Cael.*, *in Cat.*, *in Phys.*, [Simplicius] *in An.*, and Olympiodorus *in Meteor.*. Philoponus in this commentary also uses it in this technical meaning: *in GC* 74,20; 211,8; 268,32.

186. 268,33. 'The division set out before', *proektetheisês* (the Aldine has 'present' (*parousês*)); cf. 237,20ff. and diagram on p. 28.

187. 269,1. 'That the four [elements] are principles', *ta tessara arkhas einai*. Böhm's translation, '<dass> es vier Urgründe gibt' ('that there are four principles'), would require *tas tessaras*.

188. 269,1. Reading *metablêta* with the MSS where Vitelli has *metablêtika*, see n. 8 ad 237,26 above.

189. 269,11. Reading *metablêta* with the MSS for Vitelli's *metablêtika*, see n. 8 ad 237,26 above.

190. 269,20. Vitelli prints *ex hotououn <merous>*, adding *merous* following the Aldine; V does have *merous*, thus lending additional support to this conjecture, which I adopt. Cf. 273,29 at n. 215 below.

191. 269,33-4. The idea that sense perception may be insufficient to discern the diversity of microstructure in homogeneous stuffs is present already in Aristotle *GC* 1.10, 327b31ff. Some similar views, as well as the distinction between genuine homogeneous mixture and a mixture that only appears homogeneous, can be found in Galen (cf. *Elem. ex Hipp.* 1,1-9 (56,3-58,5 de Lacy, and de Lacy's commentary ad loc.)).

192. 270,2. cf. *GC* 1.5, *PA* 2.1.

193. 270,2-5. Böhm says that the proponents of this doctrine are atomists. But the last argument indicates that this is not so: the doctrine seems to involve a view of the elements as divisible, perhaps even indefinitely divisible, while at the same time qualitatively unchangeable. It is hard to say who the proponents might be. Cf. the position outlined by Simplicius in *in Cael.* 660,19ff., following Proclus' lost treatise *Examination of Aristotle's Objections to Plato's Timaeus*, discussion in de Haas 1999, 40-4. Cf. also a difficult text discussed in Stückelberger 1984, 156-9 and 195 text 96 (= Stephanus Alexandrinus, *De magna et sacra arte* 6 in Ideler 1841, 2,223f.). Stückelberger (159) suggests that *toutôn hai akrai poiotêtes* refers to the *atomoi*. (The text is notoriously difficult, and this may be uncertain; but in any case, a tendency to incorporate some version of atomic theory in the Aristotelian doctrine of elements is indeed very clear.) Philoponus in his discussion of Aristotle's Lynceus example (*in GC* 1.10, 194,5-15, cf. 193,15-20; 196,10-19; Williams 1999b, 100-4) contrasts a genuine mixture with a compound made of atoms. In the present text the objection of the 'atomists' (or the proponents of unchangeable elements) seems to be left without response by Philoponus.

194. 270,9. Reading *estai* instead of *hama* of the MSS, following V, which supports Vitelli's suggestion in the apparatus. Vitelli prints *pôs pote hama to eidos tês sarkos ê tou ostou ê tôn allôn homoiomerôn*, following his MSS, and suggests *estai* instead of *hama* in the apparatus, which is supported by V (*pôs pote estai to eidos*).

195. 270,14-15. On matter as an 'intermediate', see above 2.5, 332a35; Philoponus, 244,12-15, and below 275,1 and n. 217.

196. 271,1-272,10. This text is translated (as two consecutive passages) by R. Sorabji and F. de Haas in Sorabji 2004, vol. 2, 20(a) 6-7 (292-4).

197. 271,2-3. See Bonitz *Index*, s.v. *hulê* 3, discussion in de Haas 1997, 20-45.

198. 271,5-6. Böhm gives three synonyms for *kekolasmenon*, the term I translate as 'inhibited': 'weakened', 'blunted', and 'restrained' (*abgeschwächt*, *abgestumpft, gebändigt*). On the problem of the status of the elements in natural compounds in medieval philosophy of nature, see his n. 121 to section 11 (Böhm 1967, 450-3).

199. 271,8-9. cf. Aristotle's distinction between the first actuality ('knowledge' in the sense of disposition) and the second actuality ('exercising knowledge') in *DA* 2.1, 412a22-8; for this meaning of 'disposition' (*hexis*) in Alexander, cf. n. 203 below.

200. 271,15. 'In the seventh book of *Physics*.' Vitelli (followed by Böhm) suggests that the reference is to *Phys*. 7.3, 245b9. The Aldine has *tritôi*, 'third', instead of 'seventh'.

201. 271,16. For the discussion of the third kind of potentiality in Philoponus, see de Haas 1999.

202. 271,17. 'Being suitable', *epitêdeiotês* is used to refer to the first potentiality by Alexander of Aphrodisias. (cf. *de An.*, 84,24; 85,1.3); on the term, see Todd 1972.

203. 271,17. *to kata tên hexin*: *hexis* is used to refer to the second potentiality, first actuality by Aristotle (see Bonitz, *Index*, s.v.) and by Alexander (*de An.*), see Bruns's *Index verborum*, s.v. Cf. 286,25 and n. 298 below.

204. 271,23. Reading 'as when he is already being taught' (*hôs êdê loipon didaskomenos*), instead of 'as someone who is already being taught' (*hôs <ho> êdê loipon didaskomenos*). The addition of an article does not seem necessary: *êdê* and *loipon* in this sentence indicate that the reference is to the same subject as in the preceding sentence.

205. 271,25-272,33. German translation in Böhm 1967, 290-2.

206. 271,25-272,10. This paragraph seems to contain a correction of the position stated earlier in the commentary. At 271,2-7, the commentator speaks of the elements as potentially present in a mixture in a special, third, sense of potentiality. In the present passage, however, in reply to a 'possible' objection (with which he agrees), he explains that elements are potentially present in a mixture in the first sense of potentiality, while the extreme heat is potentially present in a third sense. Discussion in de Haas 1999, 34f., cf. de Haas 2004, IX.

207. 272,12-13. The reference is to the difficulty stated by Aristotle at 334b4-7, cf. below 274,11.

208. 272,31. Read *atomon* ('indivisible') instead of *atopon* ('out of place') with V and the Aldine. Vitelli prints *atopon* without any comment: this must be a typographical error (cf. below 277,18 and Bagolinus 119a11: '*insectile accipimus et indivisibile*').

209. 272,31-2. 'A middle in a precise sense' (*to akribes meson*), presumably, a geometrical middle point.

210. 273,1. Vitelli's text here has *einai to koinon*, which might suggest 'a common [substrate]', whereas Joachim prints 'something in common' (*ti einai koinon*), see Appendix.

211. 273,2. For the text, see the Appendix.

212. 273,6. *peri tinos koinou*, cf. n. 210 ad 273,1 above.

213. 273,15. '<Make> [them come] from one another.' *<gennôsin>* is added by Vitelli; it is omitted in Vitelli's MSS, but present in V.

214. 273,16. Reading *metablêta* with MSS instead of Vitelli's *metablêtika*. See n. 8 ad 237,26 above.

215. 273,29. 'From any part of flesh taken at random', *ex hotououn merous*, cf. 269,20 and n. 190 above.

216. 274,12. Reading *metablêta* with MSS against Vitelli's *metablêtika*, see n. 8 ad 237,26.

217. 275,1. *prosêgoria*. On the appellations of matter, cf. 270,14-15 and n. 195 above.

218. 275,2. Reading *ouk êdê* ('no longer') with V and a instead of *oukhi dê* ('not indeed') printed by Vitelli following R (whose reading could be explained by iotacism). Other MSS read: *oukh êdê* GT; *oukh hê* Z.

219. 275,5-7. cf. 271,1-7 above (the reference is probably to the distinction drawn in the *theôria* of the commentary).

220. 275,24. In *GC* 2.3, 330b30-31a3, Aristotle does speak of fire and water as being contrary towards each other. Alexander discusses the issue at several places in his work, insisting that only elemental differentiae, but not the elements themselves, can be said to be contrary (*in Sens*. 73,24-30; cf. Simplicius *in Cael*. 168,18-169,2). For discussions, see Moraux, 2001, 10-11, Kupreeva 2003, 310-11.

221. 275,26. *epêgage to ê <tôn> stoikheiôn*. Vitelli added *<tôn>* following a; V supports this addition.

222. 275,26-8. Textual remark reflecting the lack of punctuation in the MSS (Eichner notes that this parsing of the text is adopted by Averroes, see Eichner 2005, 'Kommentar', ad 122,1-5).

223. 276,5-8. The reference to the opponents is not entirely clear. Their view as described by Philoponus, according to which the elements are completely destroyed in a mixture, corresponds to the case of fusion, *sunkhusis* of the classification of mixtures found in some doxographical sources (cf. Alexander *Mixt*. 216,14-217,13, Todd 1976 ad loc.).

224. 276,14. 'In the study', cf. 271,3-7.

225. 276,15. 'Trace' (*ikhnos*). For this term in the description of the elements in the Receptacle, cf. *Tim*. 53B, with discussion in Cornford 1937, 199.

226. 276,22. 'So that pure fire is the same as the extreme hot' (*hôs einai tôi men akrôi thermôi tauton to eilikrines pur*). This phrase is missing in Vitelli's text, but is present in V; it is stylistically plausible and, moreover, helps to account for the otherwise somewhat obscure construction of the following sentence (with the particle *de*), so I adopt this reading.

227. 276,18-23. Note that this seems to be in accordance with 270,16-271,7, but not with the *epistasis* at 271,25-272,10 (cf. n. 206 above).

228. 276,23. 'More natural', *prosphuesteron*. Vitelli in the apparatus suggests the feminine *prosphuesteran*, which is certainly better grammar; but this might be an elliptical self-quotation, cf. 276,11.

229. 276,11-23. This meaning of potentiality is discussed in de Haas 1999, 36.

230. 276,31. 'Since' (*epeidê*) see Appendix.

231. 277,14. 'The first impulse' (*tên prôtên hormên*). The concept of impulse is invoked to explain qualitative change rather than locomotion. The Greek word for 'impulse', *hormê*, occurs in the *in GC* only once. On the theory of impulse in general, see Wolff 1971; Wolff 1987.

232. 277,18. 'Indivisible', *atomon*. For the discussion of Philoponus' theory of latitude and inhibited forms, see Todd 1980, 167ff., Sorabji 1983; de Haas 1997; Sorabji 2002; Sorabji 2004, vol. 2, 21 (316-26).

233. 277,20. This is not printed as a lemma by Vitelli, but it likely is one (although these words are omitted by GTZa and present only in RV).

234. 277,26. Reading *kai talla <panta> ta toiauta* Philoponus MSS; *<panta>* deleted by Vitelli. Aristotle: *ta toiauta* (= '[and] such') Joachim with F[2]EL; *talla ta toiauta* (= '[and] the rest of this kind') F[1]HJ (accepted by Vitelli).

235. 278,1. 'To produce form'. For the term *eidopoioi*, cf. Williams 1999b n. 270 (who translates it as 'specifying').

236. 278,3. 'All', *panta*; on the text, see Appendix.

237. 278,13. *Meteor.* 2.4, 359b28f.

238. 278,19. 'Earth', *gê*. For the text, see Appendix.

239. 278,28-9. On the link between moisture and the property of being easily bounded (*euoristia*), see *GC* 1.10, 328a35-b5. On air being moist *par excellence*, cf. *GC* 2.3, 331a5, also *Phys.* 4.5, 213a2.

240. 278,29-279,2. The principle involved in this explanation is that water can be *said* to possess a property E to a higher degree, although not actually possessing it in this way (for air has more E), because it has greater power of imparting this property to a compound. This principle appears to be in conflict with the Neoplatonic principle according to which a cause of a property has to possess that property in a higher degree than its effect (*propter quod alia id maximum tale*, see Lloyd 1976, Mourelatos 1984, Berryman 1999b, 4-5 and n. 13, cf. Introduction, p. 8 with n. 69 there).

241. 279,16. Transpose Vitelli's comma from after *hudôr* to after *hugrotês*.

242. 279,24. *Cat.* 5, 3b24; cf. 230,4 (Vitelli's reference).

243. 279,25-6. This can be understood either (i) as a contrast between simple and composite substances, in which case the idea would be that simple substances, viz. the elements, are outside the scope of discussion in the *Categories* (a question-begging, although, strictly, not impossible, assumption); or (ii) as a contrast between composite substance and its substantial constituents (form and matter), so that the elements on this view will be treated as composite substances (for the ambiguity of the notion of 'composite', cf. Alexander of Aphrodisias, *de An.* 3,27). The following sentence seems to support (ii).

244. 279,26-8. cf. *Cat.* 8, 9a14 sq. (where qualities are described as standing for 'powers' (*dunameis*)). For a discussion of this problem by Alexander, cf. Kupreeva 2003, 311-14.

245. 279,29. For the text (335a10) see Appendix.

246. 280,11. 'Since', *epeidê estin* (335a14) see Appendix.

247. 280,12. 'Taken together with', *to suneilêmmenon* For the text, see Appendix.

248. 280,15. *Iliad* 14.182.

249. cf. *GC* 1.5, 321b16-24.

250. 280.19. cf. *Meteor.* 4.1, 379a16.

251. 281,1-2. This lemma is printed by Vitelli as a part of Chapter 8, as it is in the editions of Aristotle's text. But in Philoponus' commentary, the discussion opened by it is a study of the whole of the argument of Chapter 9.

252. 281,13-20. Aristotle does not discuss the matter of heavenly bodies specifically in this chapter; this passage elaborates on his brief mention of the eternal bodies as an example of things which have being of necessity. Joachim comments: 'The celestial bodies (a) *qua* perceptible, involve matter as well as 'form'; but their matter is the Aether and is itself eternal: and (b) *qua* moving, they involve *hulê pothen poi* (*hulê topikê*), i.e. a something *dunaton*, viz. a *hupokeimenon* capable of occupying successively the different points on its orbit'. Cf. Williams 1982 ad loc. It is interesting that neither aether nor *hulê topikê* are mentioned in this section of Philoponus' commentary; the matter of the eternal beings is characterised in abstract terms of hylomorphic theory in a way that suggests rather that this matter *qua* matter does not differ from that of the sublunary bodies except in the way in which it is combined with the form it has. For Philoponus' later criticism of Aristotle's theory of aether, see Wildberg 1987 and Wildberg 1988.

253. 281,20. 'The third, efficient, cause', *triton aition poiêtikon*. I keep the translation 'efficient' for *poiêtikon* where possible; 'produce' and 'productive' are alternative renderings. We may notice a switch from the term *arkhai* (principles) in the description of form and matter to *aition* (cause) in the description of efficient cause. Cf. Williams 1982 ad loc.

254. 281,26. cf. n. 297 ad 285,13-14 below.

255. 281,27. Reading *apedexato* with Va (Z) and following Vitelli's suggestion in the apparatus.

256. 281,28. Deleting *hoti* with Vitelli in the apparatus.

257. 281,27-9. cf. *Phaedo* 97B8-98B6. The sentence in parentheses is commentator's addition to Aristotle's account of the *Phaedo* in *GC* 335b10-16, where Anaxagoras is not mentioned.

258. 281,29-30. cf. *Phaedo* 100C3-E3.

259. 281,30-33. This is a paraphrase of Aristotle's argument at 335b20-4: see next three notes.

260. 281,31-3. 'We don't say that the image produces what comes to be in proportion with it, but the craftsman.' Where Aristotle's text (335b20-4) has an example of knowledge and knower (*epistêmôn*), our commentary introduces a craftsman and the 'image', perhaps as a reminiscence of a different argument in *Metaph.* 1.9, 991a21 (= 13.5, 1079b25: *ti gar esti to ergazomenon pros tas ideas apoblepon;*).

261. 281,33-282,1. This is a paraphrase of *GC* 335b18-20. The commentator here reverses the actual order of these two arguments in Aristotle's text.

262. 281,34. 'Why is it that when that which partakes is present, it does not come to be directly?' The emphasis seems to be changed compared to Aristotle's argument. Aristotle asks why the Forms do not generate (*gennâi*) continuously (*sunekhôs*), where our commentator speaks about coming to be directly (*eutheôs*), i.e. immediately. This shift of meaning influences the commentator's choice of example in the next sentence, where the question is why the state of health does not come to be immediately. Aristotle's formulation would be better served by the question why there is the state of illness at all, given that there is the form of health and that which receives it.

263. 282,3. 'Because of its being changed', *autên trepomenên*. The term for 'being changed' (*trepomenê*, from *trepein*, 'to turn') is a standard Stoic epithet of matter (cf. *SVF*, *Index verborum*). Aristotle's text at this point describes matter as the source of change using the word (335b16-7) has *hoi d' autên tên hulên, apo tautês gar einai tên kinêsin*.

264. 282,4. 'Indivisible principles' (*tas atomous arkhas*), atoms. The atomist theory is not specifically mentioned by Aristotle in this chapter.

265. 282,5. I keep a translation 'movement' for *kinêsis*, but here and in all general contexts not dealing with a specific kind of movement (such as the motion of heavenly bodies), 'change' should be understood.

266. 282,14-18. This curious 'proof' is not a part of Aristotle's chapter, which only says of fire 'that it is worse than the tools' (see below under lemma 336a6-12), so we again may raise a question of the subject of 'he proves' (*deiknusi*). Cf. Williams 1982 ad loc. Aristotle's contrast between 'instrumental' means and fire is probably best understood as that between organic and inorganic parts of a living being. Fire is 'worse' in the sense of being less in control of living functions compared to the organic systems, e.g. the heart. Philoponus (or his source) understands 'worse' in axiological sense: fire is worse because it is destructive. There is no gap between the two interpretations (fire is destructive because it is itself lacking structure and order which the instruments and organs have), but there is a certain difference. Cf. Philoponus, *in An.* 277,15-23: 'But it is so far, he says, from being the cause of augmentation without qualification, that he says in the *On Coming-to-Be and Perishing* that it is a contributory cause worse than an instrument. For it is by being regulated by the account of end that instruments reach the end, and when they are left alone by the artisan they are not the cause of detriment since they cannot act at all without the artisan, whereas fire acting by itself becomes cause of destruction. For in the digestion of bread and medicine, if the digesting fire is not governed by the account of a doctor or caterer, it rather destroys and displaces [us] from the form that is our own' (Charlton trans.).

267. 282,20. This is not printed as a lemma by Vitelli, but it must be a lemma: lacking connective in the first sentence after it, and the fact that it is written as a lemma in V support this.

268. 282,22. 'Since', *epeidê*, see Appendix.

269. 282,26-7. Verrycken 1990b, 255 and n. 140, points out that this and the following passage (283,1-10) show that at the time of writing this commentary Philoponus still accepted Aristotle's theory of the fifth body, presumably because of the classification of all bodies into eternal and perishable. The exegetical context in which this classification is introduced here should not escape us.

270. 283,1-2. As opposed to 'being potentially,' see nn. 271, 273, 274 below.

271. 283,3-4. 'In a general sense (*koinôs*) is seen to be present in both.' Vitelli suggests in his *Index* that *koinôs* here means 'in accordance with the common notion' (*kata tên koinên ennoian*); but it may be useful to compare this whole passage with Alexander's *Quaest*. 1.10 (see nn. 274, 275 below): 'For this account of the principle in the substrate is more general (*koinoteros*), in that it includes both [types of] substrate in itself' (21,4-5, Sharples trans. modified).

272. 283,6. Vitelli's addition of 'which have' (*ekhonta*), omitted in all his manuscripts, on the basis of the Aldine reading (*tên diaphoran ekhonta*), is supported by V (which has *ekhonta tên diaphoran*).

273. 283,6-7. *tautên pros allêla tên diaphoran <ekhonta>, tên kata to kreitton kai kheiron. diaphora* in this case can be alternatively translated as *differentia*. (Cf. Alexander, *Quaest*. 1.10, 21,10-11, where the author discusses the *differentiae* of two kinds of matter which would give them their forms (i.e. forms characterising them as the kinds of matter they are).

274. 283,10-11. In Alexander's school treatise *Quaest*. 1.10 ('How, if there are four causes, the substrate of the divine bodies too will not be matter'), it is argued that 'it is not the case that, if the two matters are different from each other, that which is the substrate in the divine body and that which is in the things subject to coming to be and passing away, therefore they are compound. For if they [both] had some one substrate, they would need differences which would give them their forms, so that they would be different from each other while possessing the same substrate. But if they are different, it is certainly not necessary for them to differ from each other according to certain differences which give them their forms' (21,5-10, Sharples trans.) The thesis stated in our text corresponds to the position that is rejected in this *Quaestio*, with the difference that the issue of matter being compound, which is the main point of refutation in the *Quaestio*, is replaced here by the point that the difference between the two kinds of matter is due exclusively to the forms they receive. But the main assumption underlying both versions is *construed* in the same way in the two texts, i.e. as saying that divine and sublunary matter differ in kind when 'kind' is taken in a more precise sense, perhaps that of a 'genus'.

275. 283,21-3. The distinction corresponds to that drawn in Alexander's *Quaest*. 1.10, between 'the ultimate substrate which is receptive of opposites in turn' (20,33-4) and 'the ultimate substrate which in itself lacks shape' (21,2-3), although the wording is different.

276. 283,26. 'The two' (*hai duo*), for the text see Appendix.

277. 283,26. 'For making [things] come to be', *gennêsai*. For the text, see Appendix.

278. 283,29. 'Of its own nature and spontaneously' (*autophuôs kai automatôs*). This exact wording is not found in Aristotle, although the point that the matter of natural (or, more precisely, living) substances can be brought to motion without an external agency is made in *Metaph*. 7.9, 1034a9-26; cf. *Metaph*. 9.8, 1049b4-10, *Phys*. 8.5.

279. 284,4. 'For making the matter suitable to work upon.' This suggests that working on matter is distinct from making matter suitable to work on (although both may be functions of efficient cause). The example in the following sentence seems to fuse these two functions, or at least to be making a transition from one to another continuous without gaps (for the point that neither matter nor form come to be in the coming to be of a natural hylomorphic compound, see *Metaph*. 7.8, 1033a25-b10).

280. 284,19. Aristotle here does not specify what he means by 'things that necessarily are not', but he uses 'goat-stag' as an example of 'that which is not' in *Phys*. 4.1, 208a30; *Int*. 1, 16a16; *An. Pr*. 1.38, 49a24; *An. Post*. 2.7, 92b7.

281. 284,25. *hippokentauros*. The word is not used by Aristotle (*kentauros* occurs thrice (Bonitz), cf. *Poet*. 1, 1447b21; *An. Post*. 2.1, 89b32; *Insomn*. 461b20), but not as an example of an empty concept; it is used so (as referring to a non-existent object) by Alexander *in Metaph*. 82,6; 433,17; *in An. Pr*. 183,16; *in Top*. 213,18; 355,13; Ammonius *in Porph. Isag*. 39,15 (with 'goat-stag'); 40,2.4; *in Int*. 41,33; 52,15; and by Philoponus *in Cat*. 9,18; *in An. Post*. 43,5; 290,18; 360,2; 411,6. [Philoponus] *in An*. 488,18; 497,26 curiously explains the meaning of the word by 'etymology' as referring to a half-horse half-bull.

282. 285,5. *Phys*. 2.7, 198a24ff.

283. 285,12. The reference is probably to the Demiurge who is regarded as efficient cause in most ancient post-Aristotelian interpretations of the *Timaeus*. Cf. Alexander ap. Simplic. *in Phys*. 1.2, 26, 13-25; Philop. *in Phys*. 5.7ff, *Aet*. 159,5ff., discussion and references in Sharples 1995; Rashed 2001.

284. *Phaedo* 100C10-D7, Tredennick/Tarrant trans.

285. 285,14. 'Why', see Appendix.

286. 285,14. 'That' Philoponus, see Appendix.

287. 285,15-16. 'All these', see Appendix.

288. 285,17. 'Makes the object beautiful', see Appendix.

289. 285,23. 'For coming to be', see Appendix.

290. 286,2. 'Creative forms', *ta dêmiourgika eidê*, cf. Procl. *in Parm*. 731,40; 845,21; 877,26; 960,27. On the account of creation in the school of Ammonius, see Verrycken 1990a, 209-10. On this view, the creative role of the Demiurge (understood as divine Intellect) consists in eternal contemplation of its inherent creative ideas, *dêmiourgikoi logoi*. These latter act as efficient causes of sensible things, which participate in them.

291. 286,7. Read *dia touto auto* with Z V. Vitelli prints *dia touto autôi*, reporting *autôi* om. T; *auto* Z; and suggests in the apparatus that the words *tôi Platôni* could perhaps be deleted (taking *tôi Platôni* to be in apposition to *tôi*, giving the sense 'Plato himself').

292. 286,7-10. 'Assigning no causal rôle to the maker who looks at the forms and in accordance with likeness to them produces things here'. *mê aitiasamenos ton aphorônta tois eidesi dêmiourgon kai pros auta kath'homoiotêta ta têide paragonta*. The phrase is ambiguous, allowing for two interpretations: (a) a narrow 'Platonising' one, where *dêmiourgos* will refer to the Demiurge, the second God, who plays the rôle of efficient cause in contemplating the immanent 'creative forms' (*dêmiourgika eidê* or *dêmiourgikous logous*) and bringing about 'things here' (*ta têide*). This account, although it is a little vague on the details of efficient causation, would be in a good agreement with the kind of metaphysics taught by Ammonius (cf. Verrycken 1990a, 208-10). But within the present context, it does not square well with the passage that follows immediately after it, based on Aristotle's examples of 'knower' and physician, which might suggest a more inclusive metaphysical interpretation (b): 'maker' referring to any craftsman (a synonym of *tekhnitês* without any specific theological connotations), *ta têide* keeping its meaning, and 'forms' understood as essences (cf. the analysis of production by Aristotle in *Metaph.* 7.7). Such a deflationary interpretation might be expected from someone like Alexander. (Admittedly, in this commentary we might be dealing with a deliberate ambiguity.)

293. 286,11. 'The rational principles', *logoi*. The commentator uses this term to gloss Aristotle's phrase with an allusion to the Neoplatonic theory of 'creative forms' mentioned at 286,2.

294. 286,17. Reading *autên*. Vitelli writes *au tên* (the reading of Aristotle MS H and Philoponus MS V (as it seems)) and reports *autên* GRTZ, *autên tên* a; Joachim prints *autên tên*.

295. 286,17. 'From', see Appendix.

296. 286,19. *tropê*, a Stoic term for change, see *SVF* 4, *Index verborum*, s.v. and n. 263 ad 282,3 above; cf. also Aristotle, *Phys.* 1.7, 190b8-9.

297. 286,20. Philoponus refers to what follows in Aristotle's text, at 335b20-24, which he paraphrased under the previous lemma, 286,10-15.

298. 286,25. 'In accordance with acquired disposition' (*kath' hexin*) glosses 'in accordance with potentiality' (*kata dunamin*) of Aristotle's text. Note that Aristotle and Alexander use this expression to refer to the second potentiality (first actuality), see 271,17 and n. 202 ad 271,17 above.

299. 286,27. 'Were to say', see Appendix.

300. 287,5. 'Special property', *idion*. See n. 68 ad 246,34 above.

301. 287,10. Reading *energeiâi on poiei* with V which supports Vitelli's conjecture (*an poiê* GRT a: *poiei* Z).

302. 287,20-21. Philoponus seems to be referring to the 'instrumental' causes that were added by the Neoplatonists, along with the 'paradigmatic' causes, to the Aristotelian list.

303. 287,20-21. Cf. Williams ad loc. ('The suggestion is that the true explanation is to be sought in that which moves and acts upon fire, and is not itself moved or acted upon. The only satisfactory explanation is to be sought in an unmoved mover, such as Aristotle thought soul to be, which is at once form and a cause *qua* origin of movement'.)

304. 287,26-8. Cf. DK 28A24, A35. For the discussion of Alexander's attribution of this view to Parmenides, and other Presocratic parallels, see Solmsen 1960, 362 n. 38, Frohn-Villeneuve 1980, 75-85. The lemma that follows is omitted by the Aldine (cf. Introduction).

305. 287,28. 'By far the most active', *malista drastikôteron*. For other instances of *malista* used with comparative degree in Philoponus, cf. *in Categ.* 204,9; *in An. Post.* 285,25; *in An.* 406,7; with superlative: *in Categ.* 29,19; *in An.* 73,1; 83,2; 292,33; 347,39; 397,28; *in Phys.* 177,4; *Aet.* 88,22; 396,26; 397,9.

306. 288,6. cf. 282,14-17 above.

307. 288,10. Vitelli prints *to proteron*, where Aristotle manuscripts have *te*, except H which omits it. V has *te*; and *to* is not supported by Philoponus' comment under the lemma (288,15).

308. This lemma is printed by Vitelli as a part of Chapter 9, as it is in Bekker; but in Philoponus' division of the text (as in Joachim) this is the opening sentence of Chapter 10, and the discussion that follows opens the study of the argument of the whole chapter (cf. Introduction, p. 2 and n. 17).

309. 288,24-6. This reference is to *Phys.* 8.1, 250b13-15, which says (in explication of the second part of the dilemma about the eternity of movement): '[but] it always was and always will be, and this immortality and lack of cessation belongs to all existents, being as it were some kind of life to all things subsisting by nature.' We may notice that our commentator gives a loose paraphrase of the sentence changing its grammar and original meaning. The exact source of this paraphrase is difficult to track down: it could be Philoponus paraphrasing Ammonius, or Ammonius interpreting Aristotle; and it cannot be ruled out that this reference to the *Physics* is originally due to Alexander.

From Simplicius' *Physics* commentary we learn that this place was heavily commented upon. Simplicius himself interprets it in the spirit of 'harmony between Plato and Aristotle': ' "as it were some kind of life to all things subsisting by nature" is said in accordance with Aristotle's precision which is in agreement with Plato. For we say that those things live that are moved from inside by themselves. Therefore if all natural bodies have in themselves nature as the principle of movement, then they could plausibly be described as living, on account of their internal suitability for movement. And indeed (*kai gar*) nature is the last of the lives*. Therefore it has its being in the underlying physical body, and is "like living" rather than life in a strict sense. And movement in accordance with it is suitability for movement, as we shall learn in this book. And [to see] that Aristotle said "as it were life" in agreement with Plato, referring to the internal movement as natural, read what is written in the tenth book of the *Laws* about the internal movement: "If we see that this [movement] has come about somewhere in an earthen or watery or firelike [nature] either separate or mixed, what property shall we say it is in such [a nature]? Perhaps you will ask me whether we say of it that it lives, when it moves itself". But this has been said about the self-moved life in a strict sense, i.e. about the psychic life. Therefore Aristotle well said that natural movement is "as it were life", and not life without qualification, because life in a strict sense has the same relation to natural movement as soul has to nature' (*in Phys.* 1119,3-20). *Simplicius uses the term 'life' (*zôê*) in its Neoplatonic sense of 'soul', i.e. referring primarily to the world-soul, hence the statement that nature is 'the last life' is in agreement with the Neoplatonist theory of emanation.

Simplicius also reports Alexander's interpretation (which he goes on to criticise (*in Phys.* 1119,28-1120,3)): 'And Alexander says that "being as it were life to all things that exist by nature" is said to indicate that movement is immortal and unceasing. For if movement is related to natural bodies as life to ensouled bodies, then just as ensouled bodies cannot exist without soul, so too natural bodies [cannot exist] without movement. Therefore, since natural bodies are eternal *qua* natural (for they have not begun at any time, nor will they perish into non-being, since the perishing of natural bodies is into some other natural body, for when water perishes air comes to be), it is clear that movement, too, in accordance with which they are natural, is eternal' (*in Phys.* 1119,20-28). In Alexander's interpretation *zôê* seems to be treated as a term of comparison rather than as a cause of movement in natural things (cf. Moraux 2001, 173-4).

310. 289,4. 'By virtue of their direction', *têi phorâi*. In translating *phora* here as 'direction' I adopt the suggestion of Williams 1982 ad 336a30 ('The word translated "direction" is the word (*phora*) normally translated "locomotion", but it would hardly make sense so to translate it here').

311. 289,4. 'Or, at any rate, by virtue of unevenness', *êgoun têi anômaliâi*. I have been persuaded by Alan Bowen not to use the term 'irregularity' for *anômalia*, because heavenly motions in Aristotle's system are fully subject to a rational account and in that sense they are 'regular'. Their apparent irregularities have to do with varying geometrical and temporal patterns of visible movements. As Williams 1982 put it (ad 336a30), 'the defining characteristic of irregular motion is having parts that are not intersubstitutable'.

312. 289,6-9. Philoponus' text makes clear the point not stated clearly by Aristotle that in the case of contrariety by virtue of unevenness, we are dealing with *one* motion that causes diverse or even contrary effects by virtue of its uneven character.

313. 289,24. 'This' (*tautês*), i.e. the daily rotation of the fixed stars.

314. 289,27. 'Daytime-and-night-time', *hêmeronuktion*, a space of 24 hours (at 291,13 Philoponus uses the term *nukhthêmeron*).

315. 289,27-290,7. Both the difficulty and the solution correspond in all the main points to Alexander's *Quaest.* 3.4, 87.1-21, where superior substances are described as 'primary' (*proêgoumena*) and inferior ones as 'secondary and contrary to those that come to be primarily' (*deutera kai tois proêgoumenôs ginomenois hupenantia*). See Joachim, 260; Sharples 1994, 47.

316. 290,2. 'Superior elements, fire and air', cf. *GC* 2.8, 335a19; *Meteor.* 1.2, 339a18; 1.8, 345b33.

317. 290,3. *kai tôn allôn hapantôn haper tôi logôi diexelthein ou radion.* Since all the main kinds of natural substances have been listed, it is not immediately clear what this might refer to. Probably, we should think of various *powers* of substances, which Philoponus elsewhere also describes in terms of degrees of perfection (cf. *Aet.* 530,18).

318. 290,6. Vitelli's emendation of the MSS reading *hote* to *ho ge* is supported by V which has *ho ge*.

319. 290,7. 'Turns', *tropai. tropê* is used to designate solstice, frequently so by Aristotle, of winter and summer solstices (cf. *GC* 2.11, 337b12; *Meteor.* 2.6, 364b2.3; 3.5, 377a20-5; *HA* 7.13, 598b25, *GA* 2.7, 748a28; *HA* 5.30, 556b8; 5.8, 542b4.11.15, 543b12; 5.19, 552b19; 5.8, 542b6.7.20; 6.17, 570b27), but here it might refer more generally to the changes of climate following upon the solstices: cf. *in Meteor.* 10,35.

320. 290,23. 'Coming to be and perishing', see Appendix.

321. 290,25. Reading *dia tên kuklôi kinêsin aïdion ousan. hê men suntaxis tês lexeôs toiautê.* Vitelli indicates a lacuna after *ousan*, because the sentence is not complete. Two *variae lectiones*, in R and V, are scribal errors which shed no new light on the passage. A brief survey of Philoponus' use of the word *suntaxis* in its philological meaning (28 occurrences in this meaning in Philoponus' works in the TLG database to date) shows that it often refers to the grammatical structure of a short phrase (sometimes to a specific construction, such as huperbaton or conditional sentence, cf. *in An. Post.* 231,13; 216,10; *in GC* 130,3; *in Phys.* 749,17) or a particular difficult place (*in An.* 64,26). My default suggestion here is to eliminate the lacuna, and treat Philoponus' sentence as a paraphrase of Aristotle's text 336a23-5: 'Since it has been assumed, and indeed proved, that things are subject to continuous coming to be and perishing [– and we hold that locomotion is the cause of coming to be]' *hupokeitai kai dedeiktai sunekhês ousa tois pragmasi genesis kai phthora, phamen d' aitian einai tên phoran tou ginesthai*, which takes the second part of Aristotle's sentence, connected by *d'* as explicative of *dedeiktai*, rather than as introducing a new point in the argument – the new point being dealt with in the next sentence, *zêtei de* (which answers the preceding *hê men suntaxis*). The Aldine editor prints: *ousan, phaneron. kai ta hexês. hê men oun suntaxis.* This may well be a conjecture (cf. the Introduction on the Aldine text, although notably in this instance the lemma is not omitted), but if so, it is a skilled one (cf. Philop. *in An.* 156,13-16). On Philoponus' lemmata, see the Introduction. (Note that Williams 1982 analyses Aristotle's sentence differently. In his translation, 'Since it has been assumed, and indeed proved, that things are subject to continuous coming to be and perishing *and since* we hold that locomotion is the cause of coming to be' (my italics), the causal rôle of locomotion is made simply parallel to the continuity of coming to be, whereas Philoponus takes the former as substantiating the latter.)

322. 291,4-5. 'Which, he says, is indeed the case', i.e. the second horn of the dilemma just formulated. This dilemma is not in fact stated by Aristotle, and must be the work of some later commentator (cf. n. 309 ad 288,24-6 above). Notably, it is present in Averroes' *Middle Commentary* on *GC* (a fact noted by Kurland who, however, does not draw a parallel with Philoponus' commentary).

323. 291,14. cf. Alexander *Prov.* 45,1-7 Ruland: 'However, if the motion of [the sun] were on an inclined circle the way it is now, and did not have, along with this, the motion with the universe, there would be no way to retain the succession of night and day which is the cause for the living beings of the rest and recreation that follow upon work, but in one of the inhabited parts of the earth there would be heat during the whole year, or [rather] of the time it takes the sun to complete its revolution returning to its place, [viz.] one half would be night, and another, day.'

324. 291,15. cf. Aristotle's explanation of inhabitable zones in *Meteor.* 2.5, 362b5-9f.

325. 291,16. *muloeidês*, rotation of the heavens at the Earth's poles parallel to the horizon. The term 'millstone-like' is also used by Philoponus in his treatise on the astrolabe to describe the arrangement of the spheres represented by the circles (*de Usu Astrol.* 147,24 Hase in Segonds 1981).

326. 291,18. i.e. in the sphere of fixed stars. Philoponus' criticism here might suggest that Alexander denied the causal contribution of the planetary spheres to the continuity of sublunary processes of coming to be and perishing; but this can hardly be right. In all important treatments of the issues of heavenly motions and causation, Alexander seems to draw no distinction between the 'fixed' and the 'wandering' stars *in this respect*, and speaks of heavenly motion in general as the cause of continuity in nature (cf. *De Principiis Omnium*, Genequand's Glossary, s.e. W-S-L, *Prov.*, 35 Ruland, *Quaest.* 2.18). There is no reason to think that planets are implicitly excluded, although the sphere of the fixed stars may be singled out as the cause of the continuous motion of all spheres. The issue between Philoponus and Alexander in this case seems to be exegetical (but cf. Williams 1982, 188-91, and next note).

327. 291,25. 'To this [locomotion]', *tautêi*. An alternative, suggested to me by Alexander Jones, would be to translate it as 'in this way', understanding that it is followed by a comma. In any case, there remains a problem of interpretation. On both readings, the sentence can be interpreted (a) as saying that the sun is the cause of the continuity of planetary movement; or (b) as taking the sun to be the most prominent example of the planetary movement. The interpretation (a) has been taken for granted by most modern commentators (except Williams 1982), all of whom are critical of Philoponus (cf. Joachim, Mugler 1966, Migliori

1976, Moraux 2001, 257). If this interpretation, is correct, Philoponus' position is indeed difficult to support, but whether it is correct remains an open question. There are several Hellenistic texts in which the sun is described as playing causal rôle with respect to the motion of the planets (cf. Vitruv. 1.9.13, where the heat of the sun is said to be the cause of the planetary retrogradations, and Cleomedes, *Meteor.* 2.1, where the sun is described as the cause of all motion in the universe – I owe these references to Alan Bowen and Bob Todd). However, the extent to which Philoponus or his source could be influenced by such theories is uncertain. The interpretation (b), 'according to which the whole' in the 'locomotion of the whole' should include planetary motion, apparently was not taken into account by most modern commentators, except Williams 1982. For the theory of heavenly motions in Philoponus' later writings, see Scholten 1996, 308-45. I am grateful to Alan Bowen, Alexander Jones, Bob Sharples and Bob Todd for discussion of this point.

328. 292,5. I translate here *genesis* (regularly translated as 'coming to be') as 'generation' and in the next sentence *phthora* ('perishing') as 'destruction' in order to keep the link with the verbs 'generates' (*gennâi*) and 'destroys' (*phtheirei*) of Aristotle's text in the lemma, as is clearly intended by Philoponus.

329. 292,9-10. 'The transformation of the elements.' The reference is to the change of seasons over the year.

330. 292,11. One full cycle of the sun (i.e. the earth in the heliocentric system) on the ecliptic circle, i.e. one year.

331. 292,12. Read *tukhoi ti*. Vitelli's printed sentence at 292,12-13 is: *ei toinun dia pollôn proseleuseôn tou teleiou eidous tukhoi, dia pollôn apokhôrêseôn, phêsi, touto parakmazei*. The subject of both protasis and apodosis is understood to be *touto* of the apodosis omitted in the protasis; but a formal subject in the protasis seems to be more natural. Vitelli's best MSS GRT have *túkhoi te*; Z omits *te* (but it is characterised by numerous omissions and transpositions); F *tunkhánei* F; *tunkhánein, kai* a; V appears to have *tukhêi ti*. I suggest *tukhoi ti* on the basis of GRT+V (missing *te* in Z could be a scribal omission of the kind this manuscript has a few).

332. 292,14-15. This sentence is presented in the Aldine edition as an explicit aporia, replacing concessive construction with 'although he said' that our text has in the second part by a question ('How did he say that coming to be and perishing, etc.?') On the text of the Aldine edition, see the Introduction, n. 102.

333. 292,30. 'There arises no co-perception (*sunaisthêsin*).' In this case, *sunaisthêsis* refers to the co-perception by the whole of an organism of the external state of the environment, such as cold temperature in winter, whereby e.g. the growing processes may be inhibited. (The argument would be, e.g., that the animals born in autumn will not be growing slower than those born in spring.)

334. 292,30-1. As the example that follows makes clear, the reference here is to the Peripatetic theory of 'mutual replacement' (*antiperistasis*), which described the interaction between the principles of the hot and the cold. On this theory, the cold principle produces in the hot the effects of concentration, solidification, contraction, and attraction. This theory is outlined in Aristotle's *Meteorology* 4, for references and detailed analysis of relevant Aristotle passages, see Furley 1987, 132-48; for a good general discussion and the Platonic background, see Solmsen 1961, 136-7, 413-17; for discussions of this theory in Theophrastus, see Steinmetz 1964, 123-6, Federspiel 2003, and the next note; for the later Platonic tradition, see Opsomer 1999, 417-29. For the Peripatetic tradition, cf. the answer given in Alexander of Aphrodisias *Quaest.* 1.20 to the main question ('Why we are more sleepy in the summer, if sleep is on account of the change of place of our connatural heat into the interior [parts]'), 34,1-20.

335. 292,31-2. cf. Theophrastus *de Igne* 13: 'Furthermore, our bodies digest food better and are more vigorous in winter because their heat has been collected and intensified' (Coutant trans.).

336. 293, 2-3. cf. Alexander, *Prov.*, 37,1-10 Ruland: 'For if the distance from the sun to us turned out to be closer to us than it is now, and its distance from us were not such as it is found now, then it would heat the place <on> the earth which it approaches, because of the closeness of its motion, in a way that surpasses the balance and would be excessive for this place. And if the contrary [of what has been just described] took place and the distance from [the sun] to us were greater than this [present] distance, its blazing would be less. And if any of these [two] were the case, the coming to be of any kind of animals or plants would not be possible. And one can get a sufficient proof of this from some places of the earth that are called uninhabited because of the [respective] prevalence of each one of these two qualities in them.'

337. 293,9-10. 'By nature', *kata phusin*. 336b9 'in nature' Williams 1982, a little modernising.

338. 293,9. 'Take place in equal time', see Appendix.

339. 293,11-14. The idea discussed in the next paragraph, that two periods of life – before and after the prime (*akmê*) – are equal in length, does not seem to be elaborated in this precise form anywhere else in Aristotle, although he does point out the proportion between the length of life and that of the period of gestation (*GA* 4.10, 777a32-5). On dependence of the length of life on heavenly motions, see *GA* 4.10, 777b18-78a10. Cf. the discussions in Balme 1987, 277-8, King 2001, 80-6.

340. 293,15-18. For this distinction, cf. Aristotle, *de Iuventute* 5, 469b21-4, although the main point there is that both 'natural' and violent deaths have the same natural cause (lack of nourishment for the internal heat).

341. 293,19-21. 'Forced' (*biaios*) understood in a generic sense as *para phusin*.

342. 293,21-5. cf. Averroes' *Middle Commentary*: 'One should realise that if we assume this view expressed by Aristotle to the effect that the period of growth is equal to that of decay, and if we assume also what the physicians say to the effect that the span of man's youth is up to thirty-five years, then a natural course of life for him is seventy years, and anything above or below that is an exception to the rule. Therefore the man of scripture has said that a life stretches over a span of between sixty and seventy years' (126,7-11 'Alawî, Kurland trans.), with Kurland's note 42.

343. 294,2. The suggestion considered by our author is that Aristotle here, speaking about equal times required for coming to be and perishing, refers not to the processes of growth and decay undergone by a living substance as a whole (as it was suggested at 292,5 above) but to the 'absolute' coming to be, of which Aristotle's physics knows two types: (i) reversible, such as the elemental trans-formations, and (ii) 'irreversible', the coming to be and perishing of a living substance. The difficulties with this interpretation raised in our commentary are stated separately for each of these two types. (i) An elemental change from, say, air to fire, is analysed as two simultaneous processes: the coming to be of fire and the perishing of air. Since these processes are numerically identical they will also take the same time. But in this case, the subject of coming to be (fire) is not the same as the subject of perishing (air); and it is not clear from our text that Aristotle, in speaking about the processes taking equal time has given up the 'identity' requirement for the subject of changes (293,28-294,2). (ii) If we assume that the 'absolute' coming to be and perishing of a living substance is

Aristotle's model for the processes that take equal time, and take gestation to be the natural measurable process that corresponds to coming to be, it remains unclear what measurable process corresponds to perishing, and in what sense it can be said to take equal time with coming to be: so this assumption is even less helpful than the initial one (294,2-11).

344. Shorey 1921 compares Plato *Republic* 546A-C.

345. 294,14-15. 'The specific form of each particular thing', *tou hekastou eidous* of the absolute construction technically allows for a variety of translations ((i) 'the form of each thing', (ii) 'each form', (iii) 'the kind (species) of each thing', (iv) 'each kind (species)'), each of which has its own plusses and minuses. I chose (i) as a tentative 'catholic' middle ground, on the assumption that our commentator here is working within the framework of Aristotle's hylomorphic theory, but leaving room for Platonic interpretation as well. What nature 'measures' is the form that is enmattered (and thus inseparable from an individual), and that characterizes a certain *kind* of individuals in a technical (metaphysical and biological) sense. Nature does not measure material circumstances of each individual which do not depend on form (cf. below and Aristotle *GA* 4.10). (ii), unless it means the same as (i), might involve a special theory of 'each form', understood either as inseparable form of an individual, or as a Form among the Forms detached from individuals: both senses seem unlikely in this context. (iii) or (iv) 'kind' or 'species' could be appropriate, but because of the nature of the argument (see n. 348 ad 294,19 below) and since *eidos* in the next line clearly refers to 'form' as distinct from an individual whose form it is, I retain 'form', with a warning that it should not be taken to mean anything like a form of an individual *qua* this individual.

346. cf. Aristotle, *GA* 4.10, 778a5-10; on length and shortness of life in different species, *Long.*

347. 294,17-18. cf. 293,15-18 and n. 340 above.

348. 294,19. 'Species', *ta eidê*, refers to a specific form. On my interpretation, the argument is from the temporal order 'measured' by nature for the individual 'enmattered forms' to the corresponding differentiation among the species that comprise actual individuals. The point about 'individual form' could have been imported from Alexander's lost commentary: the precedence of enmattered form over species as well as the ontological distinction between an individual-*cum*-individual-properties and its inseparable enmattered form is found in several school texts (cf. *Quaest.* 1.8; 1.11; 1.17; 1.26; *Mant.* 5, with discussions in Tweedale 1984, Ellis 1994).

349. 333b19. *tês kata phusin*, 'that occur in nature' Williams 1982, cf. n. 337 ad 293,9-10 above.

350. 295,7. 'Because of the mingling of things with one another' (*dia tên pros allêla sunkrasin*). Joachim obelised this text, arguing that this word for 'mingling' (*sunkrasis*) does not occur elsewhere in Aristotle, and that 'the phrase would then only anticipate obscurely what the next phrase states clearly'. Verdenius and Waszink have argued that 'an anticipation is not impossible, and the term *sunkrasis* is not so strange, if it is borne in mind that, according to Aristotle, the degree of heat of a thing is constituted by a 'mingling' of the Hot and the Cold, so that its actual heat is equal to its potential coldness (334b8-13)' (73-4) (Migliori agrees too). On the text of this passage, see Appendix. It may be added that the noun *sunkrasis* occurs once in the whole corpus (in the pseudepigraphic *de Plantis* 1.1, 815a27), the verb *sunkerannunai* once, in *GA* 4.4, 755a21; the noun *sunkrousis* once (again in *de Plantis* 2.2, 823b12) and the verb *sunkrouein* thrice: *HA* 10.24, 604b2, *de Audibilibus* (pseud.) 800a5, and *Pol.* 5.11, 1313b17). In Averroes' *Middle Commentary* this passage is rendered as *wa* *dhâlika immâ min qibali ṭabî'ati l-mizâji l-tâbi'i li-ṭabî 'ati l-hayûlâ* (125,16-17 'Alawi): '(... either) on account of the nature of the mixture which follows upon the nature of matter'. The least clear point is *what things* are said to be in either mixture or collision. See the discussions in Joachim, Kurland, Verdenius & Waszink, Williams 1982, Migliori ad loc., and the next note.

351. 336b23-4. Reading with Williams 1982 and Mugler: *hôste sumbainei dia tên toutôn genesin allois ginesthai phthoran*. Aristotle's argument here is particularly convoluted and hard to follow. Joachim in his reconstruction of the argument writes: *hôste sumbainei* (sc. *pollakis en elattoni phtheiresthai*), *dia <to> tên toutôn genesin allois ginesthai phthoran*. He obelised the phrase 'because of mingling with one another' (see previous note), and took the argument to be that perishing sometimes happens over a shorter interval because of the matter, which makes some comings to be faster, others slower: 'Since the genesis of one thing is *eo ipso* the *phthora* of another, each abnormally rapid *genesis* will *eo ipso* involve an abnormally rapid *phthora*. Premature death, therefore, or abnormally rapid decline in some individuals is only the inevitable obverse of premature or abnormally rapid development on the part of other living things, whether of the same or of a different species.' This reconstruction seems quite plausible in itself, although there remains a problem with the text in lines 20-1 (Joachim seems to be supporting, *malgré lui*, the reading *sunkrousis*), and the emendation on line 24 does not seem really necessary to obtain this meaning. Williams 1982 notes that 'it is not easy to see why irregularities of corruption should be explained in terms of irregularities of generation rather than vice versa'. Perhaps this could be compared with the point made in Plato's description of the state of the universe ruled by the god, *Pol.* 271D6-E1: 'As for living things, divine spirits had divided them between themselves, like herdsmen, by kind and by herd, each by himself providing independently for all the needs of those he tended, so that none of them was savage, nor did they eat each other, and there was no war or internal dissent at all' (Rowe trans.), and by itself, 274B5-C1: 'Since we had been deprived of the god who possessed and pastured us, and since for their part the majority of animals – all those who had an aggressive nature – had gone wild, human beings, by themselves weak and defenseless, were preyed on by them ...' (Rowe trans.). The latter state of the universe is characterized by the growing prevalence of the corporeal element in its mixture (*sunkrasis*) (cf. 273B3-5).

352. 295,8-9. The exact reference is not entirely clear. It is possible that Philoponus here points out a distinction between the natural diversity of lifespans across the species which is caused by the unevenness of the sun's motion along the ecliptic circle, and the 'contingent' variation of individual lifespans within the natural species, caused by matter. In that case the 'above' may be referring to a brief discussion of material cause as a source of contingencies, in 2.9.

353. 295,14. 'Or collision', *ê sunkrousin* GR a; two MSS (TZ) read *ê sunkrisin*, 'or combination'.

354. 295,14. 'Written in two ways', i.e. both readings are found in the manuscripts. It is not clear whether this claim is based on Philoponus' first-hand knowledge of the manuscripts, or whether it goes back to one of his sources, Ammonius or Alexander. This report of different readings (unlike the one we have at 85,25 Vitelli, see Williams 1999a, 117 and n. 307) does not seem to be well attested in the direct tradition of the text (see Appendix). In what follows Philoponus presents three different explanations of the argument. For discussions, see Joachim and Migliori ad loc.

355. 295,14-296, 10. Averroes in the *Middle Commentary* gives a different interpretation of this reading: 'This may be so either (1) because of the nature of the blending (*al-mizâj*) which depends upon the nature of the matter, (i) for inasmuch as the blendings in the particular members of any one species differ according to more and less and are not uniform, it necessarily follows that the periods of coming to be and of perishing vary in the particular members of any one species so that some are longer, others shorter, (ii) and the perishing of anything of this kind that perishes will take place in no time (*fî ghairi l-waqti*), because every process of perishing is the coming to be of some other thing and every process of coming to be is the perishing of some other thing' (125,16-126,1 'Alawi; Kurland trans. modified). As Philoponus' first interpretation, so this one too is based on the idea of material mixture being the cause of variation within the species, although the axiological overtone, which is very distinct in both Philoponus and Alexander's *de Providentia*, is conspicuously absent here. The appendix (ii) seems to be loosely connected with the main argument (i): cf. the difficulties raised against this notion in Philoponus' commentary at 293,27 above.

356. 295,16-17. cf. Alexander *Prov.*: 'And matter, because of its peculiar and intrinsic weakness cannot suit and follow in every respect the agent and that which imprints on it its form; but in some things it is at variance and falls short of it (viz. form): thus, for things here (*li-l-ashyâ'i hâhunâ* = *ta têide*), which have their existence only from it, that is, from matter, it does not provide a cause for preserving the continuity of order in every respect, because that which can both be and not be is the underlying substrate of things' (103,2-9 Ruland). 'Again: it [matter] can receive both privation and form, and insofar as it can receive form it strives after the noble nature, i.e. the power of the heavenly body, and is formed by it, and yearns for permanence. And insofar as it can receive privation, i.e. is not anything in actuality, it neither follows the power of heavenly body, nor is affected nor formed by it, and it does not yearn for permanence, but for destruction. For this reason the error (*khata'*) often enters the earthly world, not because of the heavenly bodies, but because of matter, as we have explained' (D15 103,3-105,4 Ruland).

357. 295,19. 'The life that is being dispensed', *tên khorêgomenên zôên*. cf. 288,24-6 and n. 309 above.

358. 295,20-2. With (ii) and (iii) below, cf. Averroes, *Middle Commentary*: 'or (2) because of the difference (*ikhtilâf*) of the states of the proximate efficient cause; or (3) because of the difference in the ultimate efficient cause, for example, difference in the action of the sun due to a position whenever the planets come close to it or part from it; or (4) because of difference in the more proximate efficient cause, for example variation in the nature of the father in respect to the nature of the sun at the time of begetting and difference in appetite as the food is converted into a mixture. The common factor in all of the above is the diversification (*iftirâq*) of causes and a lack of affinity (*qillatu muwâfaqatin*) with one another among them' (126,2-3 'Alawi; Kurland trans. modified). The impression rather is that Averroes was working with some different version of the argument we find in Philoponus' commentary. After the last sentence printed by Kurland, the Arabic text has the following sentence which Kurland suppressed as a gloss made by an Arabic scribe (but reported in his notes): 'This expression is found in some manuscripts instead of "mixture" (*al-imtizâj*)' (126,6 'Alawî). Kurland thinks that the reference of *imtizâj* (which he renders as 'amalgam') is to the word *mizâj* in his penultimate sentence above, and if that were the case, the sentence would be indeed misplaced (cf. Eichner 2005, 'Kommentar' ad loc.). But it is also possible that the reference is made to the *mizâj* of the interpretation (1) cited in n. 355 ad 295,14-296,10, above, contrasted with *ikhtilâf* which renders *sunkrousis* understood as 'collision', or 'lack of agreement', the meaning explicated then by synonymous expressions rendered here as 'diversification' and 'lack of affinity' (*iftirâq* and *qillatu muwâfaqatin*). Unlike Philoponus, Averroes does not mention the material cause. (3) is comparable with Philoponus' (iii), and (iv) would be comparable with Philoponus' (ii) if there were any mention of the material cause. The example of appetite (*al-shahwa*) might loosely correspond to the *proairesis* of Philoponus' text, but it seems to be treated here as a more proximate efficient cause.

359. 295, 22-3. On this disctinction, cf. Aristotle *Metaph.* 12.5, 1071a15-17; for background, cf. *GA* 2.1, 716a16f.

360. 295,23-4. Note that *proairesis* is cited here in the series of material causes: cf. Philoponus in GC 1.1, 7,5-17 (at 7,7-10, where *proairesis* is presented as a kind of efficient cause); Philoponus' *Physics* commentary, where choice is given as an example of final cause (268-88 passim). For the use of this term in medical texts, cf. Galen *in Hipp. Prognostic.* III, XVIIIb 280,8-281,14 Kühn, esp. at 281,13.

361. 295,24. 'Seed and blood from the mother'. Because *kai*, translated here as 'and', can also be understood as epexegetic (meaning 'i.e.'), thus giving the sense 'the seed from the mother, i.e. blood', it is not entirely clear from this text whether our commentator commits himself to a Galenic (anti-Aristotelian) view that the mother does contribute seed and not just blood. In Aristotle's *GA* 5.1, we find the view that there is the female seed, but it is said there that it is too feeble to exercise influence on the embryo. On Galen's debate, see Nickel 1986, 40-9; Kollesch 1987; Accattino 1994, 1871-5.

362. 295,26. 'They say', *phasi*. The reference should be to the Peripatetics in general (cf. Galen's account of a debate over this issue among his contemporary Peripatetics, *de Semine* 1.3 (68,3-69,24 De Lacy); its significance is not entirely clear to me, but in every case it does indicate a certain distance between the commentator (who in this case is more likely to be either Philoponus himself or Ammonius) and his source(s) (cf. n. 332 ad 291,4-5 above and the Introduction, p. 2 and n. 22).

363. 295,28. On healthy and unhealthy mixtures, see Galen *Temp.* 1, [Aristotle] *Probl.* 1 (especially 1.9); 14.

364. 295,24-296,1. It is not entirely clear from this discussion whether our author contrasts material and efficient causes, as he suggests initially with his interpretation of *sunkrousis*, or whether the contrast is rather between the 'first' efficient cause (i.e. heavenly bodies) and the rest, so that the proximate efficient cause ('the father') would be included into the possible factors of individual deviations from nature's norms. It may be noted that for this particular example, the author's position on the issue in the embryological doctrine, whether the father's seed contributes matter, might be important. On Galen's view, it does (cf. *de Semine* 1, 3-6; Nickel 1986, 29-40; Kollesch 1987; Accattino 1994, 1857-62), so that, in accordance with the argument developed by our author, it could not be transmitting pure form and 'nature's norm'; on the 'canonical' Aristotelian view upheld by at least some Aristotelians of Galen's time (cf. *de Semine* 1.3, 68,2ff.) it does not; if this was the view adopted by the commentator, the proximate efficient cause could still be aligned with the 'first efficient cause' in its 'collision' with matter. On the Neoplatonic reception of Galen's debate, cf. Sorabji 2004, vol. 2, 1 (c) (44).

365. 296,2. 'If something disorderly and inappropriate', *ei atakton ti kai* *anarmoston*. The Aldine edition has here: 'if wood happened to be disorderly, etc.' (*ei xulon atakton ti*).

366. 296,3. For a parallel with Averroes, cf. n. 358 ad 295,20-2 above.

367. 296,7. For a similar usage of *sunkrousis*, cf. Damascenus, *Expositio fidei* 21,118 Kotter: *hoi men oun Hellênes dia tês tôn astrôn toutôn hêliou te kai selênês anatolês kai duseôs kai sunkrouseôs phasi panta dioikeisthai*. Here *sunkrouseôs* probably refers to an eclipse or something like a superposition.

368. 296,7-8. 'A cause of different fixed length (*prothesmias*) of life for different [living beings]'. Cf. with this passage Alexander, *Fat.* 6, 170,4 and 169,23-5, criticising the notion that a fixed length of life (*prothesmia*) is fated in accordance with heavenly motions. The term *prothesmia* is used in medical literature, notably by Galen, to refer to the expected length of life, illness, and other natural processes in the organism.

369. 296,9-10. 'Shaped', *diaplattomenon*. For the term, cf. the Galenic theory of generation and Alexander *Mant.* 1 104,30-1; for the account, cf. Philop. *Aet.* 374,22; *Opif.* 76,22; 209,27.

370. 296,14. The Greek speaks of *one* cause, using the singular, but since it is clear from the rest of the sentence that two causes are intended as distinct, I am translating using the plural, to make the construction more palatable in English.

371. 296,24-5. 'Namely, with extension (*diastaseôs*) and change of place.' For a discussion of extension as an attribute of matter, see de Haas 1997.

372. 296,27. Reading *meinai* with V instead of Vitelli's *einai* (*einai* om. R; *mê einai* GT; cf. 297,8 n. 388 below).

373. 296,19. 'Cheats its perishing', *tên phthoran hupokleptontos*. The verb for 'cheat', *hupokleptein*, is rare (one occurrence in Philoponus, and generally infrequent in philosophical or medical texts, more characteristic of late rhetoric).

374. 296,29. cf. *DA* 2.4, 415a25-b2.

375. 297,5. 'Is used', for the text see Appendix.

376. 297,8. 'In virtue of remaining the same in number' (*tôi kat'arithmon menein ta auta*), cf. 296,27 and n. 372 above.

377. 297,9. Although this distinction is indeed drawn by Aristotle, it does not seem to occur in any of the versions of his more standard division of the meanings of being (cf. Joachim, Williams 1982 ad loc). This interpretation (whether it comes from Philoponus himself or from one of his sources) seems to be designed to suit the context of the discussion that follows immediately.

378. 297,15. 'Perpetual', *endelekhê* cf. Bonitz, *Index*, 249a23.

379. 297,17. In this case 'produce' (*poiein*) cannot refer just to the agent principle in unspecified causal sense (as it sometimes does in the texts of Alexander). The possibility that the figure of god is metaphorical (the Demiurge of the *Timaeus*) is not to be ruled out completely, but the fact that this god is said to produce both things eternal that are unchangeable (in a strong sense of lacking any change including locomotion) and things eternal that are material constitutes a doctrinal difference with both the *Timaeus*, where the Demiurge looks at the eternal forms), and Aristotle's *Metaph.* 12, where divine intellect is the final, but not the efficient cause of things eternal. For discussion of this view in Philoponus' works, see Verrycken 1990, 209-10, 215-26, on this passage particularly 224, and n. 189; cf. the Introduction, p. 12.

380. 297,18. *diastata*. cf. Philoponus' earlier definition of the matter of change (n. 124 ad 259,22, cf. n. 274 ad 283,10-11 above (on the heavenly matter)).

381. 336b33-4. *dia to engutata einai tês ousias to ginesthai aei kai tên genesin*:

Joachim (followed by Forster) makes an attractive suggestion that *tên genesin* should be taken as the subject of *ginesthai*, giving the sense: 'because it is the nearest thing to being that coming-to-be should itself (*kai*) come to be perpetually'. This is not how the phrase is construed by Philoponus, and by most modern translators (Mugler, Williams 1982, Migliori).

382. 297,27. *heirmos*. The word has a single occurrence in the *corpus Aristotelicum* (*Probl.* 28.3, 916a31); it is frequently used by Alexander (*Fat.* 192,1; 195,19) who probably takes it over from his Stoic opponents (cf. *SVF, Index verborum*, s.v.).

383. 298,1. Reading with V a *aïdia diamenonta* (cf. 313,25; 314,10; 284,11). Vitelli prints *aïdia menonta* ('which remain') deleting *de* where MSS have *aïdia de menonta*.

384. 298,2. 'In its essence', *kata tên ousian*. *ousia* translated as 'essence' in order to distinguish it from *to einai* for which 'being' has been reserved; but the term 'essence' should not imply any elaborate essentialist picture at this point ('being' would have been an equally good translation for *ousia* here).

385. 298,9. Philoponus' comment that follows is only on the actually excerpted lemma (not on the text supplied in the square brackets).

386. 298,10. *ek parallêlou*, viz. 'affections' (*pathê*) and 'capacities' (*dunameis*) are the two terms that explicate one and the same concept. For the expression *ek parallêlou*, cf. Philoponus *in GC* 7,22; 189,5; also Alexander *in Metaph.* 331,1 with Madigan's note; Aspasius *in EN* 65,30; 104,1.

387. 298,10. 'Tendencies', *rhopas*. The term *rhopê* signifies 'impetus' in Philoponus' later theory of motion, on which see Wolff 1971; Wolff 1987; Sorabji 1988, 227-48. For the term, cf. Alexander *de An.* 12,10-11; *De Principiis* 4-28.

388. 298,10-12. This analysis is based on the distinction between tangible qualities and dynamic characteristics of natural bodies which is systematically drawn by Alexander of Aphrodisias in *de An.* 4,27-5,12f.

389. 298,10-13. This analysis is based on the distinction between active and passive qualities drawn in Aristotle's *Meteor.* 4.1, 378b10-26f.). The term 'powers' is used to describe the active qualities, the term 'affections' is reserved for passive ones.

390. Shorey 1922 refers to Plato, *Tim.* 58A and Plato's explanation of the process which Aristotle does not accept.

391. 298,21. i.e. the arguments for the reciprocal changeability of the elements, in *GC* 2.2; 4-6.

392. 299,1. The subject of *kinountai* here must be the planets.

393. 299,1-3. Averroes' *Middle Commentary* has at this point: 'They [the elements] are, however, transformed into one another because of the double motion, which is dual and varying, such as the movement of the inclined circle itself and the movement which is both eastward and westward at the same time' (127,15-17 'Alawî; Kurland trans. modified).

394. 299,11. 'Since', see Appendix.

395. 299,11. 'Something that causes motion', see Appendix.

396. 299,14. 'Natural change', *peri phusikês kinêseôs*. The exact reference is unclear. Aristotle uses the expressions *phusikôs kineisthai*, *kinein*, in *Phys.* 3.1, 201a24; but Philoponus could be referring, in a broader sense, to the discussion of various aspects of change in Books 1-7. I am translating as 'change' to indicate the broader scope of this term here. I am grateful to Alan Bowen for pressing for this clarification.

397. 299,19. Or 'the universe' (*tou ouranou*).

398. 299,21-9. For the discussion of the problem of multiple movers in

Alexander, see Sharples 1983, Accattino 1992, Bodnár 1997, Berti 2000, Genequand 2001, 6-16, Falcon 2001, 185-241).

399. 300,5-6. 'Because the additional assumption and the conclusion have been omitted, while the mode is hypothetical.' On the structure of hypothetical syllogism, cf. Philoponus *in An. Pr.* 242,14-243,10 (= *FDS* 682, with Hülser's discussion). 'Additional assumption', *proslêpsis*, is described by Philoponus and his sources (cf. Hülser ad loc.) as the Stoic term for the second premiss of the hypothetical syllogism (called *metalêpsis* in Peripatetic nomenclature). For discussions of hypothetical syllogism, see Lee 1984, Speca 2001, Barnes 2003.

400. 300,16. 'If the circular motions are more than one', *ei pleious hai kuklôi kinêseis*, see Appendix.

401. 300,16-17. 'All these [moving causes must be] in some way under a single principle', see Appendix.

402. 300,20-1. i.e. because the first meaning of 'under' (*hupo*) is spatial. This seems to be an oversimplified explanation of *pôs*. For discussions of the character of subordination of multiple movers to the first mover in earlier commentators, see references in n. 398 ad 299,21-9 above.

403. 300,24. 'Virtually', *têi dunamei*: for this usage, cf. Philoponus *in An. Pr.* 160,10; 242,1 (opp. *katêgorikôs*); 247,7; 256,1-8; 278,20-30; 280,1-4.

404. 337a27-8: 'The thing that moves' (not in the lemma), cf. n. 412 ad 302,3 below and the Appendix.

405. 301,8. *kinêsis* is rendered here and in the lemma as 'movement', because the reference in the argument is, initially, to change in general (subsuming changes in four main categories); because the question is about the *process*, I prefer 'movement' to 'change'. In the end, by excluding all categories but place, the scope of *kinêsis* is effectively narrowed down to 'motion', so that the conclusion is concerned, again, with change of place.

406. 301,9-10. In *Phys.* 8.8, Aristotle uses the expression *to en hôi*, translated here as 'that in respect of which', to refer to a category of change in his fourfold division (see n. 21 ad 239,24 above) which he there gives in full: 'and the third one is "that in respect of which", i.e. place or affection or kind or magnitude'. In Philoponus' commentary, *pathos* seems to be used generically for all non-substantial changes except locomotion, while *megethos* is supposed to have a special function, not restricted to the classification of changes (see nn. 409, 411 ad 301,17.19-21 below).

407. 301,13-15. The claim that growth *qua* process of change is continuous is implied by Aristotle's condition that the thing that grows should persist in the process (*GC* 1.5, 321a21-6, where the same condition is stated for the process of alteration). The argument is expounded at length by Philoponus in his commentary on *GC* 1.5 (69,26-123,27; see Williams 1999a, 99-157, especially 102,31-111,13; on the structure and sources of Philoponus' argument there, see Todd 1977; Berryman 1999a, 5-10; Kupreeva 2004, 314-16).

408. 301,15-16. *hou esti tina aei ephexês labein*. Aristotle defines a thing that moves continuously in *Phys.* 5.3 as 'that which leaves out no part, or the minimal part, of a thing (*tou pragmatos*) – not time ..., but a thing – in respect of which (*en hôi*) it moves' (227b28-31). The additional condition suggested in this commentary may be the gist of Aristotle's arguments for the continuity of circular motion alone in *Phys.* 8.7-8 (261a31-265a12): circular motion does not turn back onto the path it has already traversed in the opposite direction; so, it always has a successive point it will traverse in the same direction. See relevant discussion in Sorabji 1983, 210-31.

409. 301,17. Aristotle's argument against the continuity of quantitative change in *Phys.* 8.8 is more elaborate: the main idea is that growth and diminution repeat the pattern of motion along the straight line in that the intermediate states (viz. sizes) will be traversed repeatedly by a thing undergoing this kind of change (264b19-265a1).

410. 301,17. Unless this sentence is misplaced, *pathos* here is used in a generic sense to cover both remaining categories of non-substantial change excluding locomotion. See n. 182 ad 268,21 above.

411. 301,19-21. Aristotle's text here at 337a30 says that place *has* some magnitude, not that it *is* one, as our commentary (and Averroes' *Middle Commentary*, 129,10 'Alawî: *fa-inna l-makâna aiḍân 'iẓamun*). The notion that place *is* a kind of continuous quantity is introduced by Aristotle in the discussion of *poson* in *Cat.* 6, 4b22-4 and 5a8-14, which modern commentators find at odds with his theory of *topos* in *Phys.* 4. For discussions, see Mendell 1987; Sorabji 1988, 186. In this commentary, the proof of the continuity of place differs significantly from that in the *Categories*. There, the argument is based on a parallel between the continuity among the parts of a body and the continuity among the parts of a place occupied by a body: the parts of place are said to share a common limit with the parts of body. On this argument, any place containing a continuous body will possess continuity (cf. Philoponus *in Cat.* 87,7-20). The present commentary apparently restricts the continuity of place to that of a spherical body.

412. 302,3. 'Of this, he says, i.e. of the magnitude.' There are two problems with this exegetical claim: (i) its textual or doctrinal grounds; (ii) its consistency with the interpretation given to this text in the previous comment (301,21-31 above) and in the following two sentences, according to which 'of this' (*toutou*) of 337a30 should refer back to 'the thing moved' (*to kinoumenon*) at 337a28. (i) The ground can be purely grammatical, because 'magnitude' (*megethos*) is the preceding noun; it might have to do with the fact that Philoponus or his source seems to read the sentence 'since it has a certain size' (*megethos gar ti ekhei*) as if 'has' (*ekhei*) were omitted, giving the sense: 'since it *is* a certain size'. Philoponus' commentary above treats magnitude (*megethos*) as a quasi-genus of place (cf. 301,19 and previous note). If we assume that that line is continued in the present passage, then the question (ii) of the subject of 'he says' (*phêsi*) seems to be appropriate, for in the following sentence Philoponus claims that the phrase in question refers to the body that moves and not to place. 'Place' has not been suggested as a possible interpretation, but it might be implicit in the reference to magnitude, of which it is said to be 'a kind'. Could it be that the subject of 'he says' (*phêsi*) is not Aristotle, but again Philoponus' source (perhaps Ammonius), whose view Philoponus tries to reconcile with what he regards as a more natural reading of the passage?

413. 302,3. 'Obviously in virtue of that of the thing moved', cf. 337a27-8 above and the Appendix.

414. 302,6. 'The body which is circular', *to gar kukloteres sôma*. Joachim criticises Philoponus' interpretation of the phrase 'only in circle' (*to kuklôi monon*) (337a31), pointing out that Aristotle's standard epithet for a spherical body is *sphairoeides*, whereas here he clearly refers to a pattern of motion rather than shape. Although this is an apt stylistic remark, it should be noted that Philoponus is correct in his doctrinal point, namely that for Aristotle not just any motion along a circular trajectory will have continuity, but only that performed by a body whose surface is spherical and thus contains all the possible paths of 'circular' movement.

415. 302,8-10. This is rather puzzling as a paraphrase of Aristotle's sentence at 337a32-3, where 'this' (*touto*) is explicated as 'the body carried in a circle' (*to* *kuklôi pheromenon soma*), the interpretation which seems to be favoured by Philoponus in the previous paragraph. The subject of 'he says' (*phêsi*) in the preceding sentence again comes into question (cf. n. 412 ad 302,3 above). Averroes' *Middle Commentary* has it closer to Aristotle's text: 'Consequently, it must follow that that which produces a single continuous motion is the body which moves in a circle, and that it is this motion which makes time [continuous]' (129,11-13 'Alawî; Kurland trans. lightly modified).

416. 302,14. The following sentence (301,14-16: 'since things that move continuously ... after the first') is the protasis not of the previous one ('that continuity belongs to coming to be'), but of the following one ('he investigates whether, etc.').

417. 302,17. *tôi proterôi to deuteron*. The terminology going back to the theory of entailment in Stoic propositional logic, where *proteron* (*prôton*) refers to the antecedent of the conditional in the major premiss, and *deuteron* to the consequent of this conditional. Philoponus uses this pair of terms interchangeably with Aristotle's original *proteron/ husteron* ('earlier – later'). This parallel usage may go back to Alexander's commentary.

418. 302,19. *endekhomenên ekhei tên ekbasin*. Understand 'contingent' in a technical modal sense: 'A is contingent if and only if it is not necessary that A and it is not necessary that not-A'.

419. 302,23-4. 'From the subject matter (*pragmata*) itself'. *pragmata* ('things') is to be understood here broadly as objects of signification.

420. 302,24. The English expression 'is going to ...' may imply that the event in question *will* happen, and so is not an ideal translation for *mellei*, as Alan Lacey points out to me. It should be understood that 'is going to F' refers to the *present* state of the subject which is conducive to a future state F, whether or not the state F ever occurs in the present. Another possibility would be to render *mellei* as 'is about to', but it has the same problem of imminence, plus the connotation of immediate readiness for F, which *mellein* does not have. 'Is liable to be', suggested to me by one of the readers, may imply some non-temporal dependencies which Aristotle's expression does not intend (his own example is of someone going to take a walk, but in fact never taking one). *mellein* is used to refer to (i) a (likely) future action or state, but also (ii) to the present state which is conducive to the future one, and, (iii) more strongly, to the actions which are planned but never actually carried out (see LSJ, s.v. III).

421. 302,26. 'The things that follow of necessity', *hepomenôn* as Vitelli prints following FR; but other manuscripts have *esomenôn*, 'the things that will be of necessity', also a possible reading.

422. 302,31-2. 'By unimpeded disposition', *pros tên akôluton epitêdeiotêta*. This definition of possibility is post-Chrysippean (on Chrysippus' concept, see Bobzien 1993; Bobzien 1998, 112-16; Bobzien 1999, 115-21). We are not given any examples of 'impeded suitability' here; presumably, the distinction is between the cases when suitability has been incurably impeded and when it has not been realised because of some less grave circumstances (cf. Sorabji 1983, 78-9). On the term *epitêdeiotês*, generally and in connexion with Philo, see Todd 1972. For discussions of this view see Alexander *in An. Pr.* 183,29-184,8; Alexander *Quaest.* 1.4; 1.18; Philoponus *in An. Pr.* 169,17-23; Simplicius *in Cat.* 195,31-196,9; Boethius *in Int. ed. sec.* 234,10ff.; cf. Sharples 1982, 91-6.

423. 303,1. For the example of wood, perhaps going back to Philo the Dialectician (or Philo of Megara, but not of Larissa, as erroneously printed in Sharples 1992, passim), see Simplicius *in Cat.* 196,1-2; cf. Alexander *in An. Pr.* 184,6-10; discussions in Sharples 1982; Sharples 1992, 67-70 nn.; Bobzien, 1998, 110-12.

424. 303,2-5. The text of the sentence printed by Vitelli is corrupt. He indicates a lacuna before *legomen* which he suggests (in the apparatus) filling with *ei de*, and reports for 303,3 beside the reading *legomen* of RZ, *kai ean legômen* in GTa (from which he takes his cue). For the purposes of this translation, I adopt this suggestion. It should be noted that a reading of V: *houtô toinun ei men phaiêmen hoti meta to ear estai theros kai anankê einai pote to theros legomen tou de spermatos katablêthentos, hoti mellei phunai stakhus kai dunaton phunai, alêthous ousês*, although tortuous, can nonetheless make sense if *apopha<n>seôs* is taken as referring back to the sentence *hoti mellei ... phunai*: 'In this way, then, if we were to say that after spring there will be summer, that would mean that there must be summer at some point; and when a seed has been cast down, although the assertion that an ear of corn is going to grow, i.e. is capable of growing, is true, it can fail to grow, because the outcome was contingent.'

425. 303,8. For this distinction in Aristotle, see *Int.* 9 (19a7-22); 12-13; *Metaph.* 12.7; in Alexander, *Quaest.* 1.4; 1.18.

426. 303,30. 'For everything commonly partakes of it, and necessities [of this kind] are seen to be and are in everything' ((i) *panta gar koinôs metekhei toutou* (ii) *kai en pasi theôreitai* (iii) *kai esti anankaia*). A difficult sentence. I take *anankaia* as the subject of the last two parts of the sentence (marked as (ii) and (iii) in the Greek text). An alternative would be to take the subject of (ii) to be *touton*, and revert to *panta* in (iii), giving the sense: 'for everything commonly partakes of it, and it is seen in everything, and everything is necessary'. 'Necessary' refers in each case to conditional necessity.

427. 303,35-304,2. The meaning of 'conversion' (*antistrophê*) in this context is explained by Aristotle at 338a11-13: it is different from the concept of conversion developed in *An. Pr.* 1 in that it operates on propositions rather than terms. (For the use of *antistrephein* with respect to conditional propositions in Aristotle, see *An. Post.* 2.12, 95b38-96a7.) In Stoic propositional logic, a similar kind of operation applied to the propositional variables (e.g. p and q standing for sentences) is called *anastrophê* (Bobzien 1999, 115). In terms of modern propositional logic, the distinction can be represented as follows. Let p be 'the first', and q 'the second'. In the case where q has only hypothetical necessity, although 'if q then (necessarily) p' will be true (by assumption), the truth of 'if p, then (necessarily) q' will not follow. If we assume that 'necessarily q' and 'if q then (necessarily) p', 'if p, then (necessarily) q' will, of course, follow.

428. 304,2-7. An explanation of the nature of assumption {q} above (of necessity *simpliciter*).

429. 304,7-10. An explanation of the nature of assumption {'if q then p'} (of necessity *ex hypothesi*).

430. 304,13-14. *kataskeuazei ek diaireseôs*. The division (presented in the commentary in a much more systematic form than in Aristotle's text) is as follows: necessity *simpliciter* is not possible in a straight line either (i) infinite or (ii) finite. The proof of (i) (304,16-32) includes proofs (a) for the case of past events (304,20-8) and (b) for the case of future events (304,27-32). The proof of (ii) (304,32-305,18) includes two proofs based on two different meanings of continuous coming to be (304,35-305,3): (a) a single uninterrupted process of coming to be (305,3-9), and (b) a recurrent process (305,9-18).

431. 304,18-19. 'If p then necessarily q', but from the argument (ia) below it is clear that the intended logical form of this is 'necessarily if p then q', because the necessity *simpliciter* is supposed to be imparted by p to q. Aristotle's idea of simple necessity does not necessarily include the condition of its being imparted. But in minimal modal logic, the claim: 'if necessarily if p then q, then if p, necessarily q' is not valid; to obtain 'necessarily q' from the valid 'if necessarily if p then q, then if necessarily p then necessarily q', 'necessarily p' has to be asserted; so the form of the conditional on lines 18-19 will have to be 'if necessarily p then necessarily q'. I am grateful to Natasha Alechina for discussion of this point.

432. 304,19. *to prôton kai to husteron* (*deuteron* R). This can be taken in a temporal sense, as it probably was taken by one of Philoponus' sources which he goes on to criticise several pages down (309,17-31 below). But it may be taken in a causal sense: in this case the sentence should be read as an announcement of the two proofs, outlined in (ia) and (ib), to the effect that there can be no 'prior' and 'posterior' necessitating conditions in an infinite line. On the temporal interpretation of this passage, see Sharples 1994, and n. 438 ad 304,29 and n. 473 ad 309,20-31 below. On the use of *prôton(proteron)/husteron/deuteron*, see n. 417 ad 302,17 above.

433. 304,20. 'Without a beginning and without a limit', *anarkhon gar kai aperatôton*. *kai* is treated by our commentator here not as epexegetic (meaning 'i.e.'), which would interpret 'beginning' (*arkhê*) as 'limit' (*peras*) (as this is correctly done by Alexander in his exegesis of 337b27-9, Alexander *Quaest.* 2.22, 71,23, Bruns 1892,22; Sharples 1979, 37; cf. Joachim ad loc.), but as a real conjunction, 'and'. Aristotle at 337b25-9, gives an argument for the case of infinity going 'downwards', i.e. with respect to future events, only mentioning that the same result holds for the infinity going upwards at 338a9; this argument is expounded by Alexander in *Quaest.* 2.22 (in a way, as the title mentions, 'that differs from that in the commentary on it', 71,4). The following argument (ia) for the infinity going 'upwards' is supplied by later commentators (we may have more than one hand at work here).

434. 304,22-3. The claim that is being proven, that it is not possible to assume necessity *simpliciter*, denies the possibility of existence for *any* pair of events described by sentences p, q such that necessarily if p then q; prior and posterior refer to the ordering within a pair. But the argument is that it is not possible to find a 'prior' in the infinite series: presumably the idea is that what is necessary *simpliciter* has to be prior to the whole series, or else, if it is posterior to something else, it will not be necessary *simpliciter* but only in a derived way (cf. Sharples 1979 and n. 438 ad 304,29 below).

435. 304,23-4. This possibly reflects Philoponus' text of Aristotle at 337b26-7, see nn. 466, 468 below and the Appendix. Bruns 1892, followed by Sharples, takes this to be an evidence that Philoponus is committed to the view that there can be no hypothetical necessity on an infinite line, but this may in fact be a view of his source, cf. n. 473 ad 309,20-31 below.

436. 304, 25-8. The argument (ae) is strikingly different from the preceding one in that it invokes the concept of infinity as infinite divisibility. Cf. the argument in *in GC* 2.5 against the view that elements could be infinite in number (250,30-3 with n. 81 above).

437. 304,28. The overall structure (although not the details) of the argument seem to depend on Aristotle's explanation that one must assume an immediate nexus between the 'first' and the 'middle' cause, on pain of infinite regress, in *An. Post.* 2.12, 95b13-25, 31-5, and [Philoponus] ad loc. Cf. Aristotle, *GC* 2.11, 337b25-9.

438. 304,29. 'For there is no 'posterior' (*to husteron*) in infinity.' Again, 'posterior' can be taken in a temporal or causal sense. The argument is supposed to be similar to the previous one, although the case seems to be even less clear: how exactly does the fact that q is not the last member of the infinite series conflict with its being necessary? Philoponus, as we shall see (304,20-31 below), is unsympathetic with this argument, and perhaps some details are missing in his exposition. Cf. Aristotle, *An. Post.* 2.12, 95b25-31, 35-7; Alexander *Quaest.* 3.5, 88,22-89,2.

439. 304,32. 'Neither does it belong to things that move in a finite line.' cf. *GC* 2.11, 338a10 with n. 484).

440. 304,32-3: the following (ii) is an elaboration of *GC* 2.11, 337b29-33.

441. 304,35-7. In Alexander's *Quaest.* 3.5, we find a distinction between two types of coming to be to infinity along a straight line which correspond to the two types of 'coming to be always' distinguished by our commentator: '[something comes to be to infinity] either (a) so that it is always receiving some increment (*tên prosthêkên*), and never ceases to come to be by being completed, or (b) it comes to be so that one thing comes to be from another, never stopping' (87,32-88,4).

442. 305,4-5. 337b32-3.

443. 305,15-17. This argument seems to be derived from Aristotle's previous discussion of elemental transformations in *GC* 2.5, 322b12, cf. especially 248,3-4 above.

444. 305,24. Reading *tautês* with V for Vitelli's *autês*.

445. 305,26-7. *tôn apokatastaseôn*, cf. Philoponus *in An.* 120,16.

446. 306,1-2. This is not printed as a lemma by Vitelli, but probably is one (the opening after it is asyndetic, i.e. lacking a connective, and it is marked as a lemma in V).

447. 306,2-3. It is possible to understand Aristotle's expression at 337b34 (*en tois kinoumenois kata genesin*) as referring to his classifications of changes (*kinêseis*) by category, which include coming to be and perishing (*genesis* and *phthora*) with some qualifications; but our commentator wants this text to incorporate Aristotle's technical distinction between substantial and non-substantial change (cf. *Phys.* 5.1; *GC* 1.3), treating *kineisthai* just in the case of coming to be as referring to a concomitant non-substantial change rather than the process of coming to be itself.

448. 306,6-7. For the text, see Appendix.

449. 306,7. 'It is going to be', *to mellon*, see Appendix. For the proof from usage, see 302,24-303,6 above.

450. 306,12. 'It is going to be', *tou mellei*. Cf. previous note, 302,25 above and the Appendix.

451. 306,13. 'And', see Appendix.

452. 306,13. 'Since', see Appendix.

453. 306,16. For the proof from the nature of things, see 303,6-21 above.

454. 306,22-3. Curiously, summers and winters rather than corresponding motions of heavenly bodies are cited as an example of necessary things. Cf. Alexander's *Quaest.* 3.5, where a comparison between the well-determined events that come to be with simple necessity (such as equinoxes and solstices) and the seasons that follow upon these events leads to a distinction between the general order of seasons and the details of their actual arrival each time (these latter being affected by matter): the order apparently does have simple necessity (although the *Quaestio* does not state this explicitly), while individual details do not (89,2-18); cf. Sharples 1994, n. 255.

455. 307,2-3. Vitelli's emendation of the MSS reading *ara* to *âra* written seems to be supported by V.

456. 307,5-8: On conversion, see 303,35-304,2 and n. 427 above.

457. 307,15-16. Transposing from line 15, following Vitelli's suggestion in his apparatus. In all the MSS this lemma appears after the following one, and

Vitelli reproduces this order in his edition, making a note that it should be transposed to keep the order of Aristotle's text.

458. 307,16-18. The point will be more familiar when stated in terms of entailment in a minimal modal propositional logic: 'if necessarily p then necessarily if q then p' is valid, while 'necessarily if q then p' is not (where q is 'There are the foundations', p: 'There is a house').

459. 307,9.14. Transposing from line 9 following Vitelli's suggestion in the apparatus. See n. 457 ad 307,15-17 above.

460. 307,20. '[Then]', see Appendix.

461. 307,25. Although not printed as such by Vitelli, this must be a lemma (opening lacking connectives and the evidence of V).

462. 308,3-5. This is a metaphysical interpretation of the following logical dependencies. Let p stand for 'the first' proposition, q for the second. The question that Aristotle discusses is whether there is an entailment such that: 'necessarily if q then p' entails 'necessarily if p then q'. His answer is that the entailment in this form will not obtain, but on the addition of the premiss 'necessarily q' to the set of premisses, the following will be valid: 'necessarily q' and 'necessarily if q then p' entail 'necessarily if p then q'. In fact, 'necessarily if q then p' is in this case logically redundant, as the entailment from 'necessarily q' to 'necessarily if p then q' is valid by itself; but 'necessarily if q then p' has to be assumed in order to provide the relation between p and q with its required metaphysical meaning.

463. 308,21. 'Not because of itself'. The Aldine adds: 'but because of the excess of nourishment' (*alla dia tên polutrophian*).

464. 308,13-28. This is one of the several objections raised by the commentators that are left without answer. It is possible (although not necessary) that these are Philoponus' own contributions to the text (see Introduction, p. 2 and n. 25). For discussion of the argument see Sharples 1979, 33-4; on medical examples, Todd 1984.

465. 308,29 (= *GC* 337b25). 'To infinity downwards', i.e. into the future (for the argument, cf. Forster ad loc.)

466. 308,30-1. These words are not a part of the lemma, but we must assume them on the basis of Philoponus' report below, see 309,15-16 and n. 468. For the text, see Appendix.

467. 337b28. 'Starting point' (*arkhê*), on the meaning see n. 433 ad 304,20 above.

468. 309,15-16. 'But neither [will there be necessity] *ex hypothesi*', as he says'. cf. 304,23-4; 308,30-1 and nn. 435 and 466 above.

469. 309,10-19. This argument can be compared with the argument at 304,22-7 above. The point that there is no first and second on an infinite line (b) is an equivalent of (aa) and (ab) of that argument. In our argument, it follows from (b) that there is no necessity *simpliciter* – the point that is omitted in the earlier argument, where it is concluded (ac) that there is no necessity *ex hypothesi* (= (d) of the present argument). In the present argument no specific support is given to (d), whereas in the earlier argument it apparently is supported by the strong claim (ad) that there is no coming to be in a straight line (itself supported by (ae) borrowed for the occasion from Aristotle's discussion in *GC* 2.5, 333a1-13).

470. 309,20. 'Not well-formed to reach its goal', *mê katôrthômenon*, i.e. there is an ambiguity in the statement of the argument leaving open the possibility of a reading on which the argument is either not valid or not sound. I take *katorthoun* in its standard meaning 'to succeed', combined with a technical meaning 'definitively settled' as given by C.J.F. Williams at 98,20 (Williams

1999a, 131), where *katorthoun* is opposed to *amphiballesthai* (cf. Vitelli's *Index verborum* ss.vv.).

471. 309,23. Reading *estin* instead of *einai* as Vitelli suggests in apparatus.

472. 309,28.30. *Phys.* 4.11 (on definition of time); 8.1; 8.8 (on time being infinitely divisible).

473. 309,20-31. This may be one of Philoponus' own objections against Ammonius' interpretation of Aristotle's argument involving the infinite straight line. He draws a distinction between the two arguments: (i) that there is no coming to be along the infinite straight line because in this case there is no completion; and (ii) that there is no coming to be along the infinite straight line because there it has no starting point or limit. He accepts (i) and rejects (ii), pointing out that (ii) could not be Aristotle's argument against necessity, in so far as Aristotle admits of the order of succession in the infinite time. The distinction seems to be between the process of coming to be where the subject is persistent, and the succession of things or events which are distinct. Thus I am not sure if it is right to ascribe to Philoponus a belief 'that there cannot even be conditional necessity in an *infinite* series because of the principle that such a series allows no ordering of earlier and later terms (Philoponus *in GC* 309,17-31)', Sharples 1994, n. 120 (emphasis original). In this passage Philoponus seems to be *denying* the idea that there is no temporal order (and coming to be) in a straight line, and criticises the use of this idea in the argument against simple necessity in the case of rectilinear coming to be, pointing out that this idea conflicts with Aristotle's views. He says nothing about the hypothetical necessity.

474. 310,1-4. The problem seems to be the same as the one raised by Aristotle at 338b5 and discussed in the *lexis* below. At this point we are dealing with a *theôria*-style paraphrase of a subsequent discussion. Different examples used in the *theôria* and *lexis* might suggest that two discussions come from different sources.

475. 310,7. 'Proper attribute' (*idion*), cf. n. 68 ad 246,34 above.

476. 310,9. For the purposes of translation, reading *anakampsis* as Vitelli suggests in the apparatus (see also nn. 478, 479 ad 310,10.12 below).

477. 310,9-13. The argument which Philoponus sets out to develop here is similar to Aristotle's argument in *Phys.* 8.7-8, 261a31-265a12, that only circular motion possesses continuity. Cf. 301,15-16 and n. 408 above.

478. 310,10. Reading *anakampseôs* (instead of MSS *antikampseôs*) as Vitelli suggests in his apparatus (see n. 476 ad 310,9 above).

479. 310,12. Reading *anakampton* (instead of MSS *antikampton*) after Vitelli in his apparatus. The MSS have *antikampton*. See nn. 476, 478 ad 310,9.10 above.

480. 310,12-13. The example of moving down and then up a ladder is supposed to illustrate the idea that when a moving body traverses the same point twice, while going each time in the opposite direction, this motion is not continuous. The turning point at which the direction of movement changes to its opposite, is the ground (*edaphos*); the first step in the ascending order, which is the last step in the descent, is the one that is traversed twice.

481. 310,21-4. cf. Alexander *Quaest.* 3.5, 88,17-21: 'And even if human beings come to be always and do not cease, and the coming-to-be of these too is in a cycle, they will be coming to be of necessity insofar as they are human beings, <not> insofar as this one is Plato and that one Socrates. Or perhaps their coming to be is in a straight line to infinity, so that at each different time a different one comes to be, and never the same again' (88,17-21; trans. Sharples modified). Immediately after this, the *Quaestio* goes on to say: 'And therefore with respect to this the consequence is sound, 'if what is posterior, of necessity also what is first' (88,21-2), but Philoponus keeps silence on the matter of hypothetical necessity in the individual coming to be, and reports no problems with the text or Alexander's commentary, although if Alexander indeed had a different reading at 337b26 (see 308,30-1 and n. 466 and the Appendix), and Philoponus and Ammonius used Alexander's commentary, one might expect to see some indication at least of a textual problem. In any case, it is clear from (vi) that Philoponus does not deny either the coming to be of individuals in an infinite straight line, or the temporal ordering in an infinite series of this kind (cf. n. 473 ad 309,20-31 above).

482. 311,12. 'Exist', *sustênai*, see LSJ s.v., B IV (d).

483. 311,14-15. For this argument, cf. 304,25-7 (ae) and n. 436 above. Note also that only the argument against coming to be in an infinite straight line is given here; the 'finite' case being the subject of the comment under the following lemma.

484. 311,17. Aristotle's text here is difficult, see Appendix.

485. 311,19-21. The distinction is between the unceasing coming to be of individuals in an infinite succession within an eternal species (which is one in number and continuous, but not the same over infinity, because its subjects are different each time) and the rotations of heavenly bodies which are the same over infinity. Cf. Alexander *Quaest.* 3.5 at 310, 21-4 and n. 481 above and *Quaest.* 2.22, 71,10-12 with Sharples' note ad loc.

486. 311,21-2. Philoponus apparently takes 'nor ... while being finite' of the lemma (the words obelised by Joachim, see n. 484 ad 311,17 and Appendix) to be the second horn of the dilemma, whose first horn is 'Of these, if it is to be eternal, it cannot be in a straight line on account of there being no sort of starting point' of the previous lemma (338a6-8).

487. 311,26. 'Makes no difference', *ouden gar diapherei*. See Appendix.

488. 311,27. 'Two or more', *pleionôn*, see Appendix.

489. 312,3. Read: *tên antisrophên· tauta eipôn epeidê tên antistrophên peri duo tina etheôrêsen* on the basis of V. Vitelli's manuscripts have *kai en tautêi monêi anankaian einai antistrophên peri duo tina etheôrêsen* which is grammatically impossible; the Aldine adds *<hên>* after *antistrophên* (suggesting a small omission); Vitelli in the apparatus suggests: *antistrophên, <tên de antistrophên>*.

490. 312,13. 'Because', see Appendix.

491. 312,23-5. On seasons, cf. 306,22-3 and n. 454 above.

492. 312,25-8. cf. Alexander *Quaest.* 3.5, 89,18-24.

493. 313,1. 'Apparently', see Appendix (338b5).

494. 313,1. 'Water', see Appendix (338b6).

495. 313,2. 'If there is a cloud', see Appendix (338b7).

496. 313,2. 'It must also rain', see Appendix (338b7).

497. 338b12. cf. n. 501 ad 313, 23 below.

498. 313,5-10. Change Vitelli's punctuation in the following way: replace full stop after *antistrephei* at 313,7 with an opening parenthesis, insert a closing parenthesis at 313,8 after *proüpêrkhen*.

499. 313,9-13. cf. the discussion of these examples alongside the Aristotelian example of house and foundations in Alexander *Fat.* 24, 194,8-15.

500. 313,22. 'Makes an addition', *epipherei*: LSJ s.v. 9, cf. Alexander *in Sens.* 5,9.

501. 313,23. 'This is where the investigation begins', see Appendix (338b11-12).

502. 314,5-6. Vitelli indicates a lacuna after *menein*, but the phrase 'of whom

Empedocles was one' could also be an incorporated gloss. The Aldine text reads: 'persist the same in number (for this is the meaning of 'but if these too are the same in number'), as Empedocles said'.

503. 314,3-8. This explanation of Aristotle's obscure final remark is adopted by Joachim and Williams ad loc. Joachim: 'As Philoponos rightly explains, this is intended to meet a criticism which might be made by a follower of Empedokles. For Empedokles (cf. *15a4-8) insisted that Earth, Air, Fire, and Water were eternal and indestructible. According to him, therefore, their ousia is aphthartos: so that, even if they recur as individually-identical members of a cycle, this does not conflict with te solution which Aristotle has just given'.

504. 314,9-16. The reference is to the Stoic theory of eternal recurrence, in its 'stronger' version which presupposes individual recurrence (cf. Gannagé 2005, forthcoming, section 94). For discussions, see Barnes 1978; Long, 1985; Mansfeld 1979, Sorabji 2004, vol. 3, 6(h).

505. 314,16-17. 'If it is granted that Socrates is re-born'. This should be taken as a concession made in the light of the revisions of the eternal recurrence theory adopted by some thinkers of the Middle Stoa (not necessarily as evidence of Alexander's own treatment of individuals).

506. 314,21. 'As he said'. The subject is unclear, because the Socrates example does not occur in the text of Aristotle. Vitelli suggests that the reference might be to 338b16, where the distinction between numerical and specific recurrence is drawn; and than proposes *eipon* as a second guess. We must, I think, consider the possibility that Philoponus refers to his secondary source: most probably ultimately Alexander, although the intermediate source might still be Ammonius (cf. Introduction, p. 2 and n. 22).

Bibliography

Abbreviations

ANRW = W. Haase, H. Temporini (eds), *Aufstieg und Niedergang der römischen Welt*, Berlin, 1991-

CAGL = *Commentaria in Aristotelem Graeca. Versiones Latinae Temporis Resuscitatarum Litterarum*, hrsg. von Charles Lohr, Stuttgart/Bad Cannstatt: Frommann-Holzboog, 1990-

DK = Diels, H., *Die Fragmente der Vorsokratiker.* Griechisch und Deutsch von H. Diels. 11te Auflage, hrsg. von W. Kranz, 3 Bde, Zürich/Berlin, 1964

DPhA = R. Goulet, J.-M. Flamand, M. Aouad (eds), *Dictionnaire des philosophes antiques*, supplément, Paris, 2003

FDS = K.-H. Hülser (ed.), *Die Fragmente zur Dialektik der Stoiker: neue Sammlung der Texte mit deutscher Übersetzung und Kommentaren*, 4 vols, Stuttgart, 1987-8

FHSG = W.W. Fortenbaugh, P.M. Huby, R.W. Sharples, D. Gutas (eds), *Theophrastus of Eresus: Sources for his Life, Writings, Thought and Influence*, parts I-II, Leiden/New York/Köln, 1993

LSJ = *A Greek-English Lexicon*, compiled by Henry George Liddell and Robert Scott, revised and augmented throughout by Sir Henry Stuart Jones, Oxford, 1996

RUSCH = *Rutgers University Studies in Classical Humanities*, New Brunswick, NJ, 1983-

STCPF = *Studi e testi per il corpus dei papiri filosofici greci e latini*, Florence, 1985-

SVF = H. von Arnim, *Stoicorum Veterum Fragmenta*, Leipzig, 1903-5

Scholarly works cited

Accattino, P., 'Alessandro di Afrodisia e gli astri, l'anima e la luce', *Atti dell'Accademia di Scienze di Torino*, 126/2, 1992, 39-62

Accattino, P., 'Galeno sulla riproduzione animale', *ANRW* II 37.2, 1994, 1856-86

Bagnall, R.S. and Rathbone, D.W. (eds), *Egypt: From Alexander to the Copts; an Archaeological and Historical Guide*, London, 2004

Balme, D.M., 'Teleology and necessity', A. Gotthelf and J.G. Lennox (eds) *Philosophical Issues in Aristotle's Biology*, Cambridge, 1987, 275-85

Barnes, J., 'La doctrine de retour éternel', J. Brunschwig (ed.), *Les stoïciens et leur logique*, Paris, 1978, 3-20

Barnes, J., Bobzien, S., Flannery, K., Ierodiakonou, K. (trans.), *Alexander of Aphrodisias: On Aristotle Prior Analytics 1.1-7*, London/Ithaca NY, 1991

Barnes, J., 'Proofs and syllogisms in Galen', J. Barnes and J. Jouanna (eds), *Galien et la philosophie*, Geneva, 2003, 1-24

Berryman, S., 'Introduction' in Williams 1999a, 1-13 (= Berryman 1999a)

Berryman, S., 'Introduction' in Williams 1999b, 1-17 (= Berryman 1999b)

Berryman, S., 'The sweetness of honey: Philoponus against the doctors on supervening qualities', C. Leijenhorst et al. (eds), *The Dynamics of Aristotelian Natural Philosophy from Antiquity to the Seventeenth Century*, Leiden/Boston/Köln, 2002, 65-79

Berti, E., 'Il movimento del cielo in Alessandro di Afrodisia', A. Brancacci (ed.), *La filosofia in età imperiale*, Naples, 2000, 225-43

Besnier, B., 'De Generatione et Corruptione – tradition grecque', *DPhA*, 295-303

Bobzien, S. *Determinism and Freedom in Stoic Philosophy*, Oxford, 1998

Bobzien, S., 'Logic: The Stoics', K. Algra, J. Barnes, J. Mansfeld, M. Schofield (eds), *The Cambridge History of Hellenistic Philosophy*, Cambridge, 1999, 83-157

Bodnár, I., 'Alexander of Aphrodisias on celestial motions', *Phronesis* 42, 1997, 190-205

Böhm, W. (trans), *Johannes Philoponos Grammatikos von Alexandrien: Christliche Naturwissenschaft im Ausgang der Antike, Vorläufer der modernen Physik, Wissenschaft und Bibel*, Munich/Paderborn/Vienna, 1967

Bruns, I., *de Dione Chrysostomo et Aristotele critica et exegetica*, Kiel, 1892

Burkert, W., 'Plotin, Plutarch und die platonisiernde Interpretation von Heraklit und Empedokles', J. Mansfeld and L.M. de Rijk (eds), *Kephalaion: Studies in Greek Philosophy and its Continuations offered to Prof. C.J. de Vogel*, Assen, 1975, 137-46

Cherniss, H., *Aristotle's Criticism of Presocratic Philosophy*, Baltimore, 1971

Cornford, F.M., *Plato's Cosmology*, London, 1935; repr. Indianapolis/Cambridge, 1997

Dietrich, A., *Medicinalia Arabica. Studien über arabische medizinische Handschriften in türkischen und syrischen Bibliotheken*, Göttingen, 1966

Durling, R., 'The anonymous translation of Aristotle's *De generatione et corruptione* (translatio vetus)', *Traditio* 49, 1994, 320-30

Duffy, J., 'Byzantine medicine in the sixth and seventh centuries: aspects of teaching and practice', *Dumbarton Oaks Papers* 38, 1984, 21-7

Eichner, H., 'Ibn Rushd's Middle Commentary and Alexander's Commentary in their relationship to the Arab commentary tradition on the *De generatione et corruptione*', in C. D'Ancona and G. Serra (eds), *Aristotele e Alessandro di Afrodisia nella tradizione araba*, Padova, 2002, 281-98

Eichner, H. (ed., trans., introd., comm.) *Averroes' Mittlerer Kommentar zu Aristoteles' De Generatione et Corruptione*, mit einer einleitenden Studie versehen, herausgegeben und kommentiert von Heidrun Eichner, Paderborn, 2005

Ellis, J., 'Alexander's defence of Aristotle's Categories', *Phronesis* 39, 1994, 69-89

Évrard, E., 'Jean Philopon, son commentaire sur Nicomaque et ses rapports avec Ammonius', *Revue des Études Grecques* 78, 1965, 592-8

Falcon, A., *Corpi e movimenti. Il De caelo di Aristotele e la sua fortuna nel mondo antico*, Naples, 2001

Falcon, A., 'A late ancient discussion of celestial motion: PSI XIV 1400', *STCPF* IV, 2003, 129-41

Fazzo, S., *Aporia e sistema. La materia, la forma, il divino nelle Quaestiones di Alessandro di Afrodisia*, Pisa, 2002

Federspiel, M., 'Le soleil comme *movens repellens* dans le *De ventis* de Théophraste et la double antipéristase', C. Cusset (ed.), *La météorologie dans l'antiquité: entre science et croyance*, Saint-Étienne, 2003, 415-36

Fowler, D., *The Mathematics of Plato's Academy. A New Reconstruction*, Oxford, 1999

Frohn-Villeneuve, W., *The Sources of Alexander of Aphrodisias for the Presocratics*, PhD thesis, Laval University, 1980

Furley, D.J., 'The mechanics of *Meteorologica* IV: a prolegomenon to biology', in D.J. Furley, *Cosmic Problems*, Cambridge, 1987, 132-48

Gannagé, E., 'Alexandre d'Aphrodise *In De generatione et corruptione* apud Jâbir b. Hayyân, *K. al-Tasrîf*, *Documenti e studi sulla tradizione filosofica medievale*, 9, 1998, 35-86

Gannagé, E. (trans.), *Alexander of Aphrodisias: On Aristotle On Coming-to-Be and Perishing 2.2-5* London/Ithaca NY, forthcoming

Glasner, R., 'Ibn Rushd's theory of *minima naturalia*', *Arabic Sciences and Philosophy*, vol. 11, 2001, 9-26

Garofalo, I., 'La traduzione araba del commento di Ioannes [grammatikos] al "De pulsibus" di Galeno', A. Garzya and J. Jouanna (eds), *I testi medici greci: tradizione e ecdotica*. Atti del III Convegno Internazionale (Napoli 15-18 ottobre 1997), Naples, 1999, 195-218

Garofalo, I., 'Il sunto di Ioannes "Grammatikos" delle opera del canone di Galeno', D. Manetti (ed.), *Studi su Galeno: scienza, filosofia, retorica e filologia*, Florence, 2000, 135-47

Genequand, Ch., *Alexander of Aphrodisias on the Cosmos*, Leiden/Boston/Köln, 2001

Ghorab, A.A., 'Greek Commentators on Aristotle quoted in Al-'Amîrî's *as-Sa'ada wa l-Is'ad*', *Islamic Philosophy and Classical Tradition*, 1972, 77-88

de Haas, F.A.J., *John Philoponus' New Definition of Prime Matter. Aspects of its Background in Neoplatonism and the Ancient Commentary Tradition*, Leiden/New York/Köln, 1997

de Haas, F.A.J., 'Mixture in Philoponus. An encounter with a third kind of potentiality', J.M.M.H. Thijssen and H.A.G. Braakhuis (eds), *The Commentary Tradition on Aristotle's* De generatione et corruptione: *Ancient, Medieval and Early Modern*, Turnhout, 1999, 21-46

de Haas, F.A.J., 'Introduction', *Johannes Philoponus, Commentaria in libros De generatione et corruptione Aristotelis, Übersetzt von Hieronymus Bagolinus* (*CAGL* Bd. 10) Stuttgart/Bad Canstatt, 2004, V-XIV

Hahm, D.E., *The Origins of Stoic Cosmology*, Columbus, OH, 1977

Hasnawi, A. 'Alexandre d'Aphrodise vs Jean Philopon: notes sur quelques traités d'Alexandre "perdus" en grec, conservés en arabe', *Arabic Sciences and Philosophy* 1994, 4: 53-109

Horstschäfer, T.M., *'Über Prinzipien': Eine Untersuchung zur methodischen und inhaltlichen Geschlossenheit des ersten Buches der* Physik *des Aristoteles*, Berlin/New York, 1998

Ideler, J.L., *Physici et medici graeci minores*. Berlin, 1841; repr. Amsterdam, 1963

Joachim, H.H. (ed.), *Aristotle On Coming-to-Be and Passing-away (*De generatione et corruptione*): A Revised Text with Introduction and Commentary*, Oxford, 1922 (= Joachim)

Judycka, J., 'Préface', J. Yudycka (ed.), *Aristoteles Latinus IX,1 (de generatione et corruptione)*, Leiden, 1986, IX-LVIII

King, R.A.H., *Aristotle on Life and Death*, London, 2001

Kollesch, J., 'Galens Auseinandersetzung mit der aristotelischen Samenlehre', J. Wiesner (ed.), *Aristoteles – Werk und Wirkung, Paul Moraux gewidmet*, Bd. 2, Berlin/New York, 1987, 17-26

Kupreeva, I.V., Review of A. Alberti, R.W. Sharples (eds), *Aspasius: The Earliest Extant Commentary on Aristotle, Ancient Philosophy* 22/1, 2002, 219-25

Kupreeva, I.V., 'Qualities and bodies: Alexander of Aphrodisias against the Stoics', *Oxford Studies in Ancient Philosophy* 25, 2003, 296-344

Kupreeva, I.V., 'Alexander of Aphrodisias on mixture and growth', *Oxford Studies in Ancient Philosophy* 27, 2004, 296-334

Kurland, S. (trans.), *Averroes On Aristotle's De generatione et corruptione: Middle Commentary and Epitome, trans. from the Original Arabic and the Hebrew and Latin Versions with Notes and Introduction*, Cambridge, Mass, 1958 (= Kurland)

Lamberz, E., 'Proklos und die Form des philosophischen Kommentars', J. Pépin and H.D. Saffrey (eds), *Proclus: lecteur et interprète des anciens*, Paris, 1987, 1-20

Lee, T.S., *Die griechische Tradition der aristotelischen Syllogistik in der Spätantike*, Göttingen, 1984

Lewis, E., 'Diogenes Laertius and the Stoic theory of mixture', *Bulletin of the Institute of Classical Studies* 35, 1988, 84-90

Lloyd, A.C., 'The principle that cause is greater than its effect', *Phronesis* 21, 1976, 146-56

Long, A.A., 'The Stoics on world-conflagration and eternal recurrence', R.E. Epp (ed.), *Spindel Conference 1984*: *Recovering the Stoics, Southern Journal of Philosophy*, Suppl. 23, Memphis, 1985, 13-37

Luna, C., *Trois études sur la tradition des commentaires anciens à la Métaphysique d'Aristote,* Leiden/Boston/Köln, 2001

Mansfeld, J., 'Providence and the destruction of the universe in early Stoic thought', M.J. Vermaeseren (ed.), *Studies in Hellenistic Religions*, Leiden, 1979, 129-88

Mansfeld, J., 'Zeno and Aristotle on mixture', *Mnemosyne* 36, 1983, 306-10

Mansfeld, J., 'Heraclitus, Empedocles, and others in a middle Platonist *cento* in Philo of Alexandria', *Vigiliae Christianae* 39, 1985, 131-56

Mansfeld, J., 'Diaphônia: the argument of Alexander: *De Fato* chs 1-2', *Phronesis* 33/2, 1988, 181-207

Medri, E., 'Un testo sul moto celeste: per una nuova edizione di PSI XIV 1400', *STCPF* IV, 2003, 109-28

Mendell, H., 'Topoi on *topos*: the development of Aristotle's concept of place', *Phronesis* 32, 1987, 206-31

McCoull, L.S.B. and Siorvanes, L. '*PSI* xiv.1400: a fragment of Philoponus', *Ancient Philosophy* 12, 1992, 153-70

McKirahan, R.D., *Philosophy Before Socrates. An Introduction with Texts and Commentary*, Indianapolis/Cambridge, 1994

Migliori, M. (trans.), *La generazione e la corruzione* [*di*] *Aristotele; traduzione, introduzione e commento*, Naples, 1976 (= Migliori)

Mioni, E., *Bibliothecae Divi Marci Venetiarum, Codices graeci manuscripti, Thesaurus antiquus*, vol. 1, Rome, 1981

Mondrain, B., 'La constitution de corpus d'Aristote et de ses commentateurs aux XIIIᵉ-XIVᵉ siècles', *Codices Manuscripti*, 29, Jan. 2000, 11-33

Moraux, P., *Der Aristotelismus bei den Griechen*, 3 vols to date (vol. 1 1973, vol. 2 1984, vol. 3 2001), Berlin/New York, 1973-

Mourelatos, A.P.D., 'Aristotle's rationalist account of qualitative interaction', *Phronesis* 29, 1984, 1-16

Mueller, I., 'Mathematics and philosophy in Proclus' commentary on Book 1 of Euclid's Elements', J. Pépin, H.D. Saffrey (eds), *Proclus – Lecteur et Interprète des Anciens*, Paris, 1987, 305-18

Mueller, I. and Gould, J. (trans.), *Alexander of Aphrodisias: On Aristotle Prior Analytics 1.8-13*, London/Ithaca NY, 1999a

Mueller, I. and Gould, J. (trans.), *Alexander of Aphrodisias: On Aristotle Prior Analytics 1.14-22*, London/Ithaca NY, 1999b

Mugler, Ch. (ed., trans.), *Aristote: De la génération et de la corruption*, Paris, 1966

Nasr, S.H. and Mohaghegh, M. (eds), *Al-Biruni and Ibn-Sina: al-As'ila wa 'l-Ajwibah (Questions and Answers)*, Tehran, 1972

Nickel, D., *Untersuchungen zur Embryologie Galens*, Berlin, 1986

Opsomer, J., '*ANTIPERISTASIS*: a Platonic theory', A. Pérez Jiménez, J. García López and R. Mᵃ Aguilar (eds), *Plutarco, Platón y Aristóteles*, Madrid, 1999, 417-29

Opsomer, J., *In Search of Truth: Academic Tendencies in Middle Platonism*, Brussels, 1998

Peters, F., *Aristoteles Arabus: The Oriental Translations and Commentaries of the Aristotelian Corpus*, Leiden, 1968

Pormann, P.E., 'Jean le Grammairien et le *de sectis* dans la littérature médievale d'Alexandrie', I. Garofalo, A. Rosselli (eds), *Galenismo e medicina tardoantica: fonti greche, latine e arabe*, Naples, 2003, 233-63

Primavesi, O., 'Lecteurs antiques et byzantins d'Empédocle. De Zénon à Tzétzès', A. Laks, C. Louguet (eds), *Qu'est-ce que la philosophie présocratique?/ What is Presocratic Philosophy?* Villeneuve d'Ascq (Nord), 2002, 183-204

Puig Montada, J., 'Aristotle and Averroes on coming-to-be and passing-away', *Oriens*, 35, 1-34

Rashed, M., 'Théodicée et approximation: Avicenne', *Arabic Sciences and Philosophy* 10 (2000), 223-57

Rashed, M., *Die Überlieferungsgeschichte der aristotelischen Schrift De generatione et corruptione*, Wiesbaden, 2001 (Serta Graeca Bd. 12)

Rashed, M., 'De generatione et corruptione. Tradition arabe', *DPhA*, 304-14

Reis, B., *Der Platoniker Albinos und sein sogenannter Prologos: Prolegomena, Überlieferungsgeschichte, kritische Edition und Übersetzung*, Wiesbaden, 1999

Richard, M., '*Apo phônês*', *Byzantion*, 1950, 191-222

Ruland, H.-J., *Die arabischen Fassungen von zwei Schriften des Alexander von Aphrodisias Über die Vorsehung und Über das liberum arbitrium*. Diss., Saarbrücken, 1976. (= *Prov.*)

Schiano, C., 'Il trattato inedito "Sulle febbri" attribuito a Giovanni Filopono', I. Garofalo and A. Rosselli (eds), *Galenismo e medicina tardoantica: fonte greche, latine e arabe*, Naples, 2003, 75-100

Schmitt, C.B., 'Philoponus' commentary on Aristotle's *Physics* in the sixteenth century', R.R.K. Sorabji (ed.), *Philoponus and the Rejection of Aristotelian Science*, London/Ithaca NY, 1987, 210-30

Scholten, C., *Antike Naturphilosophie und christliche Kosmologie in der Schrift 'De opificio mundi' des Johannes Philoponos*, Berlin/New York, 1996

Scholten, C. (ed., trans.), *Johannes Philoponos, de opificio mundi (Über die Erschaffung der Welt)*, Griechisch-Deutsch, 3 vols, Freiburg, 1997

Segonds, A.P. (trans.), *Jean Philopon, Traité de l'astrolabe*, Paris, 1981

Sharples, R.W., ' "If what is earlier, then of necessity what is later"?: some ancient discussions of Aristotle *De generatione et corruptione* 2.11', *Bulletin of the Institute of Classical Studies* 26, 1979, 27-44

Sharples, R.W., 'The Unmoved Mover and the motion of the heavens in Alexander of Aphrodisias', *Apeiron* 1983, 62-6

Sharples, R.W. (trans.), *Alexander of Aphrodisias: Quaestiones 1.1-2.15*, London/Ithaca NY, 1992

Sharples, R.W. (trans.), *Alexander of Aphrodisias: Quaestiones 2.16-3.15*, London/Ithaca NY, 1994

Sharples, R.W., 'Counting Plato's principles', L. Ayres (ed.), *The Passionate Intellect*, *RUSCH* vol. VII, New Brunswick/London, 1995, 67-82

Shorey, P., 'Aristotle on "coming-to-be" and "passing away" ', *Classical Philology* 17, 1922, 334-52

de Smet, D., *Empedocles Arabus*, Brussels, 1998

Smith, J.A., '*Tode ti* in Aristotle', *Classical Review* 35, 1921, 19

Solmsen, F., *Aristotle's System of Natural World*, Ithaca NY, 1961

Sorabji, R.R.K., 'Infinity and the creation', R.R.K. Sorabji (ed.), *Philoponus and the Rejection of Aristotelian Science*, London/Ithaca NY, 1987

Sorabji, R.R.K., 'The Greek origins of the idea of chemical combination: can two bodies be in the same place?', *Proceedings of the Boston Area Colloquium in Ancient Philosophy* IV, 1988, 35-75 (= Sorabji 1988a)

Sorabji, R.R.K., *Matter, Space, and Motion: Theories in Antiquity and Their Sequel*, London/Ithaca NY, 1998 (= Sorabji 1988b)

Sorabji, R.R.K., 'Latitude of forms in ancient philosophy', Leijenhorst et al. (eds), *The Dynamics of Aristotelian Natural Philosophy from Antiquity to the Seventeenth Century*, Leiden/Boston/Köln, 2002, 57-63

Sorabji, R.R.K., *The Philosophy of the Commentators, 200-600 AD: A Sourcebook*: vol. 1: *Psychology*, vol. 2: *Physics*, vol. 3: *Logic and Metaphysics*, London/Ithaca NY, 2004

Speca, A.N., *Hypothetical Syllogistic and Stoic Logic*, Leiden/Boston/Köln, 2001

Steinmetz, P., *Die Physik des Theophrastos von Eresos*, Bad Homburg/Berlin/Zürich, 1964

Stückelberger, A., *Vestigia Democritea. Die Rezeption der Lehre von den Atomen in der antiken Naturwissenschaft und Medizin*, Basel, 1984

Todd, R.B., '*Epitêdêiotês* in philosophical literature: towards an analysis', *Acta Classica* (Cape Town), 15, 1972, 25-35.

Todd, R.B., *Alexander of Aphrodisias on Stoic Physics*, Leiden, 1976

Todd, R.B., 'Galenic medical ideas in the Greek Aristotelian commentators', *Symbolae Osloenses* 52, 1977, 117-34

Todd, R.B., 'Philosophy and medicine in John Philoponus' commentary on Aristotle's *de anima*', *Dumbarton Oaks Papers* 38, 1984, 103-10

Todd, R.B., 'Some concepts in physical theory in John Philoponus' Aristotelian commentaries', 151-70, *Archiv für Begriffsgeschichte* 24, 1980, 151-70

Tweedale, M.M., 'Alexander of Aphrodisias' view of universals', *Phronesis* 29, 1984, 191-224

Verdenius, W.J., Waszink, J.H., *Aristotle On Coming-to-Be and Passing-Away: Some Comments*, Leiden, 1946 (= Verdenius and Waszink)

Verrycken, K. 'The metaphysics of Ammonius son of Hermeias', R.R.K. Sorabji (ed.) *Aristotle Transformed*, London/Ithaca NY, 1990, 199-231 (= Verrycken 1990a)

Verrycken, K., 'The development of Philoponus' thought and its chronology', R.R.K. Sorabji (ed.) *Aristotle Transformed*, London/Ithaca NY, 1990, 233-74 (= Verrycken 1990b)

Vitelli, G., 'Indice de' codici greci riccardiani, magliabechiani e marucelliani', *Studi italiani di filologia classica* 2, 1894, 471-570

Wartelle, A. *Inventaire des manuscrits grecs d'Aristote et de ses commentateurs*, Paris, 1963 (= Wartelle)

Westerink, L.G., 'Deux commentaires sur Nicomaque: Asclépius et Jean Phi-lopon', *Revue des études grecques* 77, 1964, 526-35

Westerink, L.G., 'Ein astrologisches Kolleg aus dem Jahre 564', *Byzantinische Zeitschrift* 64, 1971, 6-21

White, M.J., 'Stoic natural philosophy (physics and cosmology)' in B. Inwood (ed.), *Cambridge Companion to the Stoics*, Cambridge, 2003, 124-52

Wildberg C. (trans.), *Philoponus: Against Aristotle On the Eternity of the World*, London/Ithaca NY, 1987

Wildberg, C., *John Philoponus' Criticism of Aristotle's Theory of Aether*, Ber-lin/New York, 1988

Wildberg, C., 'Neoplatonic philosophy of nature in PSI XIV 1400: an impression', *STCPF* IV, 2003, 143-9

Williams, C.J.F., *Philoponus: On Aristotle On Coming-to-Be and Perishing 1.1-5,* London/Ithaca NY, 1999 (= Williams 1999a)

Williams, C.J.F., *Philoponus: On Aristotle On Coming-to-Be and Perishing 1.6-2.4,* London/Ithaca NY, 1999 (= Williams 1999b)

Wittwer, R., 'Aspasius' lemmatology', A. Alberti, R.W. Sharples (eds), *Aspasius: The Earliest Extant Commentary on Aristotle's Ethics*, Berlin, 1999, 51-84

Wolff, M., *Fallgesetz und Massebegriff*, Berlin, 1971

Wolff, M., 'Philoponus and the rise of classical dynamics', in R.R.K. Sorabji (ed.), *Philoponus and the Rejection of Aristotelian Science*, London, 1987, 84-120

English-Greek Glossary

above: *anôthen, anô*
accept: *apodekhesthai*
accord, in: *sunôidos*
accordingly: *toinun*
account: *logos*; give an account:
　apodidonai, apophainein
acquire: *ktasthai, prosktasthai*
act: *poiein*
acted upon, be: *paskhein*
action, be in: *energein*
activity: *energeia*
actuality: *energeia, entelekheia*; in
　actuality: *energeiâi*
add: *epipherein, proslambanein,
　prostithenai*;
addition: *prosthêkê*
addition, make an: *epipherein*
additional assumption (in
　hypothetical syllogism): *proslêpsis*
additionally assume: *proslambanein*
address oneself to: *apoteinesthai (pros
　tina)*
adduce: *theôrein*
adequate: *hikanos*
adjacent, be: *parakeisthai*
admixture: *epimixia*
adolescent: *meirakion*
adopt: *hupotithenai*
advancement: *prokopê*
affected, be: *paskhein*
affection: *pathos*
afflicted, be: *kamnein*
afraid, be: *phobeisthai*
after that: *loipon*
after the fact: *meta apobasin*
again: *palin*
again, over and over: *palin kai palin*
aggregation: *sunkrisis*
agreement, in: *sumphônos*
aim: *skopos*
air: *aêr*

airy: *aerôdês*
all: *pas*
allocate: *aponemein*
allotted, be: *lankhanein*
allude: *ainittesthai*
already: *êdê*
already (do something, be): *phthanein*
　with participle
also: *kai, palin, eti*
alteration: *alloiôsis*
alterative (power): *alloiôtikê
　(dunamis)*
always: *aei, dia pantos*
amount: *megethos*
analysis: *skepsis*
ancients, the: *hoi palaioi; hoi
　palaioteroi*
any: *hopoiosoun*
apparently: *phainesthai*
appear: *phainesthai*
appellation *prosêgoria*
apply (of a lifespan, time-interval):
　tattein
approach: *prosengizein,
　proserkhesthai, prosienai*
approach, approaching of the sun (in
　a yearly cycle): *prosienai,
　prosodos, proseleusis (tou hêliou)*
appropriate, be: *prosêkein*
aptly: *kalôs*
argue: *legein*; against sb., sth.:
　antilegein
argument *logos, kataskeuê*
arrive: *aphikneisthai*
art: *tekhnê*
artisan's mixture: *tekhnêtê mixis*
as (of comparison in terms of
　quantity): *tosoutos*
as many as: *hosos*
as many times as: *hosakis*
asleep, be: *katheudein*

assemble: *sumphorein*
assembling: *sunodos*
assimilate: *exomoioun*
association: *koinônia, koinônein*
assume: *hupotithenai, lambanein,*
    theôrein
assumed, be: *hupokeisthai;*
    (previously): *prokeisthai*; what has
    been: *hupothesis*
assumption: *hupothesis,*
    hupotithenai; give an assumption:
    hupotithenai; be an assumption,
    according to the assumption(s):
    hupokeisthai
at all: *holôs*
attribute (v.): *apodidonai*
attribute: *idion*

back: *palin*
bad: *phaulos*
bad mixture: *akrasia*
badly: *kakôs*
battle: *makhê*
be: *einai, ekhein, ginesthai,*
    huparkhein; will be: *estai*; what
    will be: *esomenon, to*
be the case: *ekhein*
bear: *gennan, pherein*
bear analogy: *analogein*
beautiful: *kalos*
become: *ginesthai*
bed: *klinê*
before, be, do: *prolambanein;*
    phthanein
before: *pro, prôton, proteron*;
begin: *arkhein*
beginning: *arkhê, prôton*
beginning, having no: *anarkhos*
being: *einai, ousia*
belief: *doxa*
believe: *dokein (tini), nomizein,*
    oiesthai
belong: *huparkhein*
below: *hupokatô, katô, katôthen*
benefit: *apolauein*
besides: *allôs*
bestow: *enapothesthai, epitithenai*
better: *ameinôn, beltiôn, kreittôn*
between: *metaxu*
beyond: *pera*
big: *megas*
bind: *dein*
birth, give: *gennan*

bitterness: *pikrotês*
bizarre: *apoklêrotikos*
black: *melas*
blackness: *melanotês*
blow: *plêgê*
bodily: *sômatikos*; of bodily kind:
    sômatoeidês
bodily frame: *sumpêxis*
body: *sôma*
bone: *ostoun*
book: *biblion*
both: *hekateroi*
bound: *dein, periorizein*
boundary: *horos*
branch (of division): *tmêma*
breadth: *platos*
brick: *plinthos*
brief: *brakhus, suntomos*
briefly: *epi brakhu, en brakhei*
bring about: *apotelein, poiein*
bring close: *prosagein*
bring in: *eisagagein*
bring round: *periagein, peritrepein*
bring to completion: *apotelein,*
    epitelein
bring together: *sunkrinein*
bring up: *anaballesthai, epipherein,*
    pherein
broad range: *platos*
build: *oikodomein*
builder: *oikodomos*
burn (n.): *kausis*
burn: *kaiein*
by and large: *epipan*
by the same token: *êdê*

call: *kalein, legein, onomazein*
can: *dunasthai, einai, endekhesthai*
cannot: *adunaton*
capable of, be: *endekhesthai*
capacity: *dunamis*
carpenter: *tektôn*
carry: *pherein*
cast down: *kataballein*
cast down before: *prokataballein*
casting down (of seed into earth):
    katabolê (tou spermatos eis gên)
cause: *aitia, aitios;* allege as a cause,
    assign a causal role, make a cause:
    aitiasthai
cause motion, movement: *kinein*
causing to disintegrate: *diakritikos*
censure: *psegein*

censure (n.): *psogos*
centaur: *hippokentauros*
certain size, of a: *tosoutos*
chair: *thronos*
champion: *prostatês*
chance: *tukhê*
chance (v.): *tunkhanein*
change: *tropê, metabolê*
change (v.): *trepesthai, metaballein*;
   change together with:
    summetaballein
change of seasons: *enallagê tôn horôn*
changeable: *metablêtikos, metablêtos*
characterise: *kharaktêrizein*
characteristic: *idios*
charge: *epipherein*
cheat: *hupokleptein*
child: *pais*
choice: *proairesis*
choose: *axioun*
circle: *kuklos*
circle, in a: *kuklikôs*
circle, make a: *anakukleisthai*
circular: *kukloterês, kuklikos*
circular movement: *kuklophoria*
circular recurrence: *anakuklêsis*
claim: *legein, phanai, propherein*
clay: *pêlos*
clear: *prodêlon*
clearly: *enargôs, prophanôs, prodêlon*
close: *engus*
close, be: *prosengizein*
cloud: *nephos*
co-exist: *sunuphistanai*
coincidence: *suntukhia*
cold: *psukhros*
cold (n.): *psukhrotês, psuxis*
coldness: *psukhrotês, psuxis*
collision: *sunkrousis*
collocation: *parabolê*
combination: *sumplokê*
combine: *sunkrinein*; be combined
   together: *sumplekesthai*
come about: *ekbainein, proserkhesthai*
come to: *ephêkein*
come to an end: *teleutan*
come to be: *ginesthai, genesis*
come together: *sunienai,*
   sunerkhesthai
comes to be, which: *genêtos*
coming to be: *genesis*
commend: *apodekhesthai*
common: *koinos*

commonly: *koinôs*
comparability: *sumbolê*
comparable: *sumblêtos*
comparable, be: *sumballesthai*
compare: *antitithenai, paraballein*
compared: *sumblêtos*
comparison: *antiparathesis, parabolê,*
   parathesis, sumbolê, sunkrisis
comparison, be in: *paraballein*
complete (adj.): *teleios*
complete: *apotelein, epitelein,*
   sumplêroun
completely: *holôs, pantelôs, teleiôs,*
   teleôs
completion: *teleiôsis, teleion*
composed, be: *sunistasthai*
comprehend: *perilambanein*
conceive (of): *lambanein, epinoeisthai,*
   noein, theôrein
concept: *ennoia, epinoia*; merely in
   concept, *kata psilên epinoian*
conclude: *sumperainein*
conclusion: *sumperasma*
concoction: *pepsis*
concourse: *sunodos*
concur: *suntrekhein*
concurrence: *sundromê*
condensation: *puknôsis*
condense: *puknoun*
conflict, be in conflict: *antipiptein*
confluence: *surrhein*
connect together: *suneirein*
consecutively: *kata to sunekhes*
consequence: *akolouthêsis*
consequence, be a: *hepesthai*
consider: *theôrein*
considerable: *polus*
consideration: *epinoia*
considered to be present in, be:
   entheôreisthai
considered, must be: *skepteon*
consist of: *sunistasthai*
consistent: *akolouthos*
constraint: *bia*
construct an argument: *kataskeuazein*
contain: *periekhein*
content, be: *arkeisthai*
contingent, be: *endekhesthai*
contingently: *endekhomenôs*
continual, continually: *aei*
continue: *proagein, proerkhesthai,*
   proienai
continuity: *sunekheia, sunekhês*

continuous: *sunekhês*
continuous, be: *suneirein*
continuously, in a continuous way:
    kata sunekheian, kata to sunekhes,
    sunekhôs
contract: *sustellein*
contradicting, contradiction,
    contradictory: *asumphônos*
contrast: *antidiastolê*
contribute: *sumballesthai eis ti*
converse case: *empalin*
conversion: *antistrophê*
convert: *antistrephein*
convertible, be: *antistrephein*
co-ordinate: *suntattein*
co-ordinated pair: *sustoikhia*
co-perception: *sunaisthêsis*
corporeal: *sômatikos*
corresponding opposite (in the
    sustoikhia): *antistoikhos*
countable: *arithmêtos*
counterargument: *antirrhêsis*
craftsman: *tekhnitês*
create: *dêmiourgein*
creation: *dêmiourgia*
creative: *dêmiourgikos*
criticise: *dialegesthai pros tina,*
    memphesthai
criticism: *mempsis*
culminating point: *akmê*
cultured: *mousikos*
cut: *tomê*
cycle: *kuklos, periodos*

day: *hêmera*
day-and-night: *hêmeronuktion,*
    nukhthêmeron
deal with: *gumnazein, diexerkhesthai,*
    diorizein
death: *thanatos*
decay: *parakmazein*
decay (n.): *parakmê*
deceive: *apatan*
decrease: *phthinein*
deem worthy: *axioun*
defer: *hupertithenai*
deficiency: *huphesis*
define: *aphorizein, diorizein, horizein*
definition: *logos*
definition, definitive account, give:
    diorizein
demonstrate: *apodeiknunai*
demonstrate before: *proapodeiknunai*

demonstration: *apodeixis*
demonstration, give a: *apodeiknunai*
denser: *pakhumeresteros*
depart: *apokhôrein*
departure (of the sun): *apostasis (tou*
    hêliou)
depend (on): *anartan, artasthai*
dependent, be: *apartasthai*
deprived, be: *stereisthai*
derive: *gennan, lambanein*
describe: *phanai*
deserving: *axios*
desire: *ephiesthai, oregesthai*
destroy: *anairein, phtheirein,*
    apollunai
destruction: *phthora*
determine: *diorizein*
devote a long discussion: *katateinein*
    polun logon
dichotomy, the opposite member of:
    antidiairoumenon
die: *teleutan*
die prematurely: *proapollusthai*
differ: *diapherein*
difference: *diaphora*
different: *allos, diaphoros*; on
    different grounds: *allôs*
different kinds, of: *heterogenês*
different way, in a: *allôs*
differentiated: *diaphoros*
differing in kind: *heterogenês*
difficult: *aporos*
difficulty: *aporia*
dimension: *diastasis*
dimension, possessed of: *diastatos*
diminution: *phthisis*
directly: *eutheôs*
discuss: *dialegesthai*
discussion: *logos*
disintegrate: *diakrinein*
disintegration: *diakrisis*
disorder: *ataxia*
disorderly: *ataktos*
dispense: *khorêgein*
disposed, be: *ekhein*
disposition: *diathesis, hexis*
dissociate: *diakhôrizein*
dissolve: *diakrinein, dialuein*
distance: *diastêma*
distant: *porrô*
distant from, be: *aphistanai*
distinguish, make distinctions:
    diairein, diorizein

diverse: *poikilos*
division: *diairesis*
do: *poiein*
doctor: *iatros*
doctrine: *doxa*
double: *diplasios, diplous*
downwards: *katô*
draw (conclusion): *sumperainein, epagagein*
draw near: *engizein, prosengizein*
drawing board: *abakion*
drawn, be (of geometrical lines): *prospiptein*
dream: *oneirôttein*
drive out: *existanai*
dry: *xêros*
drying powder: *xêrion*
dryness: *xêrotês, xêron*

each: *hekateros kata meros*, each of the two: *hekateros*
ear of corn: *stakhus*
earlier: *proteros, proteron*
earlier, be, do something: *phthanein* (with participle)
easily: *râidiôs, râidion*
easily bounded: *euoristos*
east: *anatolai*
easy: *eumarês, râidios*
easy to dissolve: *eudialutos*
eat: *edêdesthai*
effect: *pathos*
effect (v.): *poiein*
efficient (of causes): *poiêtikos*
effluence: *aporrhoê*
either, of the two: *hekateros*
element: *stoikheion*
elephant: *elephas*
eliminate: *anairein*
elliptically: *ellipôs*
emaciation: *iskhnansis*
embrace: *emperiekhein, periekhein*
embrace by definition: *periorizein*
embryo: *embruon*
empowered, be: *dunasthai*
end: *telos*
end (v.): *teleutan*
end up at: *katantan eis*
endow with form: *eidopoiein*
enough: *epi tosouton*
ensue: *akolouthein*
environment: *periekhon*
equal: *isos*

equal amount: *isomegethês*
equal degree, in: *homotimôs*
equal importance, of: *homotimos*
equal in time to: *isokhronos*
equal, be: *isazein, exisoun, exisazein*
equality: *isos*
equality: *isotês*
equally: *isos*
equally matched, be: *exisazein*
equivalent, be: *en isôi einai, exisazein*
escape: *diadidraskein*
essence: *ousia*
essential: *ousiôdês*
establish: *kataskeuazein*
eternal, eternally: *aei, aidios*
eternity: *aidiotês*
every, everything: *hapas, pas*
evidence: *phainomena, pistis*
evident, be, evidently: *phainesthai* (with participle)
exact: *akribês*
examine: *episkopein, skopein, zêtein*
example: *khrêsis, paradeigma*
excess: *huperbolê, huperokhê*
excess of nourishment: *polutrophia*
excess, be in: *huperekhein; pleonazein*
exercise: *gumnazein*
exhalation: *anathumiasis*
exist: *einai, huparkhein, huphistanai*
exist in: *enuparkhein*
existence: *huparxis, hupostasis*
existing things: *onta, ta*
explain: *aitiasthai, apodidonai, didaskein, ektithesthai, gumnazein*
explain before: *prodiorizein*
explanation: *aitia, aitios*
explanation, give an: *apodidonai, apophainein*
explicitly: *phanerôs*
expound at length: *mêkunein*
expound: *ektithesthai, gumnazein*
extend: *ekteinein*
external: *exôthen*
extreme: *akros, eskhatos, akrotês*
extreme degree: *akrotês*
extreme, in the: *akrôs*

fail: *hupoleipein* (with participle), *dialeipein*
fall (n.): *ptôsis*
fall into: *peripiptein*
false: *pseudês*
farmer: *geôrgos*

farther away: *porrô*
father: *patêr*
fault: *hamartanein*
fewer (of time): *elattôn*
fiery: *purôdês*
fill up: *anaplêroun*
final (of cause): *telikos*
find: *heuriskein*
find out: *zêtein*
fine: *kalos*
fine structure: *leptomereia*
finite, be: *perainesthai*
fire: *pur*, of fire: *purios*
first: *proteros, prôtos*; (logical term) *proteron, prôton* (dist. *husteron deuteron*); *emprosthen*
first place, in the (be, do something): *phthanein*
first sense, meaning, in the: *kata to prôton (sêmainomenon)*
fit: *harmozein*
fixed: *aplanês*
fixed length of life: *prothesmia tou biou*
flesh: *sarx*
fleshy: *sarkôdês*
flow: *epirrhein*
follow: *akolouthein, epakolouthein, hepesthai, parakolouthein, proïenai*; (as a conclusion) *sumperainesthai*; (in succession) *diadekhesthai*
following: *ephexês*
following upon: *akolouthêsis*
follows (upon), what: *ephexês*
foolish: *euêthês*
for the sake of: *heneka, kharin*
forced: *biaios*
forgetfulness: *lêthê*
form: *morphê; eidos*
Form (Plato): *eidos, idea*
form, give: *eidopoiein*
form, make to have a: *eidopoiein*
formless: *aneideos*
foundations (of a house): *themelios*
four ingredients, of (of a drying powder): *tetraeidês*
frequently: *pollakis*
from an external standpoint, from outside: *exôthen*
from the following, from this: *enteuthen*
from there: *ekeithen*

fruit: *karpos*
fulfil: *plêroun*
further: *porrôteron, eti, eti te*
further on: *hupokatiô*
further specify: *prosdiorizein*

gathering: *sunodos*
generable: *genêtos*
general: *haplous, koinos*
general sense, in a: *koinôs*
generally: *haplôs, holôs*
generate: *gennan*
generated: *genêtos*
generating: *gennêtikos*
generation: *genesis, gennan*
gestate: *kuiskein*
gestation: *kuêsis*
get: *lambanein*
give: *didonai*
go: *ienai*
go on: *proïenai*
go over: *epexerkhesthai*
go through: *diexienai, diexerkhesthai*
goal: *skopos*
goatstag: *tragelaphos*
god: *theos*
good: *agathos, kalos*;
good reason, with: *eulogôs*
grant: *didonai*
grapevine: *ampelos*
grasp: *lambanein*
ground: *edaphos*
ground: *logos*
grow: *auxanein, phuein*
growth: *auxêsis*

half: *hêmiolios*
hand down: *paradidonai*
happen: *prospiptein, suntunkhanein, tunkhanein*
have: *ekhein*
have in mind: *aphoran*
have to: *anankaiôs* (with verb), *anankê, dein*
have what is needed: *euporein*
heal: *hugiazein*
health: *hugeia*
healthy, become: *hugiainein*
heat: *thermon, thermotês*
heavenly: *ouranios*; heavenly bodies: *ta ourania*
heavy: *barus*
heed: *ephistanai*

hence: *toinun*
here: *entautha, teôs*
hint: *ainittesthai*
hold (a view etc.): *theôrein,*
    hupotithenai, dokein tini, phanai
hold in charge: *aitiasthai*
hollow of the earth: *koilôma tês gês*
homoeomer, homoeomerous:
    homoiomerês
homonymous sense, in a: *homônumôs*
hot: *thermos*
house: *oikia*
housebuilding: *oikodomêma*
housebuilding, knowledge of:
    oikodomikê epistêmê
human: *anthrôpinos*
human being: *anthrôpos*
hypothetical: *hupothetikos, kata*
    hupothesin, ex hupotheseôs

idea: *dianoia*
if: *ean, ei, epei*
ignorance: *agnoia*
ignorant: *anepistêmôn*
ill, be: *nosein*
illness: *nosos*
image: *eikôn*
imitate: *mimeisthai*
immediately: *ephexês*
immobile: *akinêtos*
impart motion: *kinein*
impedes, that which: *empodôn, to*
impediment: *empodion*
imperceptible: *anaisthêtos*
implication,by: *akolouthôs*
implied, be: *hepesthai*
imply: *akolouthein*
import: *eisagein*
impose: *epitithenai*
impulse: *hormê*
in a certain way: *toiôsde*
in general: *holôs*
in many places: *pollakhou*
in most cases: *pollakis*
in no way: *mêdamôs*
in relation to: *pros*
in that case: *tênikauta*
in that way: *tautêi*
in the course of argument: *proïontos*
    tou logou
in turn: *palin, para meros*
in two ways: *dikhôs, dittôs*
in vain: *matên*

inappropriate, inappropriateness:
    anarmostos
in-between: *metaxu*
incapable of being composed:
    asustatos
incidentally: *ek suntukhias*
inclined circle: *loxos kuklos*
incongruous: *atopos*
incorporeal: *asômatos*
increase: *epididonai*
indeed: *amelei*
indicating: *dêlôtikos*
indicative: *sêmantikos*
indivisible: *atomos*
inevitable: *anankê*
infer: *sullogizesthai*
inferior, inferiority: *kheirôn*
infinite: *apeiros*
infinity: *to apeiron*
inflammable substance: *hupekkauma*
ingredient, be an: *sunerkhesthai*
inherent, be: *enuparkhein*
inhibit: *kolazein*
inquire: *zêtein*
inquiry: *zêtêsis*
insert parenthetically: *paremballein*
    dia mesou
insomnia: *agrupnia*
instrument: *organon*
instrumental: *organikos*
intellect: *nous*
intend: *boulesthai*
intending: *mellôn*
intensify: *epiteinesthai*
intercourse, have: *sunerkhesthai*
intermediate: *mesos, metaxu*
intermediate state: *mesotês*
interrupt: *dialambanein, epileipein*
interval: *dialeimma,*
intervals, have: *dialeipein*
interwoven, get: *sunklôsthênai*
introduce: *eisagein*
investigate: *zêtein*
investigation: *skepsis*
involve: *eisagein*
involving a problem, impasse: *aporos*
irrational: *alogos*
irrefutable: *anelenktos*
is going to be: *mellein*
is to be: *anankê*
isosceles (triangle): *isoskelês*

join: *sunaptein*

joined together, be: *sunistasthai*
judge: *krinein*
just: *prosekhôs*
juxtapose: *paratithenai*
juxtaposition: *parathesis*

keep: *têrein*
keep together: *summenein*
killing: *sphagê*
kind: *eidos*
kinship: *sungeneia*
know: *eidenai*
knowledge: *epistêmê*
knowledgeable: *epistêmôn*

lack of measure: *ametria*
ladder: *klimax*
last: *eskhatos, teleutaios*
latter, the: *ekeinos*
lay down as premiss: *hupokeisthai*
lead: *agein, pherein*
learn: *manthanein*
learning: *mathêsis*
leave: *kataleipein, leipein*
leave aside: *paraleipein*
lecture notes: *aposêmeiôseis*
legitimate: *orthos*
less: *hêttôn, elattôn*
lesser: *elattôn*
letter: *stoikheion*
life: *bios, zôê*
life-span: *bios*
lifetime: *khronos tês zôês*
lightness: *kouphotês*
like this: *toioutos*
likely: *eikotôs*
likeness: *homoiotês*
limit: *peras*
limit (v.): *perainein*
link: *prosekhein*
literate: *grammatikos*
local motion: *phora*
locomotion: *phora*
logical agreement: *akolouthia*
long (of time, discussion): *polus*
look at: *aphoran*
lose: *apoballein*
loss: *apobolê*
Love (Empedocl.): *Philia*
lower: *katô*
lump of earth: *bôlos*

maintain: *theôrein*

make: *poiein*
make come to be: *gennan*
make distant: *diistanai*
make one's way to: *hodeuein epi ti*
make reference to: *apoteinesthai*
make responsible: *aitiasthai*
Maker: *dêmiourgos*
man: *anêr, anthrôpos*;
man, of: *anthrôpeios*
manifest: *epideiknunai*
manifest (adj.): *prodêlon*
manifest facts: *enargeia*
manner of speech: *rhêsis*
manure: *koprôdês*
many: *polus*
mark: *episêmainein*
mark off: *aphorizein*
marrow: *muelos*
mass: *onkos*
master: *kratein*
material: *hulikos*
matter: *hulê*
maximum: *to megiston*
mean: *boulesthai, einai, legein, phanai*
meaning: *sêmasia*
measure: *epistatein, metrein*
measure, measurement, measuring:
    metron
medicine: *iatrikê* (*tekhnê*)
member: *meros*
memory: *mnêmê*
mention: *legein*
middle: *mesos*
militate: *makhesthai*
millstone-like: *muloeidês*
mingling: *sunkrasis*
mix: *kirnan, mignunai*
mixing: *mixis*
mixture: *migma, mignunai, sunkrasis*
mode: *tropos*
moist: *hugros*
moisture: *hugrotês*
more than: *mallon*; no more: *ou
    mallon*
moreover: *eti, eti te*
most, mostly: *malista*
mostly, for the most part: *epi pleion,
    hôs epi to pleiston*
mother: *mêtêr*
motion: *kinêsis, phora*
motion, perform: *kinein*
move: *kinein, pherein*

move away: *apagein, apienai,
    aphistanai, apokhôrein*
move over: *metienai*
movement: *kinêsis, kinein*
mover, moving cause, be a: *kinein*
moving in a circle: *kuklophorikos*
much: *polus*; as much as possible:
    malista
multiple of (this quantity):
    pollaplasiôn
must: *anankê, dein, khrê*

naïve: *euêthês*
name: *onoma*
natural: *kata phusin, phusikos*
natural for sth, be: *pephukenai*
natural, more: *prosphuês*
naturally: *prosphuês*
nature: *phusis*; by nature: *phusei*; in
    accordance with nature: *kata
    phusin*; contrary to nature: *para
    phusin*; more in accordance with
    the study of nature: *phusikôteron*
near: *engus*
necessarily: *anankaios, anankaiôs,
    anankê*
necessary: *anankaios, anankê*
necessary, be: *anankaiôs* (with verb),
    anankê, dein
necessity, of necessity: *anankaios*;
    with necessity: *anankaiôs*
need: *khreia*
need (v.): *dein*
nerve: *neuron*
never: *mêdamêi*
nevertheless: *homôs*
newborn child: *artigenês pais*
next: *eti, eti te, ephexês*
night: *nux*
nonetheless: *ouden hêtton, homôs*
not generable: *agenêtos*
not subject to affection: *apathês*
not traversable: *adiexitêtos*
notion: *ennoia*
nourish: *trephein*
nourishment: *trophê*
now: *nun, nuni, teôs, toinun*
number: *arithmos*

object: *enkalein*
objection: *enstasis*
obliquity: *enklisis*
observe: *theôrein*

obviously: *phainesthai* (with inf.)
occupy: *katekhein*
often: *pollakis*
omit: *paraleipein, parhienai*
on that account: *tautêi*
once for all: *kathapax*
one after another: *ephexês*
only: *monôs*
opinion: *doxa*
opinion, be an: *dokein*
opposite direction, in: *empalin*
opposition: *antithesis*
order: *tattein*
orderly arrangement: *kosmos*
organ: *organon*
organic: *organikos*
other: *allos, loipos*
otherwise: *allôs*
ought to: *khrê*
outcome: *apobasis, ekbasis*
outline of the argument: *kataskeuê*
overcome: *epikratein, kratein*
overstep: *huperbainein*
own: *idios, oikeios*
own nature, of: *autophuôs*

pair: *suzugia*
parentheses, in: *en mesôi*
parenthetically: *dia mesou*
part: *meros, morion*
partake: *metekhein*
partakes, that which: *methektikos*
participation: *metalambanein,
    metalêpsis*
pass: *agein, hodeuein, meterkhesthai*
pass away: *phtheiresthai*
pass through: *dierkhesthai, diodeuein*
passage: *parodos*
pause: *hêsukhia*
perceptible: *aisthêtos*
perception: *aisthêsis*
perfect: *teleios*; in a perfect manner:
    teleiôs
perform: *poiein*
perhaps: *isôs, mêpote, takha*
period (of time): *khronos, periodos*
periodic return (of the zodiac):
    apokatastasis
periphery: *perix*
perish: *phtheiresthai, apollusthai*
perishable: *phthartos*
perishing: *phthora*
permanence: *diamonê*

perpetual: *endelekhês*
perpetual coming to be: *aeigenesia*
perpetual motion: *aeikinêsia*
persist, persistence: *diamenein,*
  hupomenein, menein,
persistent, be: *hupomenein*
pertain: *huparkhein*
piece of flesh: *sarkion*
pint: *xestiaios*
place: *khôra, topos*
place, in respect of: *kata topon*
plane: *epipedos*
planet: *planêtês*
planning: *mellôn*
plant: *phuton*
plausible: *eikos, eulogos, pithanos,*
  eikotos
plausible, more: *pithanôteros*
plausibly: *eulogon*
pleonastic sense, in a: *ek parallêlou*
poet: *poiêtês*
poetic: *poiêtikos*
point: *sêmeion*
pole: *polos*
poorly mixed, be: *duskratôs (ekhein)*
posit: *hupotithenai, lambanein,*
  protithenai, theôrein
possess, be in possession: *ekhein*
possible, be: *khôran ekhein, eneinai,*
  einai, dunasthai, endekhesthai
potentiality: *dunamis,* in potentiality,
  potentially: *dunamei*
pour: *khein*
power: *dunamis*
powerful: *epikratês*
practice: *poiein*
praise: *epainein*
precede: *phthanein, proêgeisthai;*
  preceding, what precedes: *pro,*
  prolabôn
precise: *akribês;* in a precise sense:
  akribôs
preconceive: *proepinoein*
preexist: *proüparkhein*
premiss: *hupothesis*
prescribe: *tattein*
presence: *pareinai, parousia*
present, be: *huparkhein, pareinai,*
  prosienai
prevail: *huperekhein, katakratein,*
  epikratein
prevalence: *huperokhê*
prevent: *empodizein*

previous, previously: *prolabôn*
previously assume: *proüpotithenai*
previously exist: *proüparkhein*
primary: *prôtos, prôtôs*
prime: *prôtos* (of matter); *akmê* (of
  age)
principle: *arkhê*
prior: *prôtos;* prior to that: *teôs*
prior in the order, be: *protattesthai*
privation: *sterêsis*
problem: *aporia*
proceed: *hodeuein, ienai, proagein,*
  proerkhesthai, proïenai
process: *proodos*
produce (an effect): *apotelein, dran,*
  paragein, poiein
producing form: *eidopoios*
producing: *poiêtikos*
progress, progression: *proodos*
proof: *deixis, kataskeuê*
proper: *idios, oikeios*
properly: *eikotôs*
property: *idion*
property, be a: *huparkhein*
proportion: *analogia*
propose: *prokeisthai*
prove: *apophainein, deiknunai*
provide an account, explanation:
  apodidonai
providing with boundaries: *horistikos*
proximate: *prosekhês, sunengus*
pure: *eilikrinês, katharos*
purpose: *prokeimenon, to*
purpose, be a: *prokeisthai*
put forward a defence (of something
  or somebody): *huperapologeisthai*
put in a precise way: *akribologeisthai*
put to work: *prokheirizesthai*
put together: *sunaptein*
putrefaction: *sêpein*
pyramid: *puramis*

query: *zêtein*
quick: *takhus*
quicker: *thatton*

raise: *anagein;* (a problem, objection)
  aporein, epipherein
rare: *manos, spanios*
rarefaction: *manôsis*
rarefy: *manoun*
rather: *mallon*

rational: *rhêtos* (of numbers); *logikos*
    (*zôion*)
reach: *aphikneisthai, katalambanein*
read: *anagignôskein*
real: *ontôs*
realise: *eidenai, sunoran*
reason: *aitia*
reasonable, reasonably: *eikotôs,*
    eulogos, eulogôs, eulogon
reasoning: *epikheirêma*
reasoning: *logos*
rebirth: *palingenesia*
recall: *hupomimnêskein*
receive: *katadekhesthai, lambanein*
received, be: *paradidousthai*
recently: *prosekhôs*
receptive: *methektikos*
reckoning: *logos*
recognise: *eidenai*
recourse, have to: *katapheugein*
refer: *ainittesthai, apoteinesthai,*
    kalein, legein
refutation: *elenkhos*
refute: *anaskeuazein, elenkhein*
relapse: *palindromein*
related as sth to sth, be: *epekhein*
    (*logon, taxin tinos pros ti*)
relation: *skhesis*
relax: *anhienai*
relaxing: *anesis*
remain: *hupoleipein, katamenein,*
    leipein, menein
remaining: *loipos*
remote: *porrô*
remove: *exairein*
render as a cause: *aitiasthai*
repeatedly: *pollakis*
reproach: *epitiman, memphesthai*
reproduction: *palingenesia*
resolve: *epiluein, luein*
respond: *apantan*
rest: *loipos*
rest (n.): *monê*
result: *apoteleisthai,* (from) *katantan*
    (*ek*)
retain: *apotithesthai, iskhein*
retreat (of the sun): *apokhôrêsis*
return: *apokathistasthai, epanienai*
revert: *anakamptein, hupostrephein*
revoke: *anatrepein*
revolution: *periodos*
rightly: *kalôs, orthôs*
rise: *anienai*

rule: *kubernan*
ruling (order): *hêgemonikê* (*taxis*)
run back: *palindromein*
run into a problem: *aporein*

same: *autos*
same kind, of the: *homogenês*
same time length, of the: *isokhronios*
saw: *priôn*
saw (v.): *prizein*
say in defence: *apologeisthai*
say: *legein, phanai*; say something
    definite: *diörizein*
scalene: *skalênos*
science: *epistêmê*
sculptor: *agalmatopoios*
sculpture: *plastourgêma*
season: *hôra, tropê*
see: *episkopein, horan, skopein,*
    theôrein
seed: *sperma*
seek: *zêtein*
seem: *dokein, eoikenai, phainesthai*
seldom: *spaniôs*
self: *autos*
self-movement: *autokinêsis*
self-subsistent: *authupostatos*
sense: *tropos*
sense-perception: *aisthêsis*
separate (out): *apokrinein, ekkrinein,*
    diakrinein
separating: *diakrisis, ekkrisis*
sequence: *heirmos*; in sequence:
    ephexês
set apart: *diistanai*
set down (side by side): *paratithenai*
set out: *ektithenai, kataskeuazein,*
    protithenai
set out before: *proektithenai*
set up: *anatithenai*
settle on: *prosizanein*
several: *enioi*
shape (v.): *diaplattein*
shape: *morphê*
shaping (of organs): *diaplasis*
    (*organôn*)
share in: *koinônein, lankhanein*
short saying: *rhêseidion*
shorter: *elattôn*
should: *anankê, khrêsthai*
show: *deiknunai, phainesthai*
signify: *sêmainein*
silence: *siôpan*

similar: *toioutos*
simple: *haplous*
simply, *simpliciter: haplôs*
since: *epei*
sinew: *neuron*
six ingredients, of (of a drying
    powder): *hexaeidês*
skill: *tekhnê*
slip away: *diolisthanein*
slow: *bradus*
slow digestion: *bradupepsia*
smaller: *elattôn*
so much: *epi tosouton*
so on: *palin*
soar aloft: *anatrekhein*
solution: *lusis*
some: *enioi*
sooner than the prescribed time:
    endoterô tou tetagmenou khronou
soul: *psukhê*
source of motion: *kinêtikos*
sourness: *struphnotês*
speak: *legein, phanai*
speak falsely: *pseudesthai*
special: *idios*
species: *eidos*
specific, more: *idikôteros*
specifying: *eidopoios*
sphere: *sphaira*
Sphere (Empedocles): *Sphairos*
spontaneously: *automatôs, hupo tou
    automatou*
spread out: *anateinein, paraspeirein*
spring: *ear*
stand by: *ephistanai*
start (v.): *arkhein*
start, starting point: *arkhê*
starvation: *atrophia*
state (v.): *legein, phanai, propherein*
state: *hexis*
statement: *apophansis, rhêma, rhêton*
stay: *menein*
step (of a ladder): *bathmos (tês
    klimakos)*
still: *dêpou, eti, eti te, homôs*
stone: *lithos*
straight (line): *eutheia*
strengthen: *rhônnunai*
strict sense, in a: *kuriôs*
Strife (Empedocles): *Neikos*
strive: *speudein*
strong: *iskhuros*
structural differentiation: *diorganôsis*

structure: *suntaxis*
study: *theôria*
subject: *hupokeimenon, to*
subject matter: *pragma*
subject to change: *metablêtikos,
    metablêtos*
subject to coming to be: *genêtos*
subject to passing-away: *phthartos*
subsequently: *ephexês*
subsist: *huparkhein, huphistanai,
    sunistasthai*
subsistence: *huparxis*
subsistent, be: *huphistanai*
substance: *ousia*
substrate: *hupokeimenon, to*
substrate, be: *hupokeisthai*
subsume: *sunkatatattein*
succession: *ephexês, diadokhê*
such, of such kind: *toioutos*
suffice: *arkein*
sufficient by itself: *autarkes*
sufficient: *hikanos*
sufficiently: *hikanôs*
suggest: *hupotithenai*
suitability, suitable disposition, being
    suitable: *epitêdeiotês*
suitable: *epitêdeios*
sum up: *anakephalaiousthai*
summer: *theros*
sun: *hêlios*
superior, superiority: *kreittôn*
supervene: *epiginesthai*
supply: *epipherein, paratithenai*
supply in thought: *prosupakouein*
supported by evidence, be: *pistousthai*
suppose: *hupotithenai*
suppress: *kolazein*
surely: *dêpou*
surface: *epiphaneia*
surprise: *thaumazein*
surround: *periekhein*
suspect: *hupopteuein*
sustain: *diarkein*
sweetness: *glukutês*
systematic procedure: *methodos*

take: *lambanein, theôrein*
take away: *aphairein, exairein*
take place: *prosienai*
take up: *analambanein*
taken together, be: *sullambanesthai*
taking longer time: *khroniôtera*
taking the same time as: *isokhronios*

tangible: *haptos*
task: *ergon*; be a task: *prokeisthai*
teach: *didaskein*
ten parts, of: *dekaplasiôn*
ten pints, of: *dekaxestiaios*
ten times the amount: *dekaplasios*
tendency: *rhopê*
tension: *epitasis*
tenth (part): *dekaton* (*meros*)
term: *onoma*
term (v.): *kalein*
text: *lexis*
that: *ekeinos*
theorem: *theôrêma*
there: *ekei, ekeise*
therefore: *tautêi, toinun*
thing: *pragma*
things: *ta onta*
things here, things that occupy this
   (viz. sublunary) region: *ta têide*
think: *epinoeisthai, noein, oiesthai*
this, this particular: *hode*
this is why: *dioper*
this many: *tosoutos*
three times as: *triplasios*
three-dimensional: *trikhêi diastaton*
time: *kairos, khronos*
time-interval: *khronos*
times, at different: *allote*
totally: *holôs, pantêi*
towards: *pros*
trace: *ikhnos*
transcendent: *exêirêmenos*
transform: *metaballein*
transformation: *metabolê*
transposed order, in a: *huperbatôs*
traverse: *diexerkhesthai*
treat of: *dialambanein*
treating: *didaskalia*
treatise: *pragmateia*
triple: *triplasios*
turn: *tropê*
turn (v.): *trepesthai*, (to) *apoteinesthai*
turn back, backwards: *anakamptein*
turn into fire: *ekpuroun*
turn out: *tunkhanein*
turn round: *peritrepein*
turn to air: *exaeroun*
turning back: *anakampsis*
twice, two times (the amount):
   diplasios
twofold, of two kinds: *dittos*

unalterable: *analloiôtos*
unaware, be: *agnoein*
unbroken: *adiakopos*
unchangeable: *ametablêtos*
unclear: *aphanês*
uncultured: *amousos*
undergo: *hupomenein*
undergo change: *metaballein*
underlie: *hupokeisthai*
underlying: *hupokeimenon, to*
understand: *akouein, eklambanein,*
   noein, sunoran, theôrein
understanding: *ennoia*
undivided: *adiairetos*
unequal: *anisos*
uneven: *anômalos*
unevenly: *anômalôs*
unevenness: *anômalia*
unify: *henoun*
unimpeded: *akôlutos*
uninhabitable: *aoikêtos*
unintelligible: *adianoêtos*
unite: *sunkrinein*
united, be: *koinônein*
uniting: *sunkrisis*
universal: *koinos*
universal order: *kosmos*
universal sense, in a: *holôs*
universe: *kosmos, to pan*
unmixed: *akratos*
unqualified way, in: *haplôs*
unsuitability: *anepitêdeiotês*
upwards: *anô*
usage: *khrêsis*
use: *khrêsthai, prokheirizesthai*
use additionally, an additional step,
   assumption: *proskhrêsthai*
usual: *sunêthês*

variety: *diaphora*
vein: *phleps*
very: *agan*
very (adj.): *autos*
very distant: *porrôterô*
vice: *kakia*
vice versa: *empalin, palin*
view (n.): *doxa, logos*
view: *dokein*
vigorous: *eutonos*
virgin: *parthenos*
virtue: *aretê*

wander: *planasthai*

want: *boulesthai, ethelein*
wary: *dediôs*
water: *hudôr*
watering: *ardeia*
wax: *kêros*
way: *tropos*
way of life: *diaita*
weak: *asthenês*
weaken: *asthenein*
weaker: *hêttôn*
weal: *môlôps*
weight: *barutês*
well: *eu, kalôs*
well-form (the argument) to reach its
　goal: *katorthoun*
west: *dusmai*
what, what kind: *poios*
whether: *poteron*
white: *leukos*
whiteness: *leukotês*
whole: *pas, sumpas*
whole (n.): *holon, holotês*
will be: *mellein*

winter: *kheimôn*
winter, in: *kheimônos*
withdraw: *aphistanai, apienai*
withdrawal (of the sun): *aphodos (tou
　hêliou)*
without: *ektos, khôris*
without a limit: *aperatôtos*
without beginning: *anarkhos*
without end: *ateleutêtos*
without mediation: *amesôs*
without qualification: *aneu prosthêkês*
work: *pragmateia*
work upon: *ergazesthai*
world: *kosmos*
worry: *phrontis*
worth, worthy: *axios*
write: *graphein*
wrong: *plêmmeleia*

year: *eniautos, etos*

zone (geographical): *zônê*

Greek-English Index

(Ar) after the line number indicates a quotation from Aristotle, (Pl) from Plato.

abakion, drawing board, 296,2
adiairetos, undivided, 272,31
adiakopos, unbroken, 297,24; 305,31
adianoêtos, unintelligible, 294,9
adiaphoros, making no difference, 307,14
adiaphorôs, indifferently, 36,8 ad 307,14
adiexitêtos, not traversable, 254,19; 255,24
adunaton, cannot, impossible, not possible, impossibility, 239,5.9.11; 240,18; 241,25; 242,7.16.17; 243,19; 244,17(Ar).29; 245,30; 246,1; 248,4; 250,1.3.13; 251,20.22.30; 254,19.26; 255,13.26.27; 258,5.28; 260,20; 262,1.19; 270,6; 284,16.17.22(Ar).24.25.28.29; 297,13; 300,13; 302,22; 303,8.13; 304,5.12.26.28.33-5; 305,4.7.17; 306,18; 309,11; 310,26; 311,5.11
aei, always; continual; continually; eternal; eternally, 247,29; 251,15; 254,21; 263,16-18; 272,16; 281,16.18; 283,8.9.12.13.15; 286,16; 288,1; 289,7.20; 293,3; 296,11.14.18.23.28; 297,9.26; 298,3.5.23.24; 301,16.20; 304, 34-6; 305,1.3.5.7-9.15; 310,25.28-32; 311,2-5.19.22.26; 312,4; 314,10.11
aeigenesia, perpetual coming-to-be, 290,12; 291,23; 296,15; 298,7; 299,19
aeikinêsia, perpetual motion, 289,15
aerôdês, airy, 280,9
aêr, air, 237,28; 238,4.5.31; 239,10.12.19(Ar).25-7; 240,2.3.5.9.11.12.15.17.19.20.22.

24(Ar).26.28; 241,2.4.10.11.13.27; 242,3-5.8.12.13; 243,13.14; 245,4.5.14.20.21.33.34; 246,1.5.29.30(Ar); 247,6.7.9.12-15.24.28; 248,22.23.26.29.31.33.34; 249,2.7.8.9.14.17; 250,18; 251,24.32; 252,9(Ar).20; 253,4.7; 255,9.11.24.27.28; 256,7.8.12.13; 258,8-10.20.21.25.27.29.31.34; 259,2.3.10.14.15.20; 260,16.17.19.22.27(Ar); 261,8; 262,3.11.14.17.18.21.22; 268,23; 274,9; 278,28(Ar); 279,3.4.5.7(Ar).8.10.13.14.17; 280,7; 290,3; 313,2.5.15-17
agathos, good, 264,21(Ar).24; 296,19.20
agalmatopoios, sculptor, 284,5
agan, very, 295,28
agein, lead, bring, pass, 266,17; 286,6; 293,28; 294,18
agenêtos, not generable, 314,6
agnoein, be unaware, 287,2
agnoia, ignorance, 268,28
agrupnia, insomnia, 308,27
aidios, eternal, 267,25.27; 281,12.16.18.21; 282,26.30(Ar).32; 283,1.4.12.19.24; 284,16.24; 290,9.12.25; 291,7; 296,16; 297,16-18.21; 298,1.7; 299,16.21.22.25.29; 300,1.2.7.8.26; 305,10.14.18.23; 308,5.6.11; 311,10.16.18(Ar).19.29; 312,13.19-22.24
aidiôs, eternally, 291,25; 296, 17; 299,20.26; 300,2.3.7; 305,12-14.17.28; 312,23

aidiotês, eternity, 291,9;
 296,23.27.30; 297,4; 298,4.5; 312,27
ainittesthai, hint, allude, refer,
 246,4; 248,8; 250,2; 276,26; 285,10
aisthêsis, sense perception,
 perception, 260,15; 269,30.32;
 294,28(Ar)
aisthêtos, perceptible, 243,2(Ar);
 257,27; 268,25
aitia, cause; explanation; reason,
 253,6; 264,11.12.27; 265,1.10;
 266,4; 272,18; 275,13; 280,13;
 282,12.13.18; 284,26;
 285,10.13.20.22; 286,21;
 287,5.6(Ar).13.18-21;
 288,6.11(Ar).16.20.28.33; 289,3.19;
 290,11.12.17.18.26.28;
 291,5.8.10.17.19.21; 295,11.20.23;
 296,1.7.12.14.15.18;
 299,5(Ar).7.13; 300,18; 308,27;
 309,19; 314,11
aitiasthai (med. and pass.), explain,
 make a cause, assign a causal role,
 render as a cause, make
 responsible, blame, allege as a
 cause, hold in charge, 264,2.13;
 282,3; 286,8; 287,13; 288,13;
 289,18; 295,15; 301,25
aitios, cause, explanation, 263,26.29;
 264,5(Ar)9.10; 265,4.30;
 266,8.13.16.27.28; 267,27;
 281,20-2.25.27.28; 282,6.9;
 284,2-4.10.12(Ar); 285,2.4.25;
 286,3.5.6.13.18.29;
 287,1.2.8.9.12.25.29.30;
 288,6.8.12(Ar).14.30.31.35; 289,1;
 290,11.20; 291,23; 295,22.27.32;
 297,16; 299,13.15.19.20; 301,30;
 302,10; 314,10
akinêtos, immobile, 282,8;
 299,16.21.23.29; 300,3.9.10.26
akmê, culminating point, 292,6.7;
 293,23; 294,17
akolouthein, follow, ensue, imply,
 246,8; 251,28; 269,5; 290,2; 295,31;
 302,17.22; 303,20.27; 304,2.19;
 307,4.16; 308,17.20.21.24; 309,4.13
akolouthêsis, following upon,
 consequence, 302,21; 312,7
akolouthia, logical agreement,
 307,11.13; 309,2
akolouthos, consistent, 265,15
akolouthôs, by implication, 269,3

akôlutos, unimpeded, 302,32
akouein, understand, 257,8; 293,14;
 279,1; 295,8
akrasia, bad mixture, 295,15
akratos, unmixed, 245,31
akribês, exact, precise, 248,14;
 272,29.31
akribologeisthai, put in a precise
 way, 254,21
akribôs, in a precise sense, 293,5
akros, extreme, 245,11.13-15.30;
 246,26; 247,1; 248,15.19.20;
 249,29; 250,14; 270,29;
 271,17.29.31.32.35;
 272,7.13-16.22.30; 274,24.28.31;
 275,2.11; 277,25
akrôs, in the extreme, 245,34;
 270,22-4.26.28.29.31.32.34; 271,31;
 272,2.3.9; 274,27; 302,32
akrotês, extreme; extreme degree,
 270,27; 277,17.21
alloiôsis, alteration,
 239,18(Ar).22.23; 240,4; 302,12;
 306,2
alloiôtikê (dunamis), alterative
 (power), 263,7
allos, other, different, further,
 237,7.15.20.25.29;
 238,1.4.6.18.24.28.33; 239,2(Ar);
 240,3; 241,1(Ar).3.6(Ar).8;
 242,4.27; 243,7.9.10.15;
 244,19-21.24.30;
 245,2.3.8.14.20.21; 246,3; 248,31;
 249,8.9; 250,10.15.16.18.20.25.26;
 251,25.26; 252,5.21; 253,3.31;
 254,1(Ar).3.4.6.15(Ar); 255,3;
 256,24.27; 257,23.29; 258,10-12.20;
 259,35; 263,13; 264,1.13; 266,28;
 267,20; 268,2.5.33; 269,10.21;
 270,7.9; 271,31; 272,17; 273,20.26;
 274,7.31; 275,27.28; 276,4; 277,29;
 278,27(Ar).28; 280,27-9; 281,3;
 282,2.8.11.12; 285,15.17(Pl);
 286,13.23(Ar); 287,23.24;
 289,31.32; 290,7; 291,3; 293,30;
 294,1.19.20.26; 296,5.8.15.16.29;
 297,20; 299,12; 302,7; 308,12.23;
 310,16; 312,21.26
allôs, besides, otherwise, in a
 different way, except, on different
 grounds, 259,4; 262,5; 263,20;
 265,7; 267,9(Ar); 275,5; 284,27;

305,18; 312,13; *kai allôs*, in
particular, 268,27
allote, at different times, 263,13;
291,3
alogos, irrational, 283,6
ameinôn, better, 241,26; 257,7
amelei, and indeed, 287,30
amesôs, without mediation,
247,8.12.15
ametablêtos, unchangeable, 237,26;
238,10.13.15.17.22.23.27; 239,2.17;
241,2; 243,22.24; 244,18.20.27;
257,24.28.30; 258,3.5.16;
259,8.12.26.31.34; 260,25;
261,18.19.26(Ar); 262,1.4.24.28.30;
265,15; 268,27; 269,7.12.14; 270,6;
273,23.27(Ar); 274,15; 278,7;
297,17; 298,21.26
ametria, lack of measure, 295,15
amousos, uncultured, 268,23
ampelos, grapevine, 263,17
anaballesthai, bring up, 248,7
anagein, raise, 299,15
anagignôskein, read, 307,25
anairein, destroy, 246,21; 250,33;
253,19.23; 257,16.18; 266,24;
eliminate, 309,21.31
anaisthêtos, imperceptible, 244,14
anakamptein, turn back, turn
backwards, revert, revert back,
240,14; 247,23 (v. ad 24); 250,
14.17; 251,36; 252,9; 257,10; turn
backwards, 305,16; 310,13 (v. ad
12); 311,7;
313,3(Ar).12.15.18.23.25.29
anakampsis, turning back,
305,10.13; 313,16.17.24.26.31; ad
247,24; 310,9
anakephalaiousthai, sum up, 311,8
anakukleisthai, circle back, 247,30;
250,14; 298,16; 310,15
anakuklêsis, circular recurrence,
305,11.28.32; 310,13.16; 312,24 ad
248,3
analambanein, take up, 243,29;
281,7
analloiôtos, unalterable, 299,21;
300,4
analogein, bear analogy, 242,19
analogia, proportion, 258,14.32.34;
259,1.28; 261,7.13.15.23.27(Ar);
262,8
anankaios, necessary, necessity, of

necessity, necessarily, 240,25.28;
248,5; 251,23.25; 284,27;
303,18.22.25.26.29-31.33-5;
304,5-8.11.13.16-18.24.28.31;
305,21.22.31; 306,8.16.21.22.27;
307,1.8.22; 308,3.6.8.10-12.15.17;
309,1.7.10.12.14.15.18.31;
310,19.20.23.26; 311,16.19.23.28;
312,3.11.15.18; 313,6.14; rigorous,
246,19
anankaiôs, necessarily; with
necessity; have to, be necessary to,
279,18; 293,14; 303,19; 312,4.11
anankê, necessary, must, have to,
should, necessarily, is to be,
inevitable, 237,22; 238,9; 239,1.2;
240,1.29; 242,27; 243,5.17.27(Ar);
244,2.9(Ar); 245,35; 249,12.34;
251,2.4.8(Ar).33; 252,5.10;
253,2.13; 254,22; 255,29(Ar);
257,28; 258,7; 259,17.22.23;
260,12(Ar); 264,1; 273,2(Ar); 277,8;
278,24; 279,10.12; 280,7; 289,3;
290,28; 299,11(Ar).22.25.27.30;
300,1.7.19.22(Ar).28; 302,16.17.27;
303,3; 306,24(Ar).26(Ar);
307,2-4.10(Ar).12.15(Ar).18.
19-21(Ar)25.26; 308,30(Ar);
309,5.6; 310,3.25(Ar).28;
311,7(Ar).9.15.17(Ar);
312,8(Ar).9(Ar)
anaplêroun, fill up, 297, 14.19.22
anarmostos, inappropriateness,
295,16; inappropriate, 296,2
anartan, depend, 299,16
anarkhos, having no beginning,
without beginning, 304,20; 309,25
anaskeuazein, refute, 247,18
anateinein, spread out, 259,17
anathumiasis, exhalation, 278,12
anatithenai, set up, 291,20; assign,
292,20
anatolê, *anatolai*, east, 289,10.11;
299,2.3
anatrepein, revoke, 259,33
anatrekhein, soar aloft, 299,18
aneideos, formless, 243,20; 244,15;
245,7; 275,30; 276,8; 283,14
anelenktos, irrefutable, 260,1; 309,23
anepistêmôn, ignorant, 286,14.16
anepitêdeiotês, unsuitability,
295,16; 296,3
anesis, relaxing, 262,6.23

anêr, man, 297,2
anhienai, relax, 259,14.16.17
anienai, rise, 278,13
anisos, unequal, 262,20; 291,29(Ar)
anô, upwards, above, 256,6;
    266,10.11.15; 267,2(Ar).6.10(Ar);
    276,13; 282,23; 298,20.25
anôthen, above, 255,30(Ar); 256,2;
    295,17
anômalia, unevenness, 289,4.6.16;
    291,1.8.26; 292,1; 296,1
anomalos, uneven, 289, 12;
    291,7.23.29.(Ar).31.33
anômalôs, unevenly, 289,21
anthrôpeios, of man, 294,21
anthrôpinos, human, 293,23
anthrôpos, man, human being,
    263,17; 271,20; 293,23; 294,20;
    296,32; 310,3.4.5.7.8; 313,3(Ar); cf.
    294,14; 310,5
antidiairein, distinguish by
    dichotomy; *antidiairoumenon*,
    the opposite member of dichotomy,
    239,14
antidiastolê, contrast, 278,11
antithesis, opposition, 240,1;
    248,24.31.34; 249,11.13; 250,22;
    251,30; 252,1.23.28.32
antikamptein and *antikampsis*,
    see ad 247,24; 310,9.10.12
antikuklêsis, 248,3 v. ad loc.
antilegein, argue against, 286,10
antiparathesis, comparison, 259,6;
    260,8
antipiptein, conflict, be in conflict,
    280,2; 308,13
antirrhêsis, counterargument, 243,4
antistoikhos, corresponding opposite
    (in *sustoikhia*), 260,6
antistrephein, convert, be
    convertible, 303,35; 307,6; 308,25;
    309,2.4; 311,23; 313,6.14
antistrophê, conversion, 240,25;
    307,14.23; 312,3.6
antitithenai, compare, 298,4
aoikêtos, uninhabitable, 291,15;
    293,3
apagein, move away, 290,13; 292,1
apathês, not subject to affection,
    263,20
apantan, respond, 245,10
apartasthai, be dependent, 299,27
apatan, deceive, 286,20

apeiros, infinite, 247,29.35; 248,8;
    249,34; 250,3.9.27.29.32;
    251,2.3.9.18.19.21;
    254,7(Ar).9.10.11.13.17.18.23.25;
    255,1.9.11.14.22.24.26; 256,32.33;
    257,2.4; 304,14.15.17.26; 305,20;
    309,10.17.21.22.24; 310,20.26;
    311,12.14; 312,1; *apeiron, to*,
    infinity, 247,21(Ar).25.26.32.34;
    248,1.2.6; 249,31.33;
    250,2.5.26.28.30; 254,19.20;
    255,5.6.13.24; 257,3;
    304,19.23.25.26.28.29.31; 308,29;
    309,14.17.21.23.24.25; 311,20.21;
    312,1; 309,10
aperatôtos, without a limit, 304,20;
    309,25
aphairein, take away, 266,28
aphanês, unclear, 258,20
aphikneisthai, arrive, reach,
    255,1.3.5; 293,18; 294,16
aphistanai, withdraw, be distant
    from; move away, 266,17; 289,8;
    291,4.28; 296,26.28; 297,14
aphodos (tou hêliou), withdrawal
    (of the sun), 292,19; 299,1
aphoran, look at; have in mind,
    286,8.29
aphorizein, define, mark off, 237,16;
    290,5
apienai, withdraw, move away
    (intr.), 289,8; 290,4; 291,26; 295,1
aplanês, fixed (of stars),
    289,10.17.23; 291,5.10.18; 296,5;
    299,1; 312,22
apoballein, lose, 240,15; 241,20;
    283,18.19.20
apobasis, outcome; *meta apobasin*,
    after the fact, 304,8
apobolê, loss, 285,28; 286,4
apodeiknunai, demonstrate, give a
    demonstration, 249,21; 258,5;
    265,24.28; 308,9; 312,16.17
apodeixis, demonstration, 237,12;
    258,20; 278,18
apodekhesthai, accept, commend,
    248,2; 281,27
apodidonai, give, provide an
    account, explanation; attribute;
    account for; explain, 263,9(Ar);
    264,2; 272,18; 273,22; 282,12;
    285,20; 287,16(Ar); 292,13; 296,18;
    301,31

253,17.21.22.26.30.31;
255,18.23.31; 256,12; 257,24.29.33;
258,2.15; 260,15; 262,5.15.29;
263,5; 266,6.8.9; 270,6; 272,12;
278,5.9.21.25; 279,9; 282,14;
288,13; 290,8.15.17.18.22.24.25;
291,21; 299,6.7.19;
300,7.10.12.15.25.28; 302,23;
304,11.32; 305,19.30; 309,1.10;
310,18.27; 311,11.25; 312,19;
313,18.19; *deixas*, having proved
(at the opening after lemma),
237,5; 243,3; 244,18; 249,33;
256,11; 257,23; 262,28; 279,9;
302,14; 310,26; 311,28; 312,15;
314,3

dein, must, need, be necessary, have
to, 241,22; 244,27; 247,20.32.33;
254,4.15(Ar).17.25; 255,23.26;
261,24; 264,17; 265,23; 279,14;
284,1.9; 285,8; 289,2; 292,10;
313,2(Ar).3(Ar)

dein, bind, bound, 278,26; 283,28(Ar)

deixis, proof, 248,21; 249,18; 257,13

dekaxestiaios, ten pints of,
258,29.31; 259,10

dekaplasiôn, ten times the amount,
260,22; 262,2

dekaplasios, ten parts of, 259,13;
261,8

dekaton (meros), to, one tenth
(part), 259,14; 260,23; 261,9

dêlôtikos, indicating, 261,10

dêmiourgein, create, 297,23

dêmiourgia, creation, 297,21

dêmiourgikos, creative, 286,2.4.6

dêmiourgos, Maker, 286,9

dêpou, surely, still, 240,10; 248,24;
265,5

diadekhesthai, follow upon, 289,24

diadidraskein, escape, 279,5

diadokhê, succession, 297,3.21;
300,13; 310,2.5.18.21; 313,27

diairein, distinguish, 272,32; 288,
16; 297,9

diairesis, division, 237,14.21;
238,16.17; 239,16; 244,23; 268,33;
304,14

diaita, way of life, 295, 23.27

diakhôrizein, dissociate, 265,22

diakrinein, separate (out), dissolve,
disintegrate, 264,17.28;

265,6.13.21; 266,13; 267,1.4.5.23;
268,6; 287,22; 298,19.24

diakrisis, disintegration, separation,
separating, 264,5.9.16.19;
265,4.8.9; 266,13; 268,4

diakritikos, causing to disintegrate,
265,1

dialambanein, treat of; interrupt,
285,2; 305,17

dialegesthai (pros tina), discuss,
criticise, 237,10.11; 299,14

dialeimma, interval, 268,10

dialeipein, fail (with partic.),
305,30; have intervals, 314,19

dialuein, dissolve, 269,23; (pass.)
295,17

diamenein, persist, 298,1; 313,25;
314,10.20; persistence, 284,11

diamonê, permanence, 281,22;
292,31

diaplasis (organôn), shaping (of
organs), 263,24

dianoia, idea, 277,5

diapherein, differ, 248,27.29;
252,21; 253,16.33; 261,14; 262,3;
281,4; 311,26(Ar); 312,6

diaphora, difference, variety,
246,13; 249,14; 272,16.18.32;
275,12; 276,2.13.14.25;
283,6.11.17; 291,6; 303,7

diaphoros, different, differentiated,
246,15; 253,1; 262,19; 272,19;
291,1; 300,12; 305,24.27

diaplattein, shape, 296,9

diarthroun, articulate, 281,24

diarkein, sustain, 292,32; 295,18

diastasis, dimension, 263,8; 296,25

diastatos, possessed of dimension,
297,18; *trikhêi diastaton*,
three-dimensional, 246,10; 259,22

diastêma, distance, 255,2.6;
291,29(Ar); 304,26

diathesis, disposition, 292,18

didaskalia, treating, 269,2

didaskein, teach, explain, 271,23;
288,18; 291,31

didonai, give, grant, 249,11; 252,28;
256,16; 267,3.15; 314,16

diexerkhesthai, go through,
traverse, deal with, 250,1;
254,15(Ar).18.23.25; 255,24; 290,3;
304,26

diexienai, go through, 255,11; 257,13

dierkhesthai, pass through, 247,12

diistanai, make distant, set apart, 248,28; 265,22; 291,32

diodeuein, pass through, 247,15

diolisthanein, slip away, 279,6

dioper, this is why, 239,7; 247,33

diorganôsis, structural differentiation, 263,23

diorizein, define, give definition, definitive account, determine, distinguish, make distinctions, say something definite, deal with, 237,12; 265,20.23; 267,15; 272,10; 275,5.8; 288,11(Ar); 294,13(Ar).19; 301,1(Ar)

diplasios (-ôn), double, twice (the amount), 250,29.30; 257,3; 275,17

diplasiôs, two times (the amount), 275,16

diplous, double, 298,27.28; 299,1

dittos, of two kinds, twofold, 303,25; 308,31

dittôs, in two ways, 295,14; 297,6

dikhôs, in two ways, 302,23; 304,36

dokein, seem, appear, be an opinion, view; *dokei tini*, someone believes, holds that, 238,14.31(Ar); 239,19(Ar); 240,25; 246,19.29(Ar); 254,20; 255,21; 269,28.30; 273,1(Ar); 278,29; 280,2; 286,29; 292,1; 300,4; 308,13; 309,20

doxa, opinion, view, belief, doctrine, 237,9.13; 238,19; 241,10; 248,14; 257,31.32; 258,2; 259,36; 270,16.17; 274,21; 282,4; 286,21; 287,26

dran, act, produce an effect, 259,23.32; 260,7; 277,14; 282,16; 292,29

drastikos, active, 287,28

dunamis, power, capacity, potentiality, 258,8; 259, 9.11.14-16.19.21.25.29.32; 260,1; 261,3.6.7.11.13.15.27(Ar); 262,1.3.5.7.8.16.19.31; 263,7; 264,11; 271,11.12; 272,27; 277,16.29; 279,20.28; 282,12; 287,16(Ar).19.21; 283,19.20; 286,23(Ar); 288,7; 298,9(Ar).10.12; 305,14; 308,20; *dunamei*, potentially, in potentiality, 259,18; 270,13.15.25.33; 271,1-4.7.8.14.16.19.20.22;

272,4.5.9.22.23; 274,26.30.32; 275,1.3.6.7.9(Ar).13.20.31; 276,1.2.4.10.12.14.16.18.20.26.28; 277,7.8; 281,15.16; 283,8.9.15.18.22.23.25; 284,14; 299,8.9; 300,24.27

dunasthai, can, be possible, be able, be empowered, possibly, 237,14.30; 238,1.2.12; 239,7.16; 241,2.7.9; 243,3.7.10; 244,18.21.26; 245,3.9.13.15; 246,14; 247,26; 248,6; 249,1; 250,31.33; 251,6.15; 255,15.16; 257,23; 258,15.22.26; 259,3.4.12.17.27.30.31; 260,14; 261,2(Ar).17; 262,3.9.13; 269,9.13.17.22.23; 271,27; 273,12.28; 274,7.9.10; 275,26; 276,18; 278,25; 284,12(Ar).15.19.20.29; 288,14.35; 294,22.24; 296,3.23.26.28; 299,10; 302,25.29.31-2; 303,1.4.8.12.15.17; 304,20.25; 308,10; 309,22.25; 310,27; 311,12

duskratôs (ekhein), (be) poorly mixed, 295,28

dusmai, hai, west, 289,10.11; 299,2

ean, if, 248,16; 262,21; 276,19; 285,14(Pl); 295,24

ear, spring, 303,2

edaphos, ground, 310,13

êdê, already, by the same token, 253,2.6.21; 271,23; 288,15.17.30.31; 290,10.19; 310,24; 311,25

edêdesthai, eat, 308,20.26

ei, if (with subjunctive), 238,9; 245,16; 250,7; 250,13; 252,9; 252,28; 254,3; 256,9.16; 267,3; 274,2; 280,20; 283,23; 305,3.4; 305,4; elliptice *ei kai mê*, 300,24

eidenai, know, recognise, realise, 244,25; 250,9; 253,21; 271,25; 272,25; 281,10; 283,15; 289,9; 291,10; 303,25; 308,7; 309,20

eidopoiein, make to have a form, give form, endow with form, 239,22-3; 244,7; 275,5.23; 276,3; 281,17.30

eidopoios, producing form, specifying, 278,1; 279,20

eidos, form, kind, species, Form, 242,19-21; 246,13; 263,22;

10.12.17; 249,5.24.27; 250,1.8;
253,4.5.12-14.28; 254,5.18; 255,14;
256,4.5.29.33; 257,2.4.5.14;
258,18.20; 259,1.3.4.14.34;
260,7.25; 261,15; 262,16; 263,22;
265,5; 266,20; 267,6.21.24;
268,1.21.22; 269,11.33;
271,4.5.8.11.12.22; 272,6.32;
273,5.10.14(Ar); 274,10; 275,12.14;
276,15.16; 279,24.26; 281,18.19;
282,10; 283,6.9.12.13.15.18;
284,3.27; 285,15.17(Pl).26;
287,3.11.24; 288,4.24; 289,7.13;
291,7.22-4; 292,10.23; 293,3.18.27;
294,12(Ar); 295,14.20.28; 296,1;
297,4.9.19.21.28; 298,3; 299,28;
301,22.26-7; 302,7.9.19.21-2;
303,7.9-12.14.18; 304,6-8.26;
305,14.22; 306,9.15.17.19-22;
307,9(Ar).17.22; 308,6.8.12.16.17;
309,1.13.29; 310,23;
311,2.9.10.19.23.29; 312,1.2.11;
313,8.15.24.32
ekkrinai, separate out,
    269,18.19.21.26.28-9; 273,11; 278,8
ekkrisis, separation, 269,19
eklambanein, understand, 255,22
ekpuroun, turn into fire, 269,22
ekteinein, extend, 258,26; 260,26
ektithenai, set out, expound,
    explain, 237,12; 244,22; 248,15;
    269,12; 273,22; 274,13; 282,18
ektos (with genitive), without, 242,26
elattôn, smaller, lesser, less, (pl.)
    fewer, (of time) shorter, 238,7;
    261,5.11; 262,5.14.22; 272,25;
    277,1; 292,27.31; 295,6(Ar).10 etc.
elenkhein, refute, 237,10.14;
    238,18.19.26-7.32; 239,16; 241,11;
    250,4; 257,30; 258,2; 268,33; 278,6;
    280,3; 282,2; 286,22
elenkhos, refutation, 238,29; 246,20;
    248,14.16; 257,32; 286,20
elephas, elephant, 294,8
ellipôs, elliptically, 300,4
embruon, embryo, 271,21; 297,1.2;
    310,8
empalin, vice versa, in the opposite
    direction, for the converse case,
    240,14; 261,18; 269,4; 289,10;
    290,20; 299,2; 307,3
emperiekhein, embrace, 237,22
empodizein, prevent, 295,29

empodion, impediment, 271,9
empodôn, to, that which impedes,
    284,5
emprosthen (adv.), first, 249,32(Ar)
empsukhos, animate, 263,22
enallagê tôn horôn, change of
    seasons, 312,27
enapotithesthai, bestow, 295,30
enargeia, manifest facts, 305,12
enargôs, clearly, 258,18; 269,20
endelekhês, perpetual (Ar), 297,15.23
endekhesthai, can, be possible, be
    capable of; be contingent,
    242,23(Ar); 274,3; 279,18; 284,26;
    302,18-20.28.31;
    303,5.14.18.20.22.32; 305,5;
    306,9.13(Ar).15.17.19.20.23;
    309,4.24; 310,4.30; 311,4;
    314,2(Ar).8
endekhomenôs, contingently,
    303,10.14.16; 309,1
*endoterô tou tetagmenou
    khronou*, sooner than the
    prescribed time, 294,23.26
engizein, draw near, approach,
    289,7; 291,4
engus, close, near, 271,24; 296,22;
    297,25(Ar); 298,2.6
eneinai, be possible, 246,20
energeia, actuality, activity, 283,20;
    295,29; *energeiâi*, in actuality,
    250,28; 270,13.15.31; 273,12;
    274,26.29; 276,4.24; 281,17;
    283,8.13; 287,10; 299,8.9
energein, act, be in action, actualise,
    271,13.14; 282,15; 296,6
eniausiaios, annual, 305,30
eniautos, year, 289,26; 291,13; *ho
    megas*, the Big Year, 314,13
enios, some, several, 254,23; 255,23;
    282,22(Ar).23; 295,12; 302,19.21;
    306,6(Ar).9.10.13(Ar); 313,20.21;
    enioi, some, 238,31(Ar); 278,12
enkalein, object, 287,19
enklisis, obliquity, 291,27
ennoia, concept, notion,
    understanding, 244,26; 246,2;
    281,27
enstasis, objection, 273,24
entautha, here, 241,9; 277,23;
    279,26; 281,19; 283,2.21.24.29;
    287,21; 292,5; 295,3.10; 299,18

entelekheia, actuality, 270,29.33; 271,2

enteuthen, from this, from the following; at this point, 252,1; 253,30; 271,17; 288,18.26; 297,15

entha, where, at which point, including, 281,27; 290,11; 304,18

enthen, therefore, 277,18

entheôreisthai, be considered to be present in, 241,19

enuparkhein, be inherent, exist in, 273,12; 278,19(Ar)

eoikenai, seem, 268,2; 279,29(Ar)

epagein, add, draw (conclusion), 262,15 (*epagagôn*); 275,25; 284,26; 297,19; 302,4; 311,8

epainein, praise, 264,22(Ar).30; 266,3

epainetos, to be praised, 265,12

epakolouthein, follow, 295,1

epanienai, return, 269,2; 272,12

epanô, above, 256,8.10.16; 257,17

epei, if, since, 260,10; 266,1(Ar); 273,4; 278,6; 286,15; 288,34; 290,8(Ar).22(Ar); 302,11(Ar); 306,1; 311,1; since otherwise, 244,27; 249,8; 259,23; 282,21

epexerkhesthai, go over, 268,32

epeteios, annual, 292,9; 295,4

epekhein (logon, taxin tinos pros ti), be related as sth to sth, 237,27.29; 238,28; 239,3; 243,7; 247,13; 288,8.15; 290,6; 295,26

ephaptesthai, apply oneself to, 237,7

ephexês, next, following, subsequently, what follows (upon), in a succession, immediately afterwards, in sequence, adjacent, one after another, 239,4.11.15; 243,21; 246,20; 247,2.17.29; 248,7.9.20; 250,6.15.17.25.27.35; 251,35; 253,9.20.25.27; 254,24; 255,8.17-19.27; 256,19; 257,12.19.25; 273,13; 275,8.18; 278,25; 281,5; 286,21; 288,33; 298,7; 301,16.20.25; succession, 302,12(Ar).15; 304,11; 306,11; 308,9; 309,27.29

ephêkein, come to, 289,16

ephiesthai, desire, 296,19-22.28

ephistanai, attend to, heed, stand by, take note, pay due attention, 252,22; 267,4.7.13; 272,18; 302,2

epiginesthai, supervene, 274,31; 285,6

epideiknunai, manifest, 295,29

epididonai, increase, 263,8

epikheirêma, reasoning, 309,20

epikratein, prevail; overcome, 268,11; 269,24

epikratês, powerful, 277,8

epileipein, interrupt, 289,14.15.20; 296,17

epiluein, resolve, 270,16.17; 298,20; 313,10

epimixia, admixture, 245,31

epinoeisthai, think, conceive of, 294,5; 308,10

epinoia, concept, consideration, 284,18; 286,6; 289,24

epipan, by and large, 290,1

epipedos, plane, 265,26

epiphaneia, surface, 280,26

epipherein, add, supply, make an addition, raise (a problem), bring up, charge, 242,16; 267,20; 273,13; 276,1; 278,18; 298,17; 313,22

epiprostithenai, add, 263,1

epirrhein, flow, 288,24

episêmainesthai, mark, add an explanation; add by way of explanation, 275,12; 276,19; 312,4

episkopein, examine, see, 250,35; 259,8

epistasis, attention, 271,25

epistatein, measure, 282,15

epistêmê, knowledge, science, 265,24; 268,24; 271,8; 286,11.12.15.26

epistêmôn, knowledgeable, 286,13.16

epitasis, tension, 262,6.23

epitêdeios, suitable, 283,27; 284,2.4

epitêdeiotês, suitability, being suitable, suitable disposition, 271,17; 284,7; 302,32

epiteinesthai, intensify, 259,15-17

epitelein, complete, bring to completion, 292,15; 312,21

epitiman, reproach, 281,26

epitithenai, bestow, impose, 284,6; 291,11 ad 78,11

ergazesthai, work upon, 284,4

ergon, task, 265,24

eskhatos, extreme, last, 247,17.20(Ar).22-4.31;

300,13; 302,15.18.19; 303,9.24;
304,33-7; 305,1-3.12.28-30;
307,2.17; 309,3.21.28;
310,3.18.21.28-9; 312,6.8(Ar);
314,17; **ginomenos**, (a thing) that
comes to be, 240,4; 247,29;
254,17.22; 263, 15.19; 271,21;
275,30(Ar); 276,6.11.29; 277,24;
281,9; 284,1; 285,20.26; 286,3;
287,15.24; 288,4.20.29.31; 289,30;
290,18.19; 294,14;
302,12-13(Ar).16.18; 303,9.29;
305,12.30; 306,8.11; 308,5; 309,22;
310,28-9.32; 311,1; 312,11;
313,2.19
glukutês, sweetness, 259,33; 260,4;
277,29
grammatikos, literate, 271,22;
303,16
graphein, write, 258,4; 295,14
gumnazein, exercise, expound,
explain, deal with (see n. 16),
239,4; 244,22; 248,7; 250,9; 253,18

hamartanein, fault, 296,3
hapas, all, every, everything, 256,17;
260,13(Ar); 268,32; 271,18;
281,1(Ar).24; 282,19(Ar).20;
285,8(Ar); 297,13
haplous, simple, 238,32; 244,3;
245,27.29.30; 249,12; 264,11;
270,13; 271,1; 273,19-21;
275,4.7.18.20.21.31;
276,1.4-6.10.12.15.17.20.28;
277,21; 279,32; 280,1.19;
281,21(Ar); 282,20.21; 298,18
haplôs, simply, generally, general, in
a general way, absolutely, in an
unqualified way, simpliciter,
238,11; 246,10; 249,29; 256,8;
265,17(Ar).21; 266,22; 267,16;
271,28.35; 272,8; 274,24-6; 275,8;
285,16(Pl); 289,26.31;
303,26.31.34;
304,5.11.13.16-18.21.28.31.33;
305,20.22; 306,3; 307,1.5.8.15;
308,3.9.30(Ar).31;
309,7.9.12.15.18; 310,3.26;
311,6(Ar); 312,18
haptos, tangible, 240,1
harmozein, fit, 270,14
hêgemonikê (*taxis*), ruling (order),
290,6

heirmos, sequence, 297,27
hekateros, either of the two, each of
the two, either, each, both, 241,15;
242,8; 246,34; 247,2.3.34; 249,8;
256,5.9.11.15; 258,21.26; 259,5.18;
260,21; 267,28; 271,3; 273,7;
274,8.32; 275,2.6; 276,6;
277,3.15.17; 281,15; 289,19;
291,24; 292,18; 293,5.6; 298,4;
311,4
hêkein, apply (of arguments), 243,14;
260,9
hêlios, the sun, 288,12.22;
289,12.25.28; 290,1.4.5.13;
291,25.32.33; 292,8.11.16.17.19-21;
293,2-4.8.32; 295,1.2; 296,5;
303,11; 304,37; 305,29; 310,15;
312,23; 313,29; 314,20
hêmera, day, 288,23.26; 291,12
hêmeronuktion, day-and-night,
289,27
hêmiolios, half, 275,17
hênika, when, as long as (with
indic.), 245,27; 276,34; (with
subjunctive), 257,4; 277,14; 283,27
heneka, for the sake of, 285,1(Ar).3;
309,21
henoun, unify, 279,4
hepesthai, follow, be a consequence,
be implied, 237,14; 248,7; 252,24;
253,8; 255,31; 256,19; 265,14;
273,23.27; 299,1; 300,25; 302,26;
304,4; 307,24; 308,3.7.15.23.27;
309,26; 312,5
hêsukhia, pause, 305,16
heterogenês, of different kinds,
differing in kind, 259,29.32; 260,8;
261,19; 262,7
hêttôn, less, weaker, 262,24;
272,23.33; 274,19(Ar).23; *ouden
hêtton*, nonetheless, 283,5
heuriskein, find, 298,17
hexaeidês, of six ingredients (of a
drying powder), 269,34
hexis, state, acquired disposition,
disposition, 242,17; 271,9.11.17;
286,25
hikanos, sufficient, adequate,
265,17(Ar) 281,31; 283,26(Ar);
284,1.9; 285,22(Ar)
hikanôs, sufficiently, 259,7
hippokentauros, centaur, 284,25
(see n. ad loc.)

hode, this, one, given, this particular, some particular, 247,4; 249,30; 258,13; 259,29; 261,16.20(Ar); 262,2; 269,15; 274,2.3.6; 284,21; 298,23; 302,13(Ar); 303,18; 304,30; 309,28; *ta têide*, things here, things that occupy this (viz. sublunary) region, 286,9; 288,25; 289,20

hodeuein, pass, proceed, 238,6; 245,1; 292,28; *epi ti*, make one's way to, 293,17

holon, *to*, a whole, 258,25; 259,2; 271,6; 279,27; the whole, 291,17(Ar).18; 297,11.14.20.23

holotês, a whole, 258,17.32; 259,3

holôs, totally, completely, generally, in general, at all, in a universal sense, 246,14; 250,32; 259,32; 288,7; 292,32; 300,8; 302,12(Ar); 304,22.24; 305,21; 306,2(Ar).13(Ar); 309,24; 311,22

homogenês, of the same kind, 262,15; 282,32; 283,3.5.7.24

homoiomerês, homoiomerous, homoiomer, 264,1; 270,1-5.9

homoiotês, likeness, 261,14; 286,9

homotimos, of equal importance, 243,5

homotimôs, in equal degree, 249,29

homou, likewise, 279,16

homônumôs, in a homonymous sense, 262,31

homôs, nonetheless, still, nevertheless, 251,5; 252,4; 271,5; 274,3.7; 283,7; 286,12; 294,21; 309,29

hopoiosoun, any, 255,5

hôra, season, 288,21; 312,24.25.27

horan, see, 254,12; 258,29; 269,20; 271,13; 280,20; 288,22; 295,1; 302,12(Ar); 308,14

horizein, define, 250,31; 254,12; 265,25; 287,2

horistikos, providing with boundaries, 279,1

hormê, impulse, 277,14

horos, boundary, 280,21.23.24.26.27

hosakis, as many times as, 279,27

hosos, as many as, 237,13.14; 238,11; 242,4; 244,1.2; 246,12.19; 246,12; 254,5.18; 259,33; 261,2(Ar).16; 269,2.4.7; 273,1(Ar).8.10;

278,3(Ar).10.16; 279,11; 281,10.12; 282,5.8; 286,28; 288,29; 293,18.30; 294,9; 296,25; 309,30; 312,21; 313,28.30; (cf. 309,30)

hugeia, health, 281,32.35; 286,10-12

hugiainein, become healthy, 282,1; 286,14.16

hugiazein, heal, 281,32

hugros, moist, 237,18; 240,13.20.30; 242,6.11-13; 244,5; 245,33-4; 248,34-5; 249,3.13.15.26-7; 251,24.26.31; 252,12.22; 253,5; 259,20; 269,23; 270,30-4; 275,24; 277,10; 278,29; 279,15.20; 278,12; 298,13

hugrotês, moisture, 242,4.5; 249,9; 253,5; 277,27; 279,16

hudôr, water, 238,4; 241,11; 243,13; 245,4; 247,11.16; 248,26-7; 249,3.6.13; 252,20; 258,30.34; 259,3; 260,17.23; 263,1; 268,18; 271,4; 275,23; 278,24.26; 279,2.8(Ar).12.13.18.27; 280,2.3.5; 299,9; 308,22; 313,5.7.17

hulê, matter, 237,11.17.19.27.29.30; 238,2.10.23-4.28.30(Ar).33; 239,3.6.10.17.20; 241,5.8.9; 243,3.6-9.11.12.15.20-2; 244,12; 245,7; 246,7.9.11.12.14.15.18; 258,24.26.31; 259,4.13.16.18.22; 262,6.20; 263,5; 265,9; 269,3.4.7; 270,12.14.30; 271,2.3.5.10.13; 273,3; 274,16-18.25.27; 274,30; 275,1.2.4.6.29(Ar).30(Ar); 276,2.8.11.12.14.20.28; 280,11(Ar).16.18; 281,13.15; 282,3.9.10.16.31(Ar); 283,1.2.8.11.13.16.17.21.24.27; 284,2.4.6.9.12(Ar).14; 285,6; 286,17(Ar).19.21.27(Ar).28; 287,3.5.18; 288,8.9.13.14.17; 295,16.19.23.26.32; 296,1.3; 299,8; 314,10.12.22

hulikos, material, 238,18; 243,16; 281,23; 287,13; 295,21; 296,14.15

huparkhein, be, be present, belong, subsist, exist, be a property, pertain, 238,18; 239,27; 240,23(Ar); 241,25; 242,1.4-6.17.18.27.28; 244,19; 245,32; 246,15; 250,21; 251,5.8; 252,3.16(Ar).19.20.24; 253,2.3.11.23.26-8.31.33;

254,2(Ar).11.12; 255,29(Ar);
256,16.18.23; 257,1; 258,16.18;
260,1.2.3.6.12(Ar); 268,7; 270,5.28;
276,4.25; 278,16.24; 279,4.9;
280,26.27; 281,31; 283,18; 286,1;
288,30; 290,24; 291,12; 297,13;
301,18.19.21; 302,14; 303,35;
304,12.13.16.17.31; 304,21;
305,11.21.28.33; 307,5; 309,8.11;
310,19; 311,15.28.29; 312,16.18-20;
313,12
huparxis, subsistence, existence,
284,18; 297,27; 301,27
hupekkauma, inflammable
substance, 260,18
huperapologeisthai, put forward a
defence (viz. on behalf of
something or somebody), 269,34
(cf. *apologeisthai huper tinos*
286,2)
huperbainein, overstep,
294,22.24.27
huperbatôs, in a transposed order,
307,25
huperbolê, excess, 277,4
huperekhein, be in excess, prevail,
275,14; 277,1
huperokhê, prevalence, excess,
258,33; 272,14; 274,28.31;
275,15.16; 276,4
hupertithenai, defer, 268,29
hupodekhesthai, see n. 255 ad
281,27
hupokatienai, go down;
hupokatiôn, further on, 281,29
hupokatô, below, 256,8.17.24
hupokeimenon, to, the underlying
(body, substrate); substrate;
subject, 241,25; 246,9.11;
260,21.22.24.26; 261,4; 262,23;
265,7; 269,5; 273,4.5.17.19.21;
275,25; 282,17; 283,2.3.22;
284,14.20; 288,1
hupokeisthai, underlie, be assumed,
be an assumption, be according to
the assumption(s), be a substrate;
(med.) suppose, lay down as
premiss, posit, 237,19.20;
238,10.23.24; 239,21.25; 240,17.25;
241,3; 244,13.29; 248,21.32;
249,2.33; 250,17.20; 251,30.33;
252,13; 258,24; 259,13.16; 261,7;

262,16.17.20; 268,7; 269,3; 281,13;
287,24; 290,22(Ar); 309,9.10
hupokleptein, cheat, 296,29
hupoleipein, remain; fail, 257,25.30;
270,12; 293,22; 296,12(Ar); 312,2
hupomenein, persist, be persistent;
undergo,
239,12(Ar).13.14.18(Ar)21.24.27;
241,2.14.20.24; 243,13; 245,20;
268,22; 280,18; 293,12
hupomimnêskein, recall, 243,29
hupopteuein, suspect, 283,10
hupostasis, existence, 297,28
hupostrephein, revert, 310,13
hupothesis, assumption, what has
been assumed, premiss, 238,26;
239,27; 240,19; 245,9; 247,17;
249,4; 250,11.13; 251,22.28.35;
252,23; 253,9.18.20.23; 255,31;
256,19.21; 259,34; 261,12; 265,14;
266,7; 267,7.20; 269,25; *ex
hupotheseôs*, *ex hypothesi* (of
necessity), 303,25.27.28.33.35;
309,1.16.18; *kata hupothesin*,
hypothetical (of necessity) 304,7;
306,27
hupothetikos, hypothetical (mode of
syllogism) 300,6
hupotithenai, posit, hold a view,
assume, suggest, assumption, give
an assumption, adopt,
237,14.29.30; 238,8; 244,21;
245,16.30; 246,1.21.33; 247,4.31;
250,5.10.13; 257,3.14-16.18; 258,3;
265,23; 269,4; 273,3; 274,10; 282,4;
286,28; 287,19.21; 290,28; 294,7;
304,9; 305,9; 309,24; 310,26
huphesis, deficiency, 296,24
huphistanai, subsist, exist, be
subsistent, 241,8.10.14; 242,24.26;
244,15; 250,32; 254,14; 255,13.15;
276,3; 303,28

iatrikê (tekhnê), medicine, 286,26
iatros, doctor, 281,33; 282,1; 286,13
idea, form, Form, 246,15; 281,33;
285,21
idikôteros, more specific, 281,6
idios, own, proper, special
characteristic, property, proper
attribute, 246,34; 267,7; 287,5;
299,1.2; 308,4; 310,7

ienai, go, proceed, 247,21.29.34; 248,1.6; 249,31
ikhnos, trace, 276,15
isazein, be equal, 272,29; 277,2
iskhein, retain, 293,11; 298,8
iskhnansis, emaciation, 308,17.19
iskhuros, strong, 272,28
isokhronios, of the same time length, taking the same time as, 293,15; 294,10
isokhronos, equal in time to, 295,2
isomegethês, the same amount as, 258,17
isos, equal, equality, equally, 258,4.8.22.24-6.30; 259,4.14; 260,16.20.21.24; 261,4.8.10.21(Ar).23-5; 262,3.10(Ar).12.19.21; 265,27; 293,9.12.17.25.29; 294,16.30; *en isôi einai*, be equivalent, 278,15; 302,30
isôs, perhaps, 238,1; 245,21; 248,14; 250,5; 255,15; 269,25.34; 271,26; 275,26; 276,11; 279,22; 283,10; 285,17(Pl); 286,7; 292,20.27; 310,1; 313,19
isoskelês, isosceles (triangle), 265,26
isotês, equality, 258,17.20; 260,20; 261,3.12.13; 272,29

kaiein, burn, 269,22; 293,2.20; 302,32; 303,1
kairos, time, 271,22
kakia, vice, 268,29
kakôs, badly, 261,23
kalein, term, call, refer, 249,21; 264,14.17.30; 270,14; 283,22; 285,3; 287,9; 289,33; 296,7
kalos, good, beautiful, fine, 250,23; 252,2; 285,14.17.18(Pl); 292,32
kalôs, well, rightly (said), aptly, 288,24.26; 290,14(Ar); 295,3
kamnein, be afflicted, 281,35; 282,1
karpos, fruit, 288,21.23; 290,2; 292,9; 295,4; 303,24
kataballein, cast down, 303,3
katabolê (tou spermatos eis gên), casting down (of seed into earth), 303,20
katadekhesthai, receive, 283,28; 295,17.19
katakratein, prevail, 277,16
katalambanein, reach, 298,18.19

kataleipein, leave, 237,15; 269,1
katamenein, remain, 299,12
katantan (ek), result (from); *(eis)* end up (at the point), 255,25; 304,27
kataskeuazein establish; set out (to show, prove); construct an argument, 241,26; 246,28; 256,32; 280,20; 304,13; 306,11
kataskeuê, outline of the argument, argument, proof, 278,21; 300,27; 306,15
katateinein polun logon, devote a long discussion, 281,4
katapheugein, have recourse to, 285,21
katekhein, occupy, 240,7.9
kathapax, once for all, 271,34; 272,3
katharos, pure, 270,25; 271,6
katheudein, be asleep, 271,10
katô, lower, below, downwards, 256,7; 257,18; 266,10.11.14; 267,5; 298,20.23-4; 308,29(Ar)
katorthoun, well-form (an argument) to reach its goal, 309,20 (opp. *amphiballein*, see note ad loc.)
katôthen, below, 255,30(Ar); 256,2
kausis, burn, 293,20
kêros, wax, 273,25(Ar); 274,1.2
kharaktêrizein, characterise, 245,29; 264,23; 265,6
kharis, kharin, for the sake of, 251,24
kheimôn, winter, 289,25; 290,7; 306,22; *kheimônos* (adv.), in winter, 289,30; 292,31; 312,24
kheirôn, inferior, inferiority, 282,14; 283,5.7; 288,5; 289,34
khein, pour, 308,22
khorêgein, dispense, 295,19
khôra, place, 298,2; *khôran ekhein*, be possible, 304,29
khôris, without, 264,17
khreia, need, 282,1; 283,28; 284,3; 286,12
khrênai, should, must, ought to, 247,4.12.18; 248,1; 252,23; 253,22; 272,25; 273,19; 276,19; 283,16.21; 289,21; 291,10; 293,19; 294,10; 297,11; 302,2; 303,25; 309,3
khrêsis, example, 280,13; usage, 289,34; 302,23.24; 303,6; 306,11

leipein, remain, leave, 249,10; 261,5;
  274,15; 297,14.19.20; 311,15
lexis, text, 246,3; 250,35; 277,5;
  290,26
leptomereia, fine structure, 279,5
leukos, white 242,21; 248,32.33;
  249,2-4.10.13.14; 252,12; 258,13;
  259,29; 261,14.17.18; 301,11
leukotês, whiteness, 249,1; 259,33;
  260,3
lêthê, forgetfulness, 268,24
lithos, stone, 269,8.15.18; 271,20
logikos, logikon zôion, rational
  animal, 283,6
logos, account, argument, definition,
  discussion, ground, reasoning,
  reckoning, view, 238,20.22.29;
  239,4.7; 240,19; 243,10.15.29;
  246,4.12.20; 249,6.18.27;
  251,10.24; 255,13; 256,9; 257,8.25;
  259,19; 260,9; 263,5; 268,30.32;
  270,8.30; 276,5; 279,26; 280,6;
  281,4.8; 286,25; 287,18; 288,16;
  293,25; 294,29(Ar); 299,15.18.31;
  300,4; 301,1(Ar).24; 312,10;
  account, treatise, part of a book,
  en tôi prôtôi, 263,5 (referring to
  GC 1); *en tôi peri mixeôs*, 270,18
  (*GC* 1.10); (*en têi Phusikêi*) *hoi
  en ogdoôi*, 299,15 (*Phys.* 8); *en
  arkhêi l.*, 301,2; formula,
  proportion, rational principle,
  definition, 257,20; 262,16;
  263,16.19.26; 264,2; 272,20;
  275,15.16; 280,25; 285,3; 286,11;
  formula, 263,29;
  264,8.10.12.13.17.20.23.25-6;
  264,10.13; (rational) account,
  (*oude ... logôi perilabein*)
  250,31; (*ou tôi logôi
  diexelthein*), 290,3; *logon tinos
  epekhein (pros ti)*, have relation
  of, be related as (to sth), satisfy a
  definition of, stand for, 237,29;
  238,28; 239,3; 244,20; 247,13;
  288,8.14; 295,26; 301,2; *logon
  ekhein*, be reasonable, 245,28
loipos, other, remaining, rest,
  237,27; 239,6.10.17; 241,8;
  243,3.8.11.13.15; 244,6; 246,18.21;
  247,5; 248,12.16; 250,12; 255,12;
  257,25; 273,18; 277,10; 298,11;
  312,25; 313,6

loipon, after that, 271,23
loxos (kuklos), inclined (circle),
  289,11.19.25;
  291,2.7.12.19.21.27.28.31; 312,23
luein, resolve, 274,21
lusis, solution, 270,16; 298,17

makhesthai, militate, 239,26;
  260,10; 269,24
makhê, battle, 273,6
malista, mostly, most, as much as
  possible, 278,20(Ar).22; 287,28;
  297,25(Ar); on the use with
  comparative degree, see n. 305 ad
  287,28
mallon, rather, more than, 246,3.33;
  247,4; 249,21.30; 262,23; 264,26;
  265,4.10.12.14; 272,20-4.33;
  274,19(Ar).23; 275,9(Ar).13.14;
  279,7; 280,19; 282,7; 288,5; 291,32;
  292,21.22.29; 293,7.8; *ou mallon*,
  no more 249,30
manos, rare, 241,27
manôsis, rarefaction, 241,28; 260,27;
  261,11; 268,26
manoun, rarefy, 258,31; 260,22
manthanein, learn, 239,11
matên, in vain, 260,6; 273,4
mathêsis, learning, 271,22
mêdamêi, never, 284,18
mêdamôs, in no way, 260,4; 284,18
megas, big, 314,13; *to megiston*,
  maximum, 293,23
megethos, amount, 258,7.15.23;
  259,4.5.8.25; 260,14; 262,19;
  301,14.19; 302,2.8.9
meirakion, adolescent, 297,2
mêkunein, expound at length,
  mêkunthenta, lengthy exposition,
  272,12
melanotês, blackness, 260,3
melas, black, 242,21; 248,32.33;
  249,4.10.15.16.26; 252,12
mellein, will be, 237,22; 249,31(Ar);
  is going to be (dist. *estai* 'will be',
  see s.v. *einai*), 302,25.28-30;
  303,4; 306,7(Ar).12; *mellôn*, (of
  Aristotle) intending, planning,
  248,7; 281,5.7
memphesthai, reproach, criticise
  (with dat.), 286,7; (with. acc.),
  281,30; 287,8
mempsis, criticism, 282,9

275,11.26.30(Ar) ; 276,6.11.28; 279,2.6.15

mnêmê, memory, 268,23

môlôps, weal, 308,21

monê, rest, 266,23(Ar).25

monôs, only, 261,17; 262,7; 305,11.33

morion, part, 253,29; 254,10; 263,6.28; 274,6-8; 308,21

morphê, shape, form, 280,25; 285,1(Ar); 287,7(Ar).9.11

mousikos, cultured, 268,23

muelos, marrow, 272,17

muloeidês, millstone-like, 291,16

Neikos, Strife (of Empedocles), 264,4.8.9.15.28; 265,1.18.(Ar).19(Ar).21.29.30; 266,4.5.7.13.16.21-2.26-7; 267,2(Ar).4.12.21-2.25.27; 268,4.5.9.11-13.20

neuron, sinew, nerve (see n. 151 ad 263,27), 263,27; 264,1; 273,18.20

nephos, cloud, 313,2(Ar).3.7-9

noein, understand, think, conceive of, 276,29; 283,23; 294,10; 295,4; 298,3; 304,36; 305,33

nomizein, believe, 246,33; 247,32

nosein, be ill, 281,32; 286,14.16

nosos, illness, 282,1

nous, intellect, 287,13; 299,18; (in Anaxagoras) 281,28; 285,11

nun, now, 237,6.12.19; 238,20.32; 240,10; 241,11; 243,4; 244,19.22; 246,12.32; 248,7.15; 250,1.9; 253,18.20; 254,8; 262,29; 267.7,14.19(Ar).21.24; 268,1.9.11; 269,20; 271,13; 274,12; 274,21; 276,24; 278,9; 279,9.30; 280,13; 285,2.25; 288,11(Ar).15; 290,11.15; 291,24.31; 296,17; 299,19; 300,26; 301,7.15; 309,7.10; 310,27; 311,8; 312,10; 313,5; 314,4; *nuni*, 247,3

nux, night, 289,23.25; 291,12

nukhthêmeron, day-and-night, 291,13

oiesthai, think, believe, 238,15; 276,21; 285,22(Ar); 286,19; 297,16; 298,22

oikeios, proper, own, 245,28.33; 257,8; 268,8; 270,16.17; 274,21; 278,22; 280,22; 282,18; 296,20; 298,18.19.23

oikia, house, 269,9.16.17; 271,18-20; 303,16; 306,25(Ar).26(Ar); 307,2.3.16-18

oikodomein, build, 271,19

oikodomêma, house-building, 263,2

oikodomikos, oikodomikê (epistêmê), (knowledge) of house-building, 271,8

oikodomos, builder, 271,8

oneirôttein, dream, 281,24(Ar); 285,8

onkos, mass (see n. 128 ad 260, 14), 260,14.15.20.23; 261,3.9; 262,14.17.18.21-2

onoma, name, term, 248,23; 302,23

onomazein, call, 250,23; 264,16; 270,14; 303,25

ontôs, real, 244,26

oregesthai, desire, 297,12

organikos, organic, instrumental, 264,1; 287,17(Ar).19; 288,6.7

organon, organ; instrument, 263,24; 282,13-15; 287,25; 288,3.5

orthôs, rightly, legitimate, 253,10; 259,34

ostoun, bone, 263,27.31; 269,10.21; 270,5.9; 272,17; 273,13.18.20.28; 277,12(Ar).19.20

ouranios, heavenly; *ta ourania*, heavenly bodies, 283,12; 288,24; 289,15; 295,23.29.32; 296,4.16.24.31; 297,7; 312,20

ousia, substance, essence, being, 240,15; 241,20; 263,24.31; 264,5(Ar).14.23; 269,24; 279,18.23-6; 280,9; 285,3; 289,33; 297,18.26(Ar); 298,2.6; 313,30; 314,1(Ar).7.15

ousiôdês, essential, 280,25

pais, child, 271,21; 297,2; 310,8

pakhumeresteros, denser, 279,6

palaios, hoi palaioi and *hoi palaioteroi*, the ancients, 237,9.13

palin, again, vice versa, back, in turn, also, re-, so on, 238,9; 240,22(Ar); 242,9; 245,6; 247,23; 247,25.28; 249,6; 250,24.26; 252,7(Ar); 254,1(Ar).4; 256,9.11.24.27; 258,27; 259,19; 264,19; 266,6.11; 267,20; 269,2; 270,33; 271,25; 275,20; 297,2; 310,1.8; 314,12.16; *palin kai palin*, again and again, over and

310,27.29; 311,1.12.17(Ar).22;
312,1
peras, limit, 280,21.23.28; 301,21;
310,12; 311,2.9.10
peri (i) (with gen.) of, about, relating
to, 237,4(Ar).7.9.11.13.18.19;
238,11; 244,16(Ar); 247,11.14;
258,2; 259,33; 263,9; 264,20;
265,17(Ar).20.23.31; 267,16;
268,31(Ar); 269,2; 279,26;
281,4-6.8; 282,18; 285,2;
288,10(Ar).12.16-18; 290,10.11;
298,15; 299,14; 300,14; 301,23;
302,4-6; **makhê peri tinos**, battle
over something 273,6; in the titles:
peri psukhês, *On the soul*,
268,30; 299,17; **peri mixeos**, *On
mixture*, 270,18; **peri poiein kai
paskhein**, *On acting and being
acted upon*, 277,6; (ii) (with
accusative) in, belonging to,
around, upon, 239,22; 268,27;
273,3; 273,5;
278,3(Ar).10.11.16.17.22; 281,20;
282,16.28; 283,15; 284,29; 295,30;
296,2.6; 301,13; 312,1.3; **hoi peri
Parmenidên**, those around
Parmenides, 287,26
periagein, bring round, 266,6
periekhein, contain, surround,
embrace, 265,27; 301,29; 260,18;
280,28; 280,22-3; 300,20; 301,29;
periekhon, to, environment,
295,28
perilambanein, comprehend,
250,31; 251,6
periodos, revolution, cycle, period (of
time) 292,8.10.11.14; 293, 11.12;
294.3.5.8.32; 295,13; 305,26.30;
314,11
periorizein, embrace by definition;
bound 254,13; 278,26
peripiptein (atopois), fall into
(incongruities) 269,9; cf. 311,4
peritrepein (eis tounantion), turn
round, bring round 250,11; 265,3
(to a contrary claim) (cf. Philop.
ap. Simplic. *in Phys.* 1130,25 sq.)
perix, periphery 266,15.18
phainesthai, show; (with partic.)
appear, apparently, obviously,
evident, evidently; 246,3; 249,20;
251,28; 258,18; 261,26(Ar); 263,21;

267,1(Ar); 271,15; 274,10; 282,10;
283,29; 286,27; 287,27(Ar).28;
292,7.15; 294,2.28(Ar); 295,21;
313,1(Ar); (with inf.) seem, 271,10;
(verb to be supplied) 266,1(Ar);
312,14(Ar); **phainomena, (ta)**,
evidence, 239,26; 269,24; 269,28
phanai, say, state, speak, claim,
describe, mean, hold, (in periphr.)
to quote, according to s.o.,
237,28.30; 238,15.22.32;
239,4.9.20.21.24; 240,14;
241,2.7.14.24; 242,24-5.28;
243,5.12.18.22; 244,12.23;
245,13.16.23.26; 246,4.10.17.18;
247,17.22.24.30.33; 248,1.21.35;
249,21; 250,13.17.31.34; 252,9.17;
253,10.11.16.20; 254,12.14.17;
255,8-10.15.18; 256,2.22;
258,4.6.30; 259,1.29; 260,4.8;
261,4.28; 263,12.15.26.29;
264,7(Ar).8.16.23; 265,20.23.28-9;
266,4.24; 267,3.4.8-10(Ar)14.18;
268,2.3.6.8.18;
269,1.2.4-6.8.11.12.14.20.25-6;
270,2.4.7.10.12.18.19.29.31.33;
271,2; 272,5.14.30;
273,10.12.16.21.24.27;
274,1.5.13.29; 275,13.18;
277,5.13.21.24; 278,12.17.22.28;
279,10.27.31; 280,9.15.16;
281,11.20.24.29.30.33;
282,3.4.7.20.23.27.32; 283,1.3;
284,2.9.14.15.17.19.20.23.26;
285,2.26; 286,2.7.8.10.18.28;
287,2.9.25.28.30;
288,15.18.26.31.33; 289,32;
290,10.13.24.26-7; 291,4.20.24.26;
292,8.10.13.28; 295,10.13.26;
296,7.18; 297,9.14.27;
298,10.21.28; 299,22.24-5; 300,18;
301,2.15.22; 302,2.8.19.27.29;
303,2.21.23.26; 304,2.9.14; 305,5.8;
306,18.27; 307,11; 308,3.4; 309,29;
310,29; 311,2.4.9.19.20;
312,6.10.15; 313,7.8.11.22.27;
314,4-6.9.13; **pros ti, tina**,
counter, reply to, 269,25; 270,3;
284,2; 286,10; 292,28
phanerôs, explicitly, 300,24
phaulos, bad, 250,22; 252,2
pherein, bear, carry, bring up (of a
problem), move, lead, 266,14;

rhônnunai, strengthen, 292,21.25

sarkion, piece of flesh, 269,22
sarkôdês, fleshy, 308,21
sarx, flesh, 263,27; 269,15.26;
270,1.4.7; 273,13.20.28;
274,11(Ar).13; 277,12(Ar).19.20
sêmainein, signify, 261,20(Ar);
271,7.8.14.16; 272,4.8; 275,6;
276,13.16.18.20; 294,6; 297,9;
308,31; 311,1
sêmantikos, indicative, 254,20
sêmasia, meaning, 276,26
sêmeion, point, 265,25
sêpein, putrefaction, 269,22
siôpan, silence, 297,11
skalênos, scalene, 265,26
skepsis, analysis, investigation,
237,8; 313,22
skepteon, to be considered, must be
considered, 254,14.23
skhesis, relation, 238,25; 291,3.32.33
(cf. 289,12); 301,28
skopein, see, examine, 255,15; 283,2
skopos, aim, goal, 237,16; 285,5
sôma, body, 238,30(Ar).33;
241,8.10.14.18.23; 242,5.25.28;
243,9.16; 244,3; 249,12;
257,22(Ar); 261,26(Ar);
266,2(Ar).23(Ar);
268,6.8.27.31(Ar); 278,3(Ar).6.7;
281,1(Ar); 282,12.19.24.26;
287,16(Ar); 292,25-6.28.31; 293,1;
295,24; 296,10; 298,18;
301,7.12.26.28-9; 302,6
sômatikos, corporeal, bodily, 237,23;
243,6.18-20; 268,22.25
sômatoeidês, of bodily kind, 297,18
spanios, rare, *spaniôs*, seldom,
263,16.18
sperma, seed, 271,20; 295,25-6;
297,1.2; 303,3.20.24; 310,8
speudein, strive, 298,18
sphagê, killing, 308,27-8
sphaira, sphere, 273,26(Ar); 274,3-5;
291,25
Sphairos (in Empedocles' poem),
Sphere, 264,30;
265,2.5.6.8.11.12.15; 266,13;
267,5.23; 268,7
stakhus, ear of corn, 303,4.18
stereisthai, be deprived, 281,18
sterêsis, privation, 242,15.17.19.22

stoikheion, letter, 248,22; element,
237,5.17.19; 239,24; 242,25;
244,7.11.12; 250,10;
251,1.9.11.13-17.20.23.27.34-6;
252,5.28; 253,10.17;
254,3.6.8-10.19; 256,3;
257,22(Ar).23.25-6.29.31; 258,6.22;
259,8.31; 260,2.3.25; 261,22.28;
262,9.25.29.31; 263,20.31;
264,28(Ar); 265,20; 265,10.13.22;
266,14.26; 267,5.12.24;
268,7.22.27; 269,13.14.26;
270,4.14.35; 273,3.4.10.16.27;
274,13; 275,20.22; 276,3.33;
277,11; 278,8; 279,21; 288,21;
298,19.22; 314,5.7
struphnotês, sourness, 277,29
sullambanesthai, be taken
together, 280,12(Ar).17
sullogizesthai, infer, 279,30
sumballesthai, be comparable,
258,6.7; *eis ti*, contribute, 292,31
sumblêtos, comparable, compared,
258,4.6.23; 259,4.5.7.9.30;
260,13(Ar).14;
261,1(Ar).6.17.22.27(Ar).28;
262,1.9.29
sumbolê, comparability, comparison,
258,15; 260,18
summenein, keep together, 278,25
summetaballein, change together
with, 288,21
sumpas, whole, 299,31
sumperainein, conclude, draw
conclusion, follow (as a
conclusion), 243,4; 245,19.26;
246,2; 251,18.19; 254,8; 256,17;
312,10
sumperasma, conclusion, 300,6;
311,8
sumpêxis, (bodily) frame, 295,18.24
sumplekesthai, be combined
together, 244,5; 277,13; 279,7;
280,17
sumplêroun, complete, 268,32
sumplokê, combination, 251,4;
278,26; 296,9
sumphorein, assemble, 269,33
sumphônos, in agreement, 294,4;
313,27
sunaisthêsis, co-perception, 292,30
sunaptein, join, put together,
275,27; 297,11

xêros, dry, dryness,
240,13.20.27.30.31; 242,2.6.12.13;
245,32.35; 248,34-5;
249,2.14.15.26-7; 251,25; 253,5.6;
259,20; 270,31-4; 275,24; 278,12;
279,14.20; 298,13
xêrotês, dryness, 242,6; 249,9;
277,27; 279,17.23
xestiaios, pint, 258,29.30; 259,10

zêtein, investigate, seek, ask,
examine, inquire, query, find out,
245,18; 249,18; 251,10; 256,31;
257,26; 259,27; 268,1; 274,31;
280,13; 281,8; 282,28; 288,6;
289,27; 290,26; 295,12; 301,7.23;
302,16.20; 306,8; 313,23
zêtêsis, inquiry, 251,1; 255,10
zôê, life, 288,25; 293,3.17.26; 294,8;
295,18.19; 296,10
zônê, zone (geographical), 293,3
zôion, animal, 283,6; 287,4; 288,23;
290,2; 292,11; 293,1; 295,4; 312,26;
313,3(Ar).18.32

Index of Passages

Subject Index